WITHDRAWN

WITHDRAWN

LANGUAGE AND LITERACY SERIES
Dorothy S. Strickland and Celia Genishi, SERIES EDITORS

ADVISORY BOARD: RICHARD ALLINGTON, DONNA ALVERMANN, KATHRYN AU,
EDWARD CHITTENDON, BERNICE CULLINAN, COLETTE DAIUTE,
ANNE HAAS DYSON, CAROLE EDELSKY, JANET EMIG,
SHIRLEY BRICE HEATH, CONNIE JUEL, SUSAN LYTLE

(Continued)

165720
VC Grad - M.Ed.

62.00

What Counts as Literacy

Challenging the School Standard

EDITED BY
Margaret A. Gallego and
Sandra Hollingsworth

Teachers College
Columbia University
New York and London

Published by Teachers College Press, 1234 Amsterdam Avenue, New York, NY 10027

Copyright © 2000 by Teachers College, Columbia University

All rights reserved. No part of this publication may be reproduced or transmitted in any form or by any means, electronic or mechanical, including photocopy, or any information storage and retrieval system, without permission from the publisher.

Library of Congress Cataloging-in-Publication Data

What counts as literacy : challenging the school standard / edited by Margaret Gallego and Sandra Hollingsworth.
     p. cm. — (Language and literacy series)
     Includes bibliographical references and index.
     ISBN 0-8077-3973-1 (cloth : alk. paper) — ISBN 0-8077-3972-3 (pbk. : alk. paper)
     1. Literacy—Social aspects—United States. 2. Language arts—Social aspects—United States. 3. Multicultural education—United States.
     4. Critical pedagogy—United States. I. Gallego, Margaret A.
     II. Hollingsworth, Sandra. III. Language and literacy series (New York, N.Y.)
     LC151.W43 2000
     370.11'5—dc21   00-041777

ISBN 0-8077-3972-3 (paper)
ISBN 0-8077-3973-1 (cloth)

Printed on acid-free paper

Manufactured in the United States of America

07 06 05 04 03 02 01 00   8 7 6 5 4 3 2 1

Contents

PART II. Community Literacies

PART III. Personal Literacies

.

What Counts as Literacy

Challenging the School Standard

1

Introduction

The Idea of Multiple Literacies

MARGARET A. GALLEGO AND
SANDRA HOLLINGSWORTH

In the same way feminists have learned to live with multiple
meanings, so should they be initiators of multiple literacies.
                                        —Beckleman, 1991

We are collaborative colleagues and good friends. Gallego is a Mexican
American woman who, brought up in mainstream schools in Arizona,
was surprised to discover that she had a "special gift" for Spanish discourse in high school. Hollingsworth is a Caucasian woman, born in the
South and partially raised in Europe, who was surprised to discover a "special attraction" to feminist discourse as a new professor at the University
of California, Berkeley. Our life stories connected in East Lansing, Michigan, where, sitting on the carpeted, hardwood floors of Hollingsworth's
home in the late-afternoon autumn sun almost a decade ago, we found that
we both had hopes of making literacy—or communication/comprehen-
sion—opportunities in schools more socially just. Like many before us,
we wanted to connect literacy learning for school and literacy learning
for life. We were frustrated that after decades of legislation and school
reform, success for women and minorities in society was still more rheto-
ric than reality. We set out three goals for students' literacy in school—
the first two were common in the educational literature, and the third was
relatively unique:

1. To live successfully in the dominant society
2. To live successfully in minority communities and cultures
3. To live successfully in chosen and personal identities

What Counts as Literacy: Challenging the School Standard. Copyright © 2000 by Teachers College, Columbia University. All rights
reserved. ISBN 0-8077-3972-3 (paper), ISBN 0-8077-3973-1 (cloth). Prior to photocopying items for classroom use, please contact
the Copyright Clearance Center, Customer Service, 222 Rosewood Drive, Danvers, MA 01923, USA, telephone (508) 750-8400.

Identity here is viewed in terms of social relationships that are specific to time, place, and situation and that are forged in the context of ongoing relationships that exist in time and space (see Galindo, Chapter 15 in this volume).

The third goal is illustrated in a story told by Natalie Goldberg (1988) about a woman learning to write. She searched through her consciousness for a topic or concept that she personally enjoyed, not one intended for her teacher, or for her country, her career, or her family. She discovered that she loved the "taste of chocolate," and with that discovery began to articulate personal and changing lenses to help her communicate and comprehend more fully. A similar point is made by Cook-Gumperz and Keller-Cohen (1993) in describing Wanda, a beginning college student. Wanda's oral story, in the telling and retelling, becomes transformed. "Her individual voice becomes shaped to fit a public arena: that of the writing class and the requirements of a simple school-prose theme. But what if for Wanda there is more than one written voice? . . . Wanda knows that she has not only a public self as a beginning college student writing for a college audience, but also a private self, albeit in the background, that needs to be heard. It is precisely the complexity of her situation as a writer which finds expression in her written account, even if in an awkward way" (p. 349). Familiar with such literature, we hypothesized that if schools were to foster personal literacy as well as community and standard literacies, the personal development might give individuals and groups the knowledge to bridge cultural diversity and the dominant culture—and positively change society for everyone.

We viewed such work as critical *praxis*—or the dialectical relationship between thought and action, subjectivity and objectivity, and theory and practice (Freire, 1972; Weiner, 1994). Through successes and failures in various projects across the years, we have learned quite a bit about the dimensions of collaboration and praxis to reform urban schools for *multiple literacies*—a term we "invented" that afternoon in East Lansing in our attempts to frame our collaboration (Gallego & Hollingsworth, 1992; Hollingsworth & Gallego, 1996). Since that time, of course, we have discovered that many authors have written about the concept of multiple literacies (Siegel & Bressler, 1993), and we wanted to pull the various perspectives together. Thus, we invited some of the most provocative scholars on the topic to contribute to this volume.

In this introductory chapter, we articulate a nested set of literacies that have been useful for our own work as teachers, women, and scholars with personal and professional concerns for social justice. We also preview how the contributors to this volume speak to, challenge, or extend their conceptions of multiple literacies, and we address the pedagogical implications of each perspective.

MULTIPLE LITERACIES

As we prepared for this volume, we found many references to multiple literacies, but few that adequately situated and articulated our own personal and social experiences as women academics with differing backgrounds in urban educational settings. In other words, we found many definitions of *multiple literacies* addressing our first goal—the standard, schooled, or King's English—and, to a more limited extent, our second goal—the community or culturally based conceptions of literacy—but the personal perspective on multiple literacies as part of lived experiences is still largely missing in the literature. To find examples of work where all three literacies interact, we had to turn to the authors in this volume.

We have not been concerned with articulating an essential definition of the term *literacy* because we have each lived within shifting constructions of literacy informed by different personal and theoretical positions. For example, we have both had elementary through college-level school experiences based on psychological traditions that unquestionably defined *literacy* as the ability to read and write, read and speak standard English. Even our separate graduate school experiences in the 1980s concentrated on literacy (or reading, separate from writing, as it was considered then) as an empirically based, objective, individual cognitive psychological activity, distinct from its social and political contexts. Occasional references were made to "social constructions" of literacy (e.g., Goodman, Vygotsky), but they lost credibility in lecture-style presentations on literacy, were ignored as examples in research design courses, and were rarely articulated in mainstream journal publications at that time.

Later we discovered perceptions of literacy that included our concern for social and community-based literacies. Cook-Gumperz & Gumperz (1986) present the social construction of literacy by emphasizing the cultural and communicative practices associated with particular written and spoken forms among specific social groups.

Finally, discovering critical theoretical traditions that questioned the idea of representation associated with literacy, we found a conception of literacy that included our concern for political and personally based knowledge:

> perspectives of and approaches to literacy are shaped by theoretical and ideological concerns which extend beyond the classroom walls. These concerns are related to beliefs and assumptions about the nature of knowledge, of people (i.e., teachers and students), of experience, and to the relations of power and of social and cultural control which these beliefs and assumptions both construct and incorporate. (Walsh, 1991, p. 9)

Not only were power relations ignored in our graduate educations, explorations of our personal and lived experiences with literacy inside and outside of the classroom, which would have been characteristic of a critical feminist perspective (see C. Luke & Gore, 1992), were ignored as well. Our formal educational experiences stopped short of helping us understand that all views of literacy have epistemological, cultural, and political biases that are dependent on the social, economic, and experiential viewpoints of their proponents.

Beyond the fact that we were never taught alternatives, our successful progress throughout our schooling experiences, based on research from both behaviorist and cognitive psychological theories of literacy, supported such theories because we made it through school into doctoral programs, which "accidentally" matched our experiences. Our separate but similar educations did lead us to become specialists in how students could cognitively acquire a standard, or "generic," school-based literacy in classrooms, and how we, as researchers, could objectively and apolitically study that acquisition. Yet, as we tried to put the cognitive theories into practice,we found obstacle after obstacle in watching the populations of children we wanted to reach (and their teachers) struggle and fail in school, even as such practices were intended to facilitate all children's literacy. We soon had researched enough patterns to know that those children had difficulty attaining the standard literacy because of a combination of social, political, and instructional factors rather than cognitive factors alone. Only through the praxis of our work as professionals did it become clear that the lack of success was due to the political gatekeeping functions of school literacy which often limits success in standard English (and therefore schooling and subsequent citizenship) to those already fluent in it through family and community discourse practices.

Additionally, our own personal experiences as teachers of and participants in multiple discourse communities, if not in their schooling, suggested that those children seen as cognitively deficient in school-based literacies might be fully literate in community (or social) and personal (or political) literacies, which were "illegal" in school curricula. As we worked together, we have encouraged each other to question the "authority" in our schooled experiences (Rich, 1979) and to learn more about our community and personal literacies as we attempted to enact them in our teaching and research practices. Our hope was not only to conduct research into multiple literacies as they unfolded and collided, but, as a project of praxis, to explore them as possibilities for reconstructing school curricula. Following critical literacy scholars before us, we wanted to raise questions about literacies that have traditionally been excluded from the discourse of schooling and about the "generic" qualities of the dominant language of power (see Delpit, 1988). Our conceptions of multiple literacies that helped to shape our collaboration were, roughly, these:

- *school literacies*—the learning of interpretive and communicative processes needed to adapt socially to school and other dominant language contexts, and the use or practice of those processes in order to gain a conceptual understanding of school subjects
- *community literacies*—the appreciation, understanding, and/or use of interpretive and communicative traditions of culture and community, which sometimes stand as critiques of school literacies
- *personal literacies*—the critical awareness of ways of knowing and believing about self that comes from thoughtful examination of historical or experiential and gender-specific backgrounds in school and community language settings, which sometimes stands as critique of both school literacies and community literacies

The division of literacies into categories of place is not meant to be hierarchical or static. We realize that there are commonalties, shifts, and faults among the various literacy locations. The locational categories are intended as placeholders to make a complex argument for change.

SCHOOL LITERACIES

All the authors in this volume seriously question the current fidelity in the United States to a school-based conception of literacy as standard, print-based, English-only. While they are well aware (as are most teachers and parents) that standard English is still the communicative basis on which their society measures its citizens' worth, they want to explore some issues that challenge the educative and equitable merit of supporting a single standard of literacy in school. They realize that many people in their society agree that a standard national language is an appropriate goal for literacy instruction, even within a democracy (e.g., Hirsch, 1987), but they want to go further. Students who have mastered school literacy (as the ability to read and write standard English) are supposed to develop into a society of adult citizens who are "innovative, achievement oriented, productive, cosmopolitical, media and politically aware, more globally (nationally and internationally) and less locally-oriented, with more liberal and human social attitudes, less likely to commit a crime, and more likely to take education, and the rights and duties of citizenship, seriously" (Gee,

1990, p. 32; see also Cuban, 1990; Mikulecky, 1990). Harvey Graff (1979) has called this conception a "literacy myth" because these claims have clearly not been achieved. Why not?

Some scholars suggest that teachers' use of an inappropriate instructional method has been the problem in hindering the goal of a common literate society. The "great debate" in literacy (Chall, 1989) has historically been one involving the correct theoretical applications from either cognitive psychology or sociolinguistics. Some of the authors in this volume focus on instructional methods that bridge that binary debate (see Flood, Lapp, & Bayles-Martin, Chapter 4; Myers, Hammett, & McKillop, Chapter 5; also Bressler & Siegel, Chapter 9; Leland, Harste, & Helt, Chapter 6; Noll, Chapter 12; Short & Kauffman, Chapter 3). Other critics of school literacy focus less on instructional method and more on the social and political purposes of literacy (Gee & Clinton, Chapter 7; Minarik, Chapter 17; see Reyes, Chapter 13; Vásquez & Durán, Chapter 10). Some of these authors have written earlier critical texts that illuminate the political and communicative *norms* of the dominant society, then point to the hidden purpose behind standard literacy education. James Gee (1990), for example, citing Robert Bocoak and Antonio Gramsci, made a compelling argument to suggest that

> The most striking continuity in the history of literacy is the way in which literacy has been used, in age after age, to solidify the social hierarchy, empower elites and ensure that people lower on the hierarchy accept the values, norms and beliefs of the elites, even when it is not in their self interest (or "class interest") to do so. (p. 40)

Still other critics of societally foregrounded literacy analyses draw upon epistemological questions about societal norms (see Bordieu & Passeron, 1977). They point out that a socially constructed "literate bias" of school knowledge, understood through a standard language, functions to restrict access to knowledge to those students (primarily from the middle and upper classes) who enter the schools "already acquainted with school-like literacy tasks and equipped with a positive attitude toward literate culture" (Nespor, 1991, p. 175). Again, some chapters in this volume reflect that perspective (e.g., Andrade, González Le Denmat, & Moll, Chapter 16; Galindo, Chapter 15; Panofsky, Chapter 11).

As mentioned earlier, both of us have been educated in schools based on standard literacy. Hollingsworth was one of those students who benefited from the sociopolitically determined standard language bias of school literacy. Coming to school from a family discourse style of standard English, she easily gained entry into the educational "community of power."

Hollingsworth's communication skills helped her do well in school and eventually earn a doctorate. Gallego was not born into a family who used standard English as their primary discourse style. However, her family learned about the importance of standard English for school and societal success through her siblings' educational experiences before her. By the time she entered school, English was the primary language family members spoke at home, hoping to enhance school success. And Gallego did succeed—through elementary, secondary, and on to higher education. Yet, while we gained entry through our skills in standard English, we were still painfully aware of the thousands of other minority students who were not so successful (see Cordtz, 1989; Edelman, 1987).

Further, from our experiences, we learned that simple mastery of school literacy may be sufficient for entry into communities of power, but it does not necessarily sustain success, unless that literacy is used to endorse the values and structure of the dominant society. Successful literacy must not only have the "right" grammar, but the "right" values, beliefs, and attitudes (see Fine, 1993, for an argument supporting controversy in the classroom). For example, Hollingsworth's dissertation study offered support that it is the nature of teachers' beliefs regarding their prior educational experiences and the nature of their current relationships with students, not the style of text nor instructional processes, that led to students' mastery of standard English communication skills. As Hollingsworth wrote about those findings in perfectly acceptable standard English, they also stood as critique of acceptable norms about text and cognitive variables that were typically used to explain students' literacy success. Such values were "protected" by editorial staffs of the leading literacy journals, and Hollingsworth's ideas were often denied. Indeed, to get published in the early phase of her career, Hollingsworth found she had to submit manuscripts to nonliteracy journals whose editorial staffs were more tolerant of critical views.

In critiquing the single standard of literacy endorsed in school through sociopolitical analyses, we, along with the other authors in this volume, are admittedly engaged in "critical literacy" projects relative to what counts and who decides—where societal forces are predominant in determining who can read and write, how they can read and write, and what they can read and write. The person most strongly associated with the discourse of sociopolitics in the Western world (and *not* an author of this volume) is Paulo Freire. Freire, whose work was situated outside of the school and in disenfranchised communities, resisted a school-based definition of literacy that is associated with the worldview, values, and aspirations of the middle class. Freire looked critically at both the means and purposes of literacy, inside and outside of school. "Reading the world always precedes reading the word, and reading the word implies continually reading the world"

(Freire & Macedo, 1987, p. 35). He insisted that, if teachers teach students to read only the word and not the world, students could become literate in a technical sense but would remain passive objects of history rather than active subjects. For Freire, literacy instruction was the process through which students could come to reflect critically on the world and take action to transform oppressive conditions. The ultimate purpose of literacy, from a critical perspective, is personal empowerment and social transformation (see also Andrade, González Le Denmat, & Moll, Chapter 16). Freire, like others (e.g., Engle & Ochoa, 1988), saw thoughtful critique as part of the ongoing processes of a democracy.

The need to connect literacy with real people and real lives is a theme that runs through all of the chapters in this volume. In Chapter 2 (a reprint of her 1990 article), Lauren Resnick points out that "schools are not the only—or perhaps even the primary—source of literacy competence"; they are "too isolated from everyday ways of using the written word to serve as the only source of literacy competence in society." Resnick further suggests that dominant school practices are mismatched with the ways in which practical, informational, and pleasurable literacy activities take place in everyday life, activities which are learned through apprenticeships. Yet opportunities for apprenticeships are limited in schools. She concludes that we need to bring school learning out into real life and real-life learning into the classroom.

Kathy Short and Gloria Kauffman (Chapter 3) argue for expanding what counts as literacy beyond just privileging text—through multiple *sign systems* embedded within an inquiry-based curriculum. "A sign system perspective defines literacy broadly as all the ways in which humans share and make meaning, including music, art, mathematics, movement, drama, and oral and written language. We use these sign systems to think about and make meaning for ourselves and to communicate with others." Short and Kauffman envision that, as literacy education has shifted from skills and grammar to reading and writing as inquiry, it could shift again to accommodate basic sign processes, which should be available to all learners.

James Flood, Diane Lapp, and Debra Bayles-Martin (Chapter 4) are concerned about school practices in literacy as they relate to literacy practices outside of school with respect to access to information. They also argue persuasively to broaden the definition of literacy beyond text to include word and image, or visual media, and to bring more of it into classrooms.

Jamie Myers, Roberta Hammett, and Ann Margaret McKillop (Chapter 5) argue compellingly for broadening the schooled standard of literacy to include technological literacy needed for the workplace and out-of-school communication. They describe socially constructed hypermedia authoring projects that explore the students' and their community's understandings of the subject matter. The assignments are cast as technology investigations to move beyond the social construction of knowledge and to explore cultural values embedded in the text.

Christine Leland, Jerome Harste, and Christina Helt (Chapter 6) investigate multiple sign systems in special education. A change from having students with learning disabilities receive large amounts of practice on isolated literacy skills, engaging in multiple literacies is a "considerable departure from the norm." The risk is clearly needed, they argue, so that children in special education can believe they are members of the literacy club.

James Paul Gee and Kate Clinton (Chapter 7) use the concept of *multiple discourses* to convey language as a set of "social languages." Rather than question whether or not schools can successfully teach a secondary or dominant discourse to minority students whose primary or family discourse is radically different (Gee, 1990), Gee and Clinton examine the way in which the teacher can "read" a different primary discourse. In their analysis of an African American student's interactions with her teacher around a science lesson, the authors point out that students' access to science content depends on how well school practices match those they engage in at home and in their local community. Helping students who lack the "rules of the game" requires that the teacher pay more attention to their social languages in different discourse settings. Gee and Clinton advocate "recruiting" out-of-school means of children's talking and thinking as a way into school-based and academic literacies. In a provocative conclusion, they argue that a teacher's interactions with students construct the social language that determines whether students can use their primary discourses to understand the standard discourse of school content.

COMMUNITY LITERACIES

Another approach to expanding both the concept and pedagogy of school literacy is not only to make better connections between school and community, but to use literacies opposed to traditional school literacy to change, celebrate, and develop identity—as well as to act as a bridge for learning standard literacy. Thus, the second section of this book is a collection of writings about students' out-of-school, or community, literacies and how they can be accommodated in schools. We see community literacies as the appreciation, understanding, and/or use of interpretive and communicative traditions of culture and community, which sometimes stand as critiques of school literacies. Our view of community literacy approximates what Mehan (1974) referred to as communicative competence. That is, the social and content knowledge necessary to interact appropriately within a particular group. These groups are not exclusive to particular ethnically bound norms or racial or religious distinctions. Our view leans heavily on perspectives of culture from anthropology and critical sociology rather than from psychological disciplines.

As we have worked together to articulate this concept of literacy, we have drawn upon our personal experiences as much as other scholars' interpretations of the need to include community (or family, or cultural) literacies in school settings. The point is best made through Gallego's story of her bilingual cultural communities—as she tells it herself in the following biographical narrative.

GALLEGO'S STORY

The term culture has become such an overused term, it's hard to pin down an appropriate definition and difficult to tease out particular cases of its influence in my life—because of its persistence and also its subtlety. Mine is not a story of pain and despair often portrayed as "the minority's challenge against adversity," overcoming the enormous obstacles of poverty, racism, illness, and so forth. I certainly don't belittle these as actual lived experiences for many; yet, in my case, I didn't know I was culturally different from others in the community of school until it was over.

Living in Tucson, Arizona, for all but the past five years of my life, I enjoyed the slow, warm lifestyle. Not until I left to work at a university in the midwest did I realize that there were alternative lifestyles. I missed the sun, the easygoing "mañana" attitude promising all would get done in time, and community acceptance for an afternoon siesta—a luxury that I continue to indulge in despite collegial norms to burn the candle at both ends.

As a student in Tucson, I remember hastily dressing and watching an episode of the Andy Griffith show before walking to school. I was one of four children in a working-class home: My father is a blue-collar specialist, specifically a pipe fitter/welder, not to be confused with a plumber, and my mother is a homemaker, a quiet and slow-to-laugh woman who was briefly employed prior to her marriage. My parents tell me that I learned to speak Spanish first; in fact Spanish was our home language until my older brother entered the world of school. With new boundaries extending their family community into that of the school, my family quickly learned about acceptable "speech communities." All of us attended a Catholic school where English had a great influence in shaping our lives and our understandings of who we were. As the competing agendas of school norms necessary for success became clearer, family members—including my extended family of cousins who were my playmates—began to become linguistically and culturally assimilated. As a result, there were fewer audiences, opportunities, and reasons for meaningful communication in Spanish.

Eventually, speaking Spanish was a controlled task, limited to a few scripted topics. Reading Richard Rodriguez's (1982) *Hunger of Memory*, I recalled my own experiences. I particularly remember the painful sound of silence around the lunch table during my family's weekly visits to my grandparents' home where Spanish was required. I managed these visits by delivering well-practiced speeches in Spanish on shopping bargains (translated from the K-Mart flyer in the newspaper) or television reruns (*Bonanza* was my grandmother and grandfather's favorite).

Except for the formulaic phrases, I lost the ability to speak Spanish by my freshman year of high school. Conscious of the perceived need to appear mainstream rather than ethnic, I chose to participate in the National Honor Society and the Pep Squad rather than the Spanish Club. Later, in search of an "easy A," I enrolled in Spanish class, taught by a very Anglo middle-aged woman from the midwest. It was in that class that I discovered I had an "innate" language ability in Spanish. My experiences with monolingualism (Spanish), then bilingualism, then monolingualism (English), then bilingualism once again have made me a complex advocate for bilingual education. Ironically, the taboo area of my early life, bilingualism, was my proverbial ticket in academia, my credential in linguistic diversity. I was hired as a bilingual graduate research assistant at the University of Arizona and, after graduation, as an assistant professor.

During a recent trip home, I attended a University of Arizona forum on family literacy. The weekend was hectic—full of meetings—and left little time for visiting. Plans to meet my extended family for dinner didn't materialize, and my mother and I found ourselves in the rare situation of being alone for the evening. Working together in the kitchen, we compared salsa recipes (mine is never as good as hers, even though I use the same ingredients) and chatted about the incredible rate at which the grandchildren are growing.

A lull in the conversation brought a seemingly simple question. My mother asked about the forum I had attended: "What do you talk about all day?" This was the first time she had ever asked me about my work—I didn't know where to begin. Going beyond the days' events, I told her about my place in the university as a bilingual person, about the politics of education, about the inequities and biases in the system, and about the need for change. I told her about this book, about my insecurities in telling my story, and about my desire to contribute as myself—alongside of, but separate from, Hollingsworth. We talked for 3 hours.

My mother filled in the gaps of my story. She told me how she and my father spoke Spanish exclusively during their courtship, how she endured much embarrassment growing up not speaking English, how she wanted to save her children from that embarrassment, and how school officials advised her to speak English "for the sake of the children." We cried, talked, and cried again. She began to understand my work, and I began to understand the decisions she had made to support my education.

Sometimes I'm embarrassed that my story lacks the heartache and adversity usually associated with minority education. My story is more subtle than the hard-luck tales of others on the margin, but it has proven to be no less powerful than other more visible and obvious barriers to learning and trusting one's self as culturally different. I've come to understand that as a woman, a Mexican American, a bilingual person, and a teacher-researcher, I have sacrificed—and continue to sacrifice—more of myself than I first realized.

The Case for the Praxis of Community Literacies in School

Gallego's struggle with her identity was clearly exacerbated by the exclusion of her native community literacy from school; at the same time, her proficiency in school literacy facilitated her success in the mainstream world. Although Hollingsworth's story is clearly different, she could also tell different-from-school experiences as a member of an international community. Both her knowledge of a worldwide community and the sense of identity she had gained living with her parents in Europe was inappropriate in U.S. schools in the late 1950s, when isolationist views were promoted. Hollingsworth would have been isolated had she challenged the idea of a "unified American nation" or the requirement to unquestioningly support the concept of "nationalism"—both of which were meaningless to the sense of herself as an international community member. Later on, working as a professional academic in international contexts, Hollingsworth had a similar experience of discovering how her community literacy had been excluded from school.

The tensions associated with incongruence between school and community literacies have been well documented in the literature (e.g., Au & Mason, 1981; Erickson & Mohatt, 1982; Foster, 1992; Heath, 1983,1991; Piestrup, 1973). No one, of course, advocates the elimination of school literacy in favor of community literacy—at least, not as long as societal values and practices still favor the dominant community language over all others. Our experiences, however, suggest that the tension between competing practices of literacy might be resolved best through praxis, not through instructional practice alone. In other words, simply practicing either school or community literacy without a perspective of praxis (or the use of critical theory in practice to achieve social justice and transformation) seems to leave the inequities of both school and community literacies firmly in place.

Gloria Ladson-Billings's notion of culturally relevant teaching as a "pedagogy of opposition that recognizes and celebrates African and African American culture" is an example of literacy practice as community-based praxis. (A reprint of her 1992 article opens Part II as Chapter 8.) Ladson-Billings argues that the primary issue in literacy instruction for African American students is not whether teachers use "whole language" or traditional literacy approaches to instruction replicating the dominant culture's literacy, but whether they use a culturally relevant approach to teaching that "fosters and sustains the students' desire to *choose* academic success in the face of so many competing options." The key is not to fit the school's culture to the students' culture, but to use the students' culture "as the basis for helping students understand themselves and others, structure social interactions, and conceptualize knowledge. . . . The primary goal of culturally relevant teaching is to empower students to examine critically the society in which they live and to work for social change."

If teachers merely advocate literacy instruction as practice in the dominant community without a perspective of praxis, then those whose primary discourse closely approximates the secondary discourse have an imbalanced advantage. Often we find that schools' attempts to include community in literacy practices are merely supplemental and still privilege the dominant community. In this section of the book we find excellent pedagogical suggestions for bringing community literacies into the classroom as well as for taking school literacy to families who practice other-than-standard literacy in their communities.

Darlene Bressler and Margorie Siegel (Chapter 9) report a study of portfolio assessment in a rural school. They describe an interactive process for linking the literacy of the child-with-family to the literacy of the child-with-school through personal interactions around a lifelike literacy assessment practice. In their examples, parents from different socioeconomic groups learn to observe and reflect upon their children's literacy experiences at home, then give feedback to their children in a portfolio conference at school. The varying responses of each child's parent to their portfolio revealed that the closer the out-of-school or community discourse approached the schooled discourse, the more likely the children were to succeed at schooled literacy. Bressler and Siegel advocate a pedagogical praxis to achieve alternative outcomes.

Without instructional praxis, students whose primary or community discourse is different from school literacy seem to be either faced with denying their cultural identities or maintaining community literacies and failing in school. Finally, students taught without a perspective of praxis seldom question the school's definition of who can be knowledgeable or school literate, but are more likely to question their own knowledge and knowledge resources and deem them inadequate. Other examples of praxis are found in Part II of this volume.

Olga A. Vásquez and Richard Durán (Chapter 10) describe an afterschool computer-based program where children's cultural and linguistic resources are integral to their academic success, unlike standard schooling in which these same attributes produce failure.

Carolyn Panofsky (Chapter 11) argues provocatively that even the seemingly politically neutral advice from schools to "read to children" at home implies that communities who do not read to children are deficient and privileges the dominant group, because the practice of reading to children is based on what the dominant community does.

Teacher-Student Relationships and Praxis

Another interesting example of praxis in the literature suggests that the social relationship between teachers and students could not only help teachers become aware of students' struggles with their own literate authority but also facilitate their students' success in literacy (see Erickson's review, 1984; Gee & Clinton, Chapter 7). Hollingsworth's 11-year relationship with a group of teachers in California taught her many things about the praxis of literacy instruction. She saw how important it was for them to develop open relationships with students and their families, both to learn about alternative community literacies and to gain insights on ways they might modify their instruction to value community literacies in the classroom. Hollingsworth named that form of instructional praxis *relational knowing* (Hollingsworth, Dybdahl, & Minarik, 1993). Since she learned the importance of relationships from these teachers, she has consciously applied her new understandings in her own university classrooms. She now engages teacher-students in sustained conversation about their lives and experiences, helping her validate both community and personal literacies as they reconstruct "standard" course content (Hollingsworth, 1994).

Elizabeth Noll (Chapter 12) writes about the role of literacy in the lives of Lakota and Dakota adolescents. She reveals the importance of multiple sign systems—language as well as art, music, and movement (dance)—in the ways that the adolescents construct and express personal meanings. Furthermore, Noll explores the impact of Native American culture, popular culture, and school culture on the adolescents' literacy expressions.

In the final chapter of this section (Chapter 13), Elba I. Reyes describes the power of teachers coanalyzing students' telling-a-story writing to change their beliefs about and relationships with Native American students enrolled in special education. After acknowledging that some students might be *nonwriters* because their cultures and communities did not include a written tradition, teachers looked at children's oral stories that were written down "so they don't forget." One teacher confessed, "I didn't know she knew any stories," and another teacher echoed that discovery: "I had him for two years and I never knew."

PERSONAL LITERACIES

In Part III, we argue that an instructional perspective of praxis that is informed by teacher-student relations can be accomplished not only by recognizing and dialectically incorporating community literacies, as shown in Part II, but also through identifying, drawing upon, and validating students' personal literacies or particular ways of knowing, being, and communicating that honor the strength of the self beyond school and community evaluations.

For us, personal literacies involve the critical awareness of ways of knowing and believing about self that comes from thoughtful examination of historical or experiential and gender-specific backgrounds in school and community language settings, and can stand as critiques to both school and community literacies. Personal literacies reflect both the ways students believe they *should* join in socially accepted discourse communities and the private ways they know they *can* and would *like* to be able to participate across communities, as well as the tensions between these views.

More than simply "images of self," personal literacies affect the way students fix or give interpretive meaning to texts. The historical reality of urban students' failure to become "school literate" through standard text-process interactions (Cordtz, 1989) becomes a personally self-fulfilling prophecy, unless educators take personal responsibility for identifying and celebrating community *and* personal literacies and make available texts that support alternative interpretations of the world. For instance, a female student might struggle to reconcile participating in class in a manner deemed appropriate for school success (quietly, respectfully) with a personal desire to challenge and critique. The exclusion of personal literacies in school is perpetuated as students who have not explored their own personal literacies become teachers, for they, in turn, are destined to suppress their students' personal literacies. Instead of feeling "wrong" because of personal (and often private) ways of reading the world, teachers who are aware of their own personal literacies might help students see that the "correct" interpretation of a textual event depends upon the boundaries of interpretive possibilities. Neither of us had such a teacher in school. Hollingsworth reveals how she came to know personal literacies in the following autobiographical story.

Hollingsworth's Story

I'm told that I started reading at about 18 months of age. While that is probably exaggerating the facts, I can't remember *not* being able to read. And, before I started school at the age of 4, I do remember doubting the "facts" in print. For example, I played with Betsy, the young daughter of my family's housekeeper, almost every day. One afternoon, while reading a stack of storybooks, Betsy and I started looking through the pictures to see if any of the people in the stories had the same color skin as Betsy. We couldn't find any. So I asked my grandmother why there were no stories about dark-skinned people. She told me that the "white" people in the story were really a "neutral" color and could be "read" as any color—just like when the Bible talks about "mankind," it really implies both men and women of all colors. I remember hearing the words, but not really understanding.

When I was about to turn seven, I invited Betsy to come to my birthday party. My grandmother held me close as she told me that "colored" children couldn't attend "white" children's parties. "Why?" I asked. "Just because that's the rule. You'll understand when you grow up." But I never did.

When I was editor of the high school newspaper in this small Texas town, I wondered why I was in a new school while Betsy's old high school had so many broken windows, and why the white high school's outdated band uniforms went to the black high school as "new." I remember reading about "separate but equal," yet our schooling experiences seemed grossly inadequate. I helped Betsy's father, the janitor for a local car dealer, put together a petition to enroll her in the white high school. After a gang of men hung her father upside down in a tree and beat him with chains, he withdrew the petition.

I went to college and graduate school. Betsy didn't . We lost track of each other somewhere along the way. Like Betsy's experience with my storybooks, I couldn't find myself in the academic literature based on "objective" research. It wasn't until I was out of graduate school and in my first position as a professor at Berkeley that I had the luxury time to explore beyond the texts I was required to read in school. Then, for the first time, I felt my personal lived experience in feminist literature. I couldn't stop reading. I began to "read" the traditional cannon through a personal and critical view. In time, I came to learn that even most of the traditional feminist literature was based on white women's experiences like mine, and I read more widely. I wondered if Betsy had ever discovered the writings of bell hooks.

Hollingsworth's long-term relationship with the teacher research group in California taught her even more about personal literacies. Group member and teacher Jennifer Davis Smallwood was often criticized by well-meaning school supervisors for not meeting school standards for directing students' interactions. Hollingsworth found that by respecting her colleague enough to suspend her personal judgment as she watched (but did not understand) Smallwood's teaching, she could discover new ways of supporting African American children's community and personal literacies. Working closely with Smallwood and Gallego, who were quite aware of how their personal ways of interacting were "right," even though they may have disagreed with community and school standards, Hollingsworth learned the feminist critique of education that suggest that teachers who are not conscious of their own personal literacies can oppress women and men from every culture and class.

The Case for Personal Literacies in School

Though many sociolinguistic and sociocultural scholars have recognized the need for community-based literacies in school, few who focus on school success speak to the need for personal literacies. Some notable exceptions are found in this volume (e.g., Gee & Clinton, Chapter 7; Myers, Hammett, & McKillop, Chapter 5; Reyes, Chapter 13). To gather a full sense of the ways in which the existence of personal literacies critiques the purpose and method of allegiance to both school and community-based literacies, it is helpful to move beyond critical ethnographies in anthropology and sociology. For Hollingsworth, the feminist literature that crosses all disciplinary boundaries has the most utility. Situated within the current transformation of Western culture, the questions about societal organizations, traditions, and processes brought by feminists are only part of a sense that the "shape of life" and literacy as they knew it is growing old.

> Something has happened, is happening, to Western societies. . . . The demise of the old is being hastened by the end of colonialism, the uprising of women, the revolt of other cultures against white Western hegemony, shifts in the balance of economic and political power within the world economy, and a growing awareness of the costs as well as the benefits of scientific and technological "progress." (Flax, 1990, p. 5)

While nonfeminist postmodernists have often pointed to these ruptures in society as causes for them to become skeptical about and deconstruct ideas of truth, knowledge, power, history, and language, they are deficient in their treatment of issues of gender and self. Feminist critiques of literature and language categories have led to interpretations of self across shifting points of view within and across discourse communities. Unitary essences about common experiences are shattered through the multiple and shifting relations of gender (see Collins, 1990). In other words, the feminist self is not essentially "authentic," but changes as roles and relationships change. Many feminist critics of standard literacies would claim the centrality of gender relations in the constitution of all categories of self, person, community, knowledge, standards, and power. Other feminists, particularly African American scholars, say it is not gender that is central, but race or class. The difference in perspective comes from differently lived experiences. Acknowledging these differences keeps feminist theory from becoming a new "master narrative," as it informs the praxis of literacy instruction. In other words, to develop personal literacies in itself is an act of personal praxis.

There is a compelling societal issue to consider if we do not begin to validate personal literacies. An example comes from the recently discovered failure of adolescent girls to maintain a personal sense of confidence and self-knowledge because they become "too competent" in conforming to a standard school literacy (Gilligan, Lyons, & Hanmer, 1990). That is, by practicing school-approved communication skills to a level of mastery, young girls often submerge and forget their own personal (and multiple) ways of speaking and relating to others. They lose their own "voices," identities, courage, and morals. Although not as well researched, the loss of personal literacy may also have a similar effect on the socialization of boys and young men. Therefore, the descriptor "feminist" should be read here in the broad sense; it not only means white, middle-class, heterosexual women, but any and all people (both male and female) who are joined by experiences of marginalization and oppression in their common struggle for social change leading to personal validation.

In Part III of this volume, several authors speak to different perspectives on personal literacies. Lisa Delpit (whose 1992 classic article is reprinted as Chapter 14) addresses the important element of identity, even as she advocates that effective teachers can and should teach minority students standard English because it is within the dominant discourse that the individuals "have the ability to transform dominant Discourses for liberatory purposes . . . [to use] European philosophical and critical standards to challenge the tenets of European belief systems." Delpit challenges personal beliefs (such as Gee's 1990 perspective might have supported) that "people who have not been born into dominant Discourses will find it exceedingly difficult, if not impossible, to acquire such a Discourse. Gee argue[d] that Discourses cannot be 'overtly' taught, particularly in a classroom, but can only be acquired by enculturation in the home or by 'apprenticeship' into social practices." By changing their personal experiences and expectations that all students can and will learn standard English, Delpit hopes to "set teachers free to teach, and thereby to liberate. When teachers are committed to teaching all students, and when they understand that through their teaching change *can* occur, the chance for transformation is great." James Gee and Kate Clinton (Chapter 7) validate Delpit's hope.

René Galindo's critique (Chapter 15) of "family literacy" is another hopeful example of the development of personal literacies. Many school-based efforts to connect families and schools, as authors in Part II point out, are based on deficit perspectives of minority families. Galindo challenges that view as he analyzes Chicana/o bilingual teachers' autobiographies to examine the connections between literacy, culture, and education in their life histories. He suggests that community literacies necessarily involve critique of the standard literacy, giving us a pedagogical challenge. He tells of teachers learning literacy listening to grandfathers at their kitchen tables, developing the courage of personal identities through the development of community literacies:

> My grandfather . . . didn't read storybooks, but would read newspapers, magazines, or whatever print was available. He would read an article and turn it into a story. He spoke Spanish but would often read from an English

newspaper, then translated it into Spanish for us. He delighted in reading Jehovah's Witnesses pamphlets and questioning their view of the Bible. He would often question us to see if we were listening to his stories. As I recall those precious times, we could never get away without analyzing and critiquing each and every story.

In these sensitive and compelling stories, the development of the teachers' personal literacies "at the kitchen table" comes alive.

Rosi Andrade, Hilda González Le Denmat, and Luis C. Moll (Chapter 16) show how an after-school literature club for (mostly) women parents led to the *Señoras'* building personal knowledge of their own culture, a closer relationship between parent and teacher, and "the process of individual self-discovery, in essence to promote literacy much in the same way as in intellectual groups." Like Galindo, Andrade, González Le Denmat, and Moll argue that instead of school indoctrination of parents to standard literacy (which is often demeaning and intimidating), the invitation from the school should be for the personal development of multiple literacies necessary to succeed in both the school and community contexts; then parents can mentor the education of their children via their own personal development. This approach to parental involvement in children's literacy development is far different from the traditional advice for parents, advice critiqued by Panofsky (see Chapter 11).

The last two chapters of Part III look at the joys and dilemmas of pedagogically developing personal literacies in selves and students. Leslie Minarik (Chapter 17) reflects on the complex task of the teacher to develop multiple literacies in children. She describes the children's "failure" at standard literacy and their "success" at personal literacies in life settings.

> I see now what was failing them: (1) a teacher who had not yet learned to recognize success in other forms, (2) a structure that continued to be alien to them and which they did not need to access to survive in their life outside of school, (3) a curriculum that was not authentic, or motivating enough to hook them into practice and mastery, and (4) role models that had not shown them that the skills or tools they have used to master drawing, debating, and basketball could be applied to reading and writing within a classroom.

Minarik's careful reflection of her own biases and capabilities as a teacher led to a revision in her personal literacies and her teaching of literacy for success.

In the final chapter, we reflect on the value of the construct of multiple literacies, given the current conservative societal climate. In every paper in this volume, the most critical and focal point is challenging a single standard of literacy to benefit *all* children. We also argue that *teachers'* self-awareness will ultimately have a greater impact on children, schooling, and society. This chapter illustrates the importance of ending, as well as beginning, with the personal.

IF SCHOOLS/SOCIETY SHARED OUR PERSPECTIVE ON LITERACY, HOW MIGHT PEOPLE'S LIVES BE DIFFERENT?

To make the text more interactive and related to real life, we asked the authors writing for this volume to read our introductory chapter and then to answer briefly this question which was suggested to us by one of our reviewers. Their answers appear at the end of their respective chapters.

Our own answer is that we imagine all students would become proficient at standard or school literacy. Students at school would also have a better sense of identity—culturally, communally, and personally. The combination of those factors would result in adults who have opportunities to choose their careers and life paths from fully informed places. We also imagine that some of the students might become teachers who would, in turn, challenge norms and restructure their living and work environments. This would result in a "balance of rights" (Au & Mason, 1981) among school, community, and personal literacies. And the relational understanding that might follow years of school where differences were not only tolerated but celebrated could lead to a more just and peaceful world.

REFERENCES

Au, K., & Mason, J. (1981). Cultural congruence in classroom participation structure: Achieving a balance of rights. *Discourse Processes, 6,* 145–167.

Beckleman, D. (1991). Defining a feminist literacy. *Canadian Women's Studies/Les Cahiers de la Femme, 9*(3/4), 133.

Bordieu, P., & Passeron, J. C. (1977). *Reproduction in education, society and culture.* London and Beverly Hills: Sage.

Chall, J. (1989). Learning to read: The great debate 20 years later. A response to "Debunking the great phonics Myth." *Phi Delta Kappan, 70,* 521–538.

Collins, P. H. (1990). *Black feminist thought: Knowledge, consciousness and the politics of empowerment.* New York: Routledge.

Cook-Gumperz, J., & Gumperz, J. (1986). *Social construction of literacy.* New York: Cambridge University Press.

Cook-Gumperz, J., Gumperz, J., & Simon, H. (1981). *School-home ethnography project.* Final report to the National Institute of Education. Washington, DC: U.S. Dept. of Education.

Cook-Gumperz, J., & Keller-Cohen, D. (1993). Alternative literacies in school and beyond: Multiple literacies of speaking and writing. *Anthropology and Education Quarterly, 24*(4), 283–287.

Cordtz, D. (1989). Dropouts: Retrieving America's labor lost. *Financial World, 158*(7), 36–46.

Cuban, L. (1990). Four stories about national goals for American education. *Phi Delta Kappan, 72*, 264–271.

Delpit, L. D. (1988). The silenced dialogue: Power and pedagogy in educating other people's children. *Harvard Educational Review, 58*(3), 280–292.

Delpit, L. D. (1992). Acquisition of literate discourse: Bowing before the master? *Theory Into Practice, 31*(4), 296–302.

Edelman, M. (1987). *Families in peril: An agenda for social change.* Cambridge, MA: Harvard University Press.

Engle, S., & Ochoa, A. (1988). *Education for democratic citizenship: Decision making in the social studies.* New York: Teachers College Press.

Erickson, F. (1984). School literacy, reasoning and civility: An anthropologist's perspective. *Review of Educational Research, 54*(4), 525–546.

Erickson, F., & Mohatt, G. (1982). Cultural organization and participation in two classrooms of Indian students. In G. Spindler (Ed.), *Doing the ethnography of schooling* (pp. 131–174). New York: Holt, Rinehart & Winston.

Fine, M. (1993). "You can't just say that the only ones who can speak are those who agree with your position": Political discourse in the classroom. *Harvard Educational Review, 63*(4), 412–433.

Flax, J. (1990). *Thinking fragments: Psychoanalysis, feminism, and postmodernism in the contemporary West.* Berkeley: University of California Press.

Foster, M. (1992). Sociolinguistics and the African-American community: Implications for literacy. *Theory Into Practice, 31*(4), 303–311.

Freire, P. (1972). *Pedagogy of the oppressed.* London: Penguin.

Freire, P., & Macedo, D. (1987). *Literacy: Reading the word and the world.* South Hadley, MA: Bergin & Garvey.

Gallego, M. A., & Hollingsworth, S. (1992). Multiple literacies: Teachers' evolving perceptions. *Language Arts, 69*(3), 206–213..

Gee, J. (1990). *Social linguistics and literacies: Ideology in discourses.* New York: Falmer Press.

Gilligan, C., Lyons, N. P., & Hanmer, T. J. (1990*). Making connections: The relational worlds of adolescent girls at Emma Willard School.* Cambridge, MA: Harvard University Press.

Goldberg, N. (1988). *Writing down the bones: Freeing the writer within.* Boston: Shambahala.

Graff, H. (1979). *The literacy myth: Literacy and social structure in the 19th century city.* New York: Academic Press.

Heath, S. B. (1983). *Ways with words: Language, life and work in communities and classrooms.* Cambridge, U.K.: Cambridge University Press.

Heath, S. B. (1991). The sense of being literate: Historical and cross-cultural features. In R. Barr, M. L. Kamil, P. B. Mosenthal, & P. D. Peterson (Eds.), *Handbook of reading research, Vol. 2* (pp. 3–25). New York: Longman.

Hirsch, E. D., Jr. (1987). *Cultural literacy: What every American needs to know*. Boston: Houghton Mifflin.

Hollingsworth, S. (1994). Feminist pedagogy in the research class: An example of teacher research. *Educational Action Research, 2*(1), 457–479.

Hollingsworth, S., Dybdahl, M., & Minarik, L. T. (1993). By chart and chance and passion: Learning to teach through relational knowing. *Curriculum Inquiry, 23*(1), 5–36.

Hollingsworth, S., & Gallego, M. A. (1996). Toward a collaborative praxis of multiple literacies. *Curriculum Inquiry, 26*(3), 265–292.

Ladson-Billings, G. (1992). Reading between the lines and beyond the pages: A culturally relevant approach to literacy teaching. *Theory Into Practice, 31*(4), 312–320.

Luke, C., & Gore, J. (1992). *Feminisms and critical pedagogy*. New York: Routledge.

Mehan, H. (1974). Accomplishing classroom lessons. In A. V. Cicourel, K. H. Jennings, S. H. M. Jennings, K. C. W. Leither, R. McKay, J. Mehan, & D. Roth (Eds.), *Language use and school performance* (pp. 76–142). New York: Academic Press.

Mikulecky, L. (1990). National adult literacy and life-long learning goals. *Phi Delta Kappan, 72*, 304–309.

Nespor, J. (1991). The construction of school knowledge: A case study. In C. Mitchell & K. Theyiler (Eds.), *Rewriting literacy: Culture and the discourse of the other* (pp. 169–188). Toronto, Can.: Ontario Institute for Studies in Education [OISE] Press.

Piestrup, A. M. (1973). *Black dialect interference and accommodation of reading instruction in the first grade* (Monographs of the Language Behavior Research Lab). Berkeley: University of California.

Rich, A. (1979). Claiming an education. In A. Rich (Ed.), *Lies, secrets and silence* (pp. 231–237). New York: Norton.

Rodriguez, R. (1982). *Hunger of memory*. New York: Bantam Books.

Siegel, M., & Bressler, D. (1993, December). *Researching multiple literacies*. Research workshop at the National Reading Conference, Charleston, S C.

Walsh, C. E. (1991). *Literacy as praxis: Culture, language, and pedagogy*. Norwood, NJ: Ablex.

Weiner, G. (1994, April). *Educational research and pedagogy in an unjust world: Developing feminist praxis*. Paper presented at the annual meeting of the American Educational Research Association, New Orleans, LA.

Williams, R. (1983). *The year 2000*. New York: Pantheon.

PART I

School Literacies

We have defined *school literacies* as:

> the learning of interpretive and communicative processes needed to adapt socially to school and other dominant language contexts, and the use or practice of those processes in order to gain a conceptual understanding of school subjects.

Lauren Resnick's classic article, "Literacy In School and Out," opens Part I. It helps the reader clarify the notion that literacy, as taught in school, is not the only legitimate form of literacy. Resnick and the other authors in this section speak to the richer and fuller ways students can aquire literacy in school to help them wholly participate in life outside of school.

2

Literacy In School and Out

LAUREN B. RESNICK

To understand the literacy crisis and imagine possible solutions, it is essential to examine the nature of literacy practice outside school as well as within. Schools are too isolated from everyday ways of using the written word to serve as the only source of literacy competence in society. Young people need to function as apprentices in communities where people use the written word for practical, informational, and pleasurable purposes. To change our general levels of literacy, efforts to provide such literacy apprenticeships in the community and at work, as well as in the schools, are needed.

We are told there is a literacy crisis in the United States. Nearing the end of the twentieth century, we have still not succeeded in educating a fully literate citizenry, a goal that was articulated by our founding fathers and that motivated creation of what is probably the most inclusive public education system in the world. As the structure of the economy changes, America's declining ability to compete is attributed to workers' inadequate literacy and numeracy. All of this fuels demands for educational reform, mostly calling for tougher standards and higher rates of high school completion. It is assumed that school is the agency responsible for the nation's level of literacy, and that if schools just did their jobs more skillfully and resolutely, the literacy problem would be solved.

I will challenge that assumption in this essay. School is only one of many social forces, institutionalized and not, that determine the nature and extent of the nation's literacy. To understand the literacy crisis and imagine possible solutions, it is essential to examine the nature of literacy practice outside school as well as within. Continuing an earlier analysis of the relationship between mental work as it is performed outside school and the practices of the schools (Resnick, 1987), I examine here several different ways in which people engage with the written word. Since literacy

Chapter 2, Literacy In School and Out, by Lauren B. Resnick reprinted by permission of *Dædalus*, Journal of the American Academy of Arts and Sciences, from the issue entitled, "Literacy in America," spring 1990, Vol. 119, No. 2. Used by permission.

practice outside school has been the object of very little systematic research, my analysis is suggestive rather than definitive. Nevertheless, it is possible to see that there are important discontinuities between school literacy practices and literacy outside school. These discontinuities make it doubtful that schools alone can successfully address the problem.

In most discussions of the literacy crisis, it is assumed that literacy is an acquired ability that characterizes individuals; people either possess literacy skills or they do not. The *practice* of literacy, the social conditions under which people actually engage in literate activities, is not examined. Although cognitive scientists and other students of literacy have done much to reveal the invisible mental processes involved in reading and making sense of written texts, most have worked on a widely shared assumption that these processes are, at most, only peripherally affected by the social contexts in which people read and write. It is assumed that individuals carry literacy skills in their heads. As a result, the nature of the situation in which people "do" literacy is not thought to alter the nature of the process.

I adopt here, as a heuristic for understanding literacy more deeply, a shift in epistemological perspective. Instead of asking what constitutes literacy competency or ability, terms that invite efforts to list the skills and knowledge possessed by individuals who are judged literate, I want to examine literacy as a set of cultural practices that people engage in. Taking this perspective does not deny that people engaging in literate activity must be knowledgeable and skillful in particular ways. However, examining literacy as a set of cultural practices rather than as skills or abilities leads to questions that are not often posed in discussions of the literacy crisis. These are questions about the kinds of situations in which literacy is practiced, that is, in which people engage with written texts. *Who* are the actors—both readers and writers—in these situations? How do they define themselves in relation to the texts they engage with, to each other, to other people who may also engage with those texts? *Why* are they reading and writing? What are they attempting to do with the written word? What kinds of institutional or broadly social invitations, permissions, and constraints influence their activities? *How* do people read and write? What are the processes, cognitive and social, that define literate practices? Finally, *what* do people read and write? What are the texts themselves like, and how do their characteristics facilitate particular forms of literate practice?

The shift in perspective from personal skill to cultural practice carries with it implications for a changed view of teaching and instruction. If literacy is viewed as a bundle of skills, then education for literacy is most naturally seen as a matter of organizing effective lessons: that is, diagnosing skill strengths and deficits, providing appropriate exercises in developmentally felicitous sequences, motivating students to engage in these exercises, giving clear explanations and directions. But if literacy is viewed as a set of cultural practices, then education for literacy is more naturally seen as a process of socialization, of induction into a community of literacy practicers. The best model (*metaphor* is perhaps a more accurate term) we have for such induction into communities of practice is the ancient one of apprenticeship. *Apprenticeship* has largely dropped out of our educational vocabulary but warrants revival in new forms.

The heart of apprenticeship as a mode of learning is coached practice in actual tasks of production, with decreasing degrees of support from the master or more advanced colleagues. This practice takes place in the context of preparing a product that is socially valued. In traditional craft apprenticeships, there was far less direct instruction than we are used to in schools and relatively little decontextualized practice of component skills. Instead, by working collaboratively, often on tasks they could not yet accomplish entirely on their own, apprentices practiced in a context that both motivated work and gave it meaning. A series of increasingly complex production tasks through which apprentices progressed provided the equivalent of a curriculum. The conditions of work and learning made it possible to rely on considerable self-correction, with apprentices judging their own products against criteria established through extensive observation and discussion of the group's products. Several recent experimental programs have demonstrated possibilities for adapting elements of traditional apprenticeship forms to education in complex cognitive practices of literacy and mathematics (Collins, Brown, & Newman, 1989). These programs attempt to establish communities of literate practice in which children can participate under special forms of guidance. Such programs try to make usually hidden mental processes overt, and they encourage student observation and commentary. They also allow skills to build up bit by bit, yet permit participation in meaningful work even for the relatively unskilled, often as a result of sharing the tasks among several participants.

In this essay I consider briefly several different kinds of literacy practice and attempt to characterize each in ways that respond to the *who, why, how,* and *what* questions raised earlier. For each, I begin by sketching skilled adult practices as a way of setting a "developmental target"—a possible educational goal. I then try to imagine "beginner" forms of that practice, forms that might characterize the early stages of apprenticeship in literacy. This educational thought experiment provides a template for assessing school literacy practice. How much apprenticeship opportunity does the school typically provide? How might the school be organized to provide more such opportunity? How much of the job of educating a literate citizenry can the school alone be expected to do? In light of this analysis of literacy as situated activity, I then reexamine the nature of the literacy crisis and propose some institutional responses that may be necessary for change.

THREE FORMS OF LITERACY PRACTICE

Literacy is practiced in situations in which people engage with written texts. The range of literacy situations is vast and varied. In earlier work (Resnick & Resnick, in press), we identified, without claiming to be exhaustive, six major categories of literacy activity: the sacred (using print in religious practice and instruction); the useful (using print to mediate practical activities); the informational (using print to convey or acquire knowledge); the pleasurable (reading for the fun of it); the persuasive (using print to influence the behavior or beliefs of others); and the personal-familial (using letters to stay in touch with family and friends). Here I consider three of these categories that are most frequently cited as literacy objectives of the school—the useful, the informational, and the pleasurable.

Useful Literacy

A common type of literacy practice is the use of written texts to mediate action in the world. Some everyday examples of such practical literacy include reading recipes, following instructions for assembling or manipulating equipment, and consulting bus or airline schedules. These are among the kinds of activities that appear on functional literacy tests such as the recent National Assessment of Educational Progress. The class of useful literacy practices would also include writing letters of inquiry, filling out job applications, and leaving notes for coworkers. Readers come to functional literacy practice of this kind with very immediate goals, usually assuming that the text is authoritative and can successfully guide action. They willingly follow the author's plan of action in order to accomplish a specific task.

   This action-oriented stance shapes the nature of the reading process. Consider, for example, texts that provide instructions for action on physical systems. To engage successfully as a reader of such texts, one must relate each proposition in the text to a specific set of physical objects, infer relationships among those objects, and plan actions on them. In the simplest form of practical literacy, this is done with the objects present. Under these conditions, the physical objects substantially assist the reader in making sense of the text. Research on the processes of following directions shows that readers of such texts shift attention back and forth between the text and the physical display. Furthermore, there is evidence that diagrams, when available, are relied on to a great extent, and that readers often favor the information in diagrams when text and figures conflict. In this kind of literacy activity, the reader needs to construct only a limited mental representation of the situation described by the text, because the elements of the situation are physically present, and it is possible to act directly on them. Furthermore, the physical results of one's actions often provide continuous (if only partial) information about whether one has correctly interpreted the text and diagrams.

A more cognitively demanding form of practical literacy requires readers to make inferences about the state of a physical system from textual materials, without being able to see or interact with the physical system directly. In these situations, a more complete mental representation must be constructed by the reader, with less supportive help from the physical environment. This kind of processing is necessary, for example, when texts are read in anticipation of action—that is, preparing to do something without actually doing it. Some simple examples of anticipatory practical reading are using a bus schedule to decide when to go to the bus stop, and reading a recipe to determine if a shopping trip is needed before cooking can begin. More complex examples can be found in automated work situations in which the actual physical labor is done by machines, while workers monitor and adjust those machines on the basis of their readings of various indicators (Zuboff, 1988). To perform such tasks, workers need a complex mental model of the physical system on which they are operating, a model whose immediate states can be updated on the basis of indicator readings. As such jobs proliferate, a new standard of technical literacy is developing. As in more "hands-on" practical literacy, the reader must be able to act on a physical environment, but a much greater effort of purely mental representation is required.

Practical literacy also includes uses of texts to help one act in and on social systems. Tax forms and job applications are of this type. Such forms are used much like instructions for physical systems—that is, in step-by-step fashion, reading a line, then immediately following the instructions given. To participate effectively in this form of literacy, one needs only to understand each line of the instructions and to be willing to persist through many steps. A more general mental model of a situation—of tax rules, for example, or of what a potential employer might be seeking—can help in this step-by-step interpretation but is not strictly necessary. Thus, in this kind of literacy, there is only a limited requirement for mental representation. There are also less formulaic texts that help people act in a social system. Such texts might, for example, guide one in using services of a health care system, initiating grievance proceedings against an employer, or choosing among insurance options. When using these texts, the reader needs to construct a mental model of the system as a whole before it becomes possible to decide how to act.

How do people learn to engage in practical literacy? It is not difficult to imagine an apprenticeship in the functional use of texts occurring within families. With a parent or other older person, a child as young as 4 or 5 can participate in an activity in which a text is used to guide physical acts (assembling a game or following a recipe, for example). Very young children cannot yet read the texts themselves, but they can observe important aspects of the practical literacy form such as the ways in which one alternates between reading the text and carrying out a physical act, or the fact that the text is used to verify accuracy of action. By 8 or 9 years of age, a child participating with an adult might do some or even all of the reading but would not be expected to figure out alone exactly what actions were prescribed. Later, the child might do most of the work alone, calling for occasional help in interpreting certain difficult words or steps. This kind of "scaffolded" learning has been well analyzed and described for a number of typical family activities as well as for learning in traditional craft apprenticeships. Regular engagement in such activities in the family or other extra-school settings probably helps children develop a generalized pattern of interacting with texts ("read-do, read-do") and a broad confidence that enables them to use texts to guide practical activity on their own (Lave, 1988; Rogoff, 1990).

Such practical literacy apprenticeships, however, are largely absent from school. The reading done in school seldom mediates any practical action in the world, and there is hardly ever a chance to work side by side with a more skillful partner toward a shared goal. An exception may be found in the science laboratory. Science educators often complain that too much time is spent setting up experiments and too little on interpreting them. Yet students may learn something about a very basic form of practical literacy from these exercises—to the extent that they get to participate in them. Much elementary-level science instruction proceeds from textbooks rather than laboratories, and the students whose functional literacy is a source of public worry almost never take upper-level science courses. Vocational courses offer another potential site for functional literacy practice in school. Often, however, functional literacy skills are *prerequisite* to entering vocational courses, rather than what can be learned in them. A result is that the students most in need of this form of literacy practice are excluded from the opportunity for practice. Significant opportunities for functional literacy activity also occur in some extracurricular school activities. There is evidence, however, that, with the exception of sports, extracurricular participation in high school is largely limited to the more academically inclined and successful students and does not include those for whom functional literacy development is a concern.

These observations suggest that, if school were the only place in which people learned literate practices, we would probably observe far less functional literacy in the general population than we do. It seems likely that the many people who become competent at various forms of functional literacy develop their initial competence outside school, through participation with family members and friends. If functional literacy practices are learned mainly outside school, however, certain students—those from families who do not practice much literacy in the home or do not engage their children in such activities—can be expected not to learn them.

Informational Literacy

People also read to learn about the world when there is no immediate practical utility for the information acquired. In this kind of literacy activity, the only likely immediate activity after reading is discussion with others. The reader's main task is to build a mental representation of the situation presented in the text and to relate the new information to previously held knowledge. This process of text comprehension has been intensively studied by cognitive scientists. From their research, we know that building mental *situation models* on the basis of a text requires much more than an ability to recognize the words—a level of literacy ability that few people in this country lack. Rather, it depends crucially on the reader's prior knowledge, along with certain general linguistic abilities. It is also highly sensitive to aspects of the text structure, including rhetorical devices, signals about the relationships among sections of the text, and the extent to which suppositions and arguments are laid out explicitly.

One aspect of informational reading that has not been much studied is how the reader interprets the author's intention and what knowledge the reader attributes to the author—what we might call building an *author model*. Furthermore, cognitive science has paid almost no attention to what the reader expects to do with the information gained from the text, or to the social context of either the reading or subsequent information use. All of these can be expected to influence reading activity substantially.

A wide range of intentions, from personal interest and wanting to know what people are talking about to needing background knowledge for one's profession, can motivate informational reading. Some forms of informational reading can have eventual practical aims, even though immediate action is neither called for nor possible. For example, many advice and "how-to" texts—ranging from household hints and Ann Landers columns to books offering guidance in personal finance or business management—are geared not to individual situations, but to prototypical situations that many people encounter. When reading such texts, people have to imagine themselves in others' situations in order to find useful information for themselves. To do this, they must not only build a mental representation of the situation described in the text, but also relate the situation described to their own.

In everyday life, probably the most frequent kind of informational literacy activity is newspaper and magazine reading. For most people, reading the news is a matter of "keeping up"—finding out what is going on in the world, updating one's mental accounts of ongoing events. Although such reading appears to be a private activity, it is socially defined in two important senses. First, informational reading is often followed by discussion with others of like interests, and what one chooses to read in a news-1paper probably depends to an important degree on what kinds of conversations one anticipates. People may keep up with sports, for example, in order to join the talk at work or follow local news because that is discussed at parties or while attending to business in town. What we find it necessary to "keep up with" is determined partly by the people with whom we associate and the conversational habits of that group. If one is not in a social circle that discusses national and international political events, those parts of the newspaper will probably not receive attention. Thus, everyday informational reading is a function of the social groups with whom one interacts.

A second sense in which reading is socially defined is that the kind of mental representation constructed from the reading depends on the kinds of intentions one ascribes to the authors. American newspaper readers expect journalists to be both knowledgeable and neutral, to convey the facts fully and without bias. Except when reading signed columns and editorials, readers do not devote much attention to determining the newswriters' persuasive intentions, what political positions are represented, or what might have been left out of the communication. In contrast, continental European newspaper readers do not assume neutrality; newspapers and newswriters have known political positions, and readers interpret their articles in this light. People trying to get the whole picture of some important event are likely to read several different news reports because they expect an interpretive slant in each report. In countries with active press censorship, readers must go even further to read between the lines in order to learn what is happening in the world. These different social assumptions can cause differences in the cognitive processes involved in reading. The American assumption of a neutral press, together with a relative absence of political discussion in everyday life, probably has the effect of providing our people with minimal practice in critical textual interpretation. Americans have little experience in looking for authors' intentions or hidden meanings or tracking down missing parts of an argument. Although many become fluent at constructing text and situation models, they have little practice at building author models.

Imagined author-reader relations also play a role in the process of writing informational texts. In actual literacy practice, authors writing informational texts have, in the best cases, a lively sense of their audience. They are used to crafting their communications to appeal to imagined readers. Definitions of what constitutes a well-crafted text vary among social communities of readers and writers. Broad distinctions between popular and scholarly writing do not do justice to the variety and distinctiveness of what have come to be called "discourse communities." The readers of different segments of the popular press expect different forms of writing. In recent years, a lively analysis of the varied ways in which different scholarly disciplines shape their written discourse has emerged, and students of literacy have begun to speak of processes of initiation into these discourse communities, referring both to practices of interpretive reading and to those of authoring.

Informal, family-based opportunities for apprenticeship in these informational literacy practices are probably less available than are practical literacy apprenticeship opportunities. Not all families regularly read and discuss the information in newspapers or magazines, and most such reading is limited to particular narrow segments of the press. Reading of informational books occurs in only a limited number of families. And even among children growing up in our most literate families, few ever get to observe—much less participate in—the process of actually creating an extended informational text for an interested audience.

More than for practical literacy, it seems, we depend on the school as the place in which informational literacy will be cultivated. School is the time and place in most people's lives when they are most intensively engaged in reading for information. Indeed, other than newspapers, textbooks provide most Americans' only practice of informational literacy. A populace with the capacity and taste for engaging in informational literacy activities, particularly as they bear on public and civic issues, is part of the Jeffersonian vision of democracy. It is a major reason for treating universal public education as a requirement for a democratic society. But as education has developed, very little literacy practice in school engages students in activities from which they might learn the habits and skills of using texts to understand public issues and participate in public decision making. A consideration of the actual activity of textbook reading in school shows that it is a very different form of literacy practice from the informational reading that might be envisioned as part of the Jeffersonian ideal. Differences can be found in the intentions that people bring to school-text reading as opposed to other kinds of informational texts, in the nature of the texts themselves, in the kinds of background knowledge they bring to the reading, and in the rhythm of the activity itself.

When texts are assigned in school, they are almost always on topics new to students, for which the students must build initial mental representations. Textbook reading thus provides little experience in updating mental models, as occurs when keeping up with the news. Worse still, school textbooks are often badly written, a jumble of bits of information without the coherence needed to support this initial building of a representation (Beck, McKeown, & Gromoll, 1989; Tyson-Bernstein, 1988). Finally, and perhaps most important, students in school read textbooks because of an assignment or a test to be passed, not because they are personally interested in the topic or expect lively conversation about it with others. In many classrooms, there is a catechetical flavor to the way that texts are assigned and used. Small sections are read, and students are expected to give specific, generally noninterpretive answers to questions posed by the teacher. Informational writing experience is, if anything, more restricted. For the most part, if students write informational or analytical texts at all, it is to show teachers that they have done the required reading and absorbed the canonical interpretation. The normal relationship between author (as someone who knows something of interest) and reader (as someone who would like to learn about that something) is absent or seriously attenuated. The typical audience for student writing is only the teacher, who already knows (or is thought to know) all the information conveyed. For the large majority of students, then, no place—neither home nor school—provides an extended opportunity to engage in high levels of authentic informational literacy practice.

Pleasurable Literacy

Being literate can also mean reading for pleasure, a form of literacy practice in which reading is its own end. The kinds of texts that people read for the fun of reading are diverse, and the cognitive and social processes engaged are equally different. Narratives—texts with a story line, whether fictional or based in reality—are generally considered to be the material of pleasurable reading, although some people read expository texts that might be classed as information just for the fun of it. Engagement with the text is the primary requisite for pleasurable literacy, and many kinds of texts—from pulp crime stories and Gothic romances to high literature—are capable of providing that engagement. Different kinds of texts, of course, require differing degrees and types of interpretive activity; what is engaging for some may be too difficult or too simple to engage others.

Cognitive scientists have given substantially less attention to the processes involved in pleasurable reading than to the processes of informational and practical literacy, although some psychologists with more interest in motivation and consciousness (including Mihaly Csikszentmihalyi, 1990) have tried to understand the nature of psychological engagement with a story. The nature of fiction reading is also, of course, a major concern of literary theory and criticism. Proponents of a recent literary theory are now exploring the many personal goals served by pleasurable reading—from escape and imagining oneself in more satisfying conditions (as in reading romance stories; see Radway, 1984) to stimulating and resolving curiosity (as in reading mysteries) to penetrating cultures and life situations to which one does not have personal access. Psychologists and literary scholars seem to agree that readers of popular stories—mysteries, romances, and the like—focus all energies on understanding the situation described and perhaps on imagining themselves in that situation. This engagement with the story contrasts with what some would reserve as truly "literary" reading, which involves deliberate attention to language and expressive device. This aspect of literary reading distinguishes it from more popular forms of pleasurable literacy in which language is "transparent," unattended to in its own right, just a vehicle for conveying a story.

At first look, pleasurable literacy seems to fare better than informational literacy in terms of apprenticeship opportunities. For many children, pleasurable literacy practice begins in being read to by parents. The process by which children who are regularly read to gradually appropriate the reading act for themselves is often used as a model of how apprenticeship in cultural practice might work for literacy. Encouragement of parents to read to and with their children and extensive reading aloud to children in preschools and kindergartens represent efforts to extend these forms of apprenticeship opportunity to more children.

Similar efforts are made throughout the elementary grades in many schools. Finding pleasure in reading is frequently stressed as a goal of reading instruction. In support of this goal, books of interest to children are made available, and children are encouraged to read them. Time is allowed in the school week for free-choice reading programs and reading for which children are not formally accountable, although they are encouraged to discuss or even write about their reading. Many civic programs aimed at supporting literacy development in schools also stress the pleasurable aspects of literacy. Such programs, which include bookmobiles and other community access programs organized by public libraries, programs that distribute children's books to families at no or low cost, and programs in which volunteers either read to schoolchildren or listen to the children read, focus either implicitly or explicitly on the pleasures of reading.

The motivation for such emphasis on reading for pleasure is partly based on sound pedagogy. We know that reading skill develops best when there is massive practice in reading, and children (like adults) are more likely to read a lot when they enjoy the process of reading as well as its possible practical or informational outcomes. But educators and civic organizations also stress reading for pleasure because they recognize it as an authentic form of literacy practice; a more literate nation would engage in more reading for its own sake. With respect to pleasurable literacy, then, more than for the useful or the informational, many schools and surrounding institutions seem to be reaching for authentic forms of practice.

Yet the programs that seem to provide some pleasurable literacy apprenticeship opportunities represent a very limited part of the school experience of most students. For most Americans, the only extended discussion of literature they are likely to encounter is in school. But even a brief consideration of the ways in which literature reading is organized in school suggests a fundamental discontinuity with the features of pleasurable reading as we engage in it outside school.

A key—perhaps the defining—feature of pleasurable reading is that one picks up and puts down a book or a story at will. There is no need to prove to others that one has read, although sharing opinions about books is not uncommon among those who read for pleasure. In schooling, by contrast, literature is usually doled out in daily assignments. Not only what one is to read, but also the pace of the reading is imposed. Reading ahead if one is captivated and engaged by the story is not encouraged and may be subtly punished. Proving that one has read the assigned material by answering questions about it or writing book reports is central to school literacy. Not infrequently, literature study is turned into a kind of catechism—a canonic set of readings, standard questions, and expected answers. These activities implicitly carry a message that reading is not a pleasure in its own right. As a result, students who have not acquired a sense of the pleasures of reading elsewhere may not easily acquire it through standard schooling practice, especially after the primary grades.

LITERACY APPRENTICESHIPS

The preceding analyses suggest that the schools are not the only—or perhaps even the primary—source of literacy competence. As we have seen, dominant school practice is so mismatched to the ways in which practical, informational, and pleasurable literacy activities take place in everyday life that it seems highly unlikely that schools alone are responsible for the levels of literacy practice we observe in society. We must understand the nation's literacy—or lack of it—in terms of the kinds of literacy apprenticeships that are available to young people. For many, these apprenticeship opportunities are severely limited. In order to substantially change literacy practices in the nation, we cannot simply call for raising school standards. Without a broad cultural shift in the direction of more interpretive literacy activity in all segments of adult society, we cannot expect young people to acquire the skills and habits of literacy practice.

Schools could become sites for true literacy apprenticeship, but fundamental shifts in school practice would be required. What is called for are school activities in which students have extensive reason to use written texts in the ways that characterize out-of-school practical, informational, and pleasurable literacy. A number of experimental programs now in use point to the possibilities. These programs share features of apprenticeship environments: children work to produce a product that will be used by others (e.g., they produce a book on a history topic that is then used to teach others, or they collect data that are used to produce a scientific report); they work collaboratively, but under conditions in which individuals are held responsible for their work; they use tools and apparatus appropriate to the problem; they read and critique each other's writing; they are called upon to elaborate and defend their own work until it reaches a community standard. We know considerably more about how to design and manage such environments than we do about how to get schools to adopt and maintain them. Educational programs are often adopted enthusiastically by a few schools during an experimental phase and then abandoned in favor of conventional school literacy forms, often in the wake of calls for a return to "the basics" and the practices that adult citizens recall from their own school days. Apparently, the school system cannot move far ahead of the general culture.

To "bootstrap" ourselves into new levels of literacy participation, I believe we must actively develop other institutions for literacy practice. These can function jointly with schools in the best circumstances or independently when necessary. We need multiple apprenticeship sites where children and youth can spend significant amounts of time working among people who are using the written word for practical, informational, and pleasurable purposes. For younger children, community centers, churches, and other agencies could play this role. Many children now attend after-school and weekend programs at such centers, and there is some evidence that participation in community programs is positively related to school and later work performance. For the most part, however, these agencies offer child care and recreational programs but make no attempt to provide literacy-related activities. When after-school or summer programs are offered with the intention of improving school performance, they usually mimic school conditions rather than provide truly alternative occasions for literacy practice. We need new forms of community programs aimed at developing literacy through apprenticeship. For older students—at least from the beginning of high school—participating (preferably with pay) at real work sites is probably the best way to experience literacy practice, along with training in a variety of social skills and habits that are essential to work performance. Such on-the-job participation would not only provide natural apprenticeships for literacy, but might also solve important motivational problems resulting from some students' belief that even good school performance will not assure them access to jobs and other forms of economic participation.

These proposals follow from the shift in perspective with which I began this essay. When we stop thinking about literacy as a collection of skills and begin to view it as a form of cultural practice, we are led to consider the multiple ways in which young people are socialized into the practices of their societies. Although there is room for improvement, schools appear to be doing reasonably well at teaching the basic skills of literacy. But, at least as currently organized, schools are too isolated from everyday ways of using the written word to serve as the only sites for learning literacy practice. For some young people, family, community life, and, eventually, work provide informal apprenticeship opportunities for various literacy practices. For many others, though, these apprenticeship opportunities are unavailable. Unless organized efforts are made to provide literacy apprenticeship environments for these young people, there seems to be little hope of change in our general levels of literacy participation. There is historical precedent for looking outside schools for major changes in literacy levels in a population. Europe's earliest literacy drives took place in homes and churches. Recent literacy campaigns—for example, in Cuba and China—have looked to institutions such as citizen armies for literacy education. In past efforts of this kind, only very basic forms of literacy were sought. Today's challenge is greater, and the relatively simple forms of literacy activity that sufficed for basic literacy campaigns cannot be expected to succeed. But with imagination and perseverance, we should be able to develop places and forms for apprenticeship that can effectively reshape literacy practice in our society.

REFERENCES

Beck, I. L., McKeown, M. G., & Gromoll, E. W. (1989). Learning from social studies texts. *Cognition and Instruction, 6*(2), 99–158.

Collins, A., Brown, J. S., & Newman, S. E. (1989). Cognitive apprenticeship: Teaching the crafts of reading, writing, and mathematics. In L. B. Resnick (Ed.), *Knowing, learning, and instruction: Essays in honor of Robert Glaser*. Hillsdale, NJ: Earlbaum.

Csikszentmihalyi, M. (1990, Spring). Literacy and intrinsic motivation. *Daedalus, 119*(2), 115–140.

Lave, J. (1988). *The culture of acquisition and the practice of understanding* (Report number IRL 88–0007). Palo Alto, CA: Institute for Research on Learning.

Radway, J. A. (1984). *Reading the romance: Women, patriarchy and popular literature.* Chapel Hill: University of North Carolina Press.

Resnick, L. B. (1987, December). Learning in school and out. *Educational Researcher, 16*(9), 13–20.

Resnick, D. P., & Resnick, L. B. (in press). Varieties of literacy. In A. E. Barnes and P. N. Sternes (Eds.), *Social history and human issues in human consciousness: Interdisciplinary connections*. New York: New York University Press.

Rogoff, B. (1990). *Apprentices in thinking: Children's guided participation in culture.* New York: Oxford University Press.

Tyson-Bernstein, H. (1988). *A conspiracy of good intentions: America's textbook fiasco.* Washington, DC: Council for Basic Education.

Zuboff, S. (1988). *In the age of the smart machine: The future of work and power.* New York: Basic Books.

3

Exploring Sign Systems Within an Inquiry System

KATHY G. SHORT AND GLORIA KAUFFMAN

The students sat quietly, lost in their own thoughts, as the last words of *The Barn* (Avi, 1994) reverberated through the classroom. Gloria had chosen to read aloud this short chapter book to her intermediate multiage students because of their interest in immigration and the topic "Having a Better Life." Their intent faces showed that this story of three children who build their dying father a barn in 1855 had touched them deeply. "Oh, I just *need* to draw," sighed Ramon. Gloria responded, "Do you need time to think through your feelings and connections before we talk?" Students nodded their heads. She suggested that they respond in any way they needed in order to think about the book and reminded them of the many sign system tools available—musical recordings, the keyboard, art materials, journals, masks, puppets, dress-up clothing, and mathematical manipulatives.

The students quickly spread throughout the room. Cynthia wrote in her log about her feelings related to the father's death and the children's loneliness. Camille put on the headphones and composed music on the keyboard to get at the feeling of the cold place where the father was buried. Reuben, Matthew, and Tommy looked through musical recordings and chose a pastoral piece by Beethoven, which they played as they discussed scenes from the book that were important to them. They then moved to pen and ink drawings of the same scenes while the music continued to play. Other children used watercolors, tempera paint, pastels, chalk, charcoal, or pencil sketches to visually portray images from the book that reflected their emotional responses. Ramon experimented with pastels, gradating colors from cool to warm in his picture of a lamp spreading warmth across the dying father. Several children reread the ending of the book, and an-

What Counts as Literacy: Challenging the School Standard. Copyright © 2000 by Teachers College, Columbia University. All rights reserved. ISBN 0-8077-3972-3 (paper), ISBN 0-8077-3973-1 (cloth). Prior to photocopying items for classroom use, please contact the Copyright Clearance Center, Customer Service, 222 Rosewood Drive, Danvers, MA 01923, USA, telephone (508) 750-8400.

other small group talked about the father's death and the children's need to create community. The next day, the class gathered for a meeting to talk about their responses to the novel.

Several weeks later, Kathy and Gloria interviewed the children, asking them whether responding first in many different sign systems influenced their thinking. Camille was the first to comment: "I can express my feelings and try out ideas I have in my mind about the book." Adam added, "I can learn more about the book and understand how it felt to live during that time." Michelle commented, "I can make more connections." "Yes," Matthew agreed, "I can experience the emotions of the children in the story." The students felt that trying out ideas in their minds and in the various sign systems helped them understand more about the book and changed how they talked about the book with each other.

These children's responses demonstrate the significance of multiple sign systems within an inquiry curriculum. Our current focus on sign systems and inquiry grew out of our collaboration with students and their need to have many ways of thinking and sharing available to them in order to engage more fully in pursuing questions within the classroom that are significant in their own lives. In this chapter, we define what we mean by sign systems and provide an overview of some of our initial efforts to bring a sign system perspective into the classroom. Out of those efforts, we have developed a curricular model that supports our current approach to sign systems within inquiry. This model will be discussed using examples from Gloria's classroom, which we collaboratively collected through fieldnotes, teaching journals, videotaping, audiotaping, student artifacts, and interviews.

THE ROLE OF SIGN SYSTEMS AND TRANSMEDIATION IN LEARNING

Part of being human is our ability to use literacy to think and communicate. Sign systems are all the ways in which humans share and make meaning, including music, art, mathematics, movement, drama, and oral and written language. We use these sign systems to think about and make meaning for ourselves and to communicate with others (Short & Harste, 1996).

While schools have focused almost exclusively on language, we believe that all sign systems are basic processes that should be available to all learners. These sign systems are not special talents possessed by a few gifted people. Although there are differences in abilities in a particular system, all students possess the potential for using these as ways of making and sharing meaning in their daily lives. We do not expect everyone to become professional writers, but we do expect that our students will use reading and writing as they go about their lives. The other sign systems should have this same availability without the expectation that students will become professional musicians or theoretical mathematicians.

Students' discomfort with some sign systems is the result of a lack of exposure to, and use of, those systems in schools. If our students were immersed in all of these systems in the same ways they are surrounded with language throughout the school day, they would be able to use these systems in more powerful and meaningful ways in their lives.

Not having the potential to use multiple sign systems limits students' understandings of the world and makes learning difficult and incomplete. Elliot Eisner (1994) argues that each sign system makes available different potentials for meaning. If the systems were redundant in their meaning potentials, there would be no reason for all of them to continue to exist. There are parts of the world our students will never know and understandings that they can never communicate to others without the availability of multiple sign systems.

Flexibility in sign system use is important to becoming a successful learner just as flexibility in cueing systems is important to becoming a proficient reader (Harste, 1994). We know that readers need to use flexibly a range of appropriate cueing systems within a reading event. The same is true with sign systems. Within an experience, learners need to use more than one sign system at a time to be effective in their meaning making and to create more complex meanings. They need to choose the sign systems that are most effective for a particular message or to support their understandings about an issue.

Outside of school, students rarely use only language to communicate. They naturally integrate art and movement with language as they tell stories and play. The flexible use of multiple sign systems supports students in bringing their personal and sociocultural strengths as meaning makers into school and gives them access to a wider range of connections from their lives outside of school. Literacy should not be a different event in school than in their lives in the community and in their homes.

Sign systems also form the basis for creative and critical thought processes (Eco, 1976). In the process of taking their ideas public through a sign system, students create new ideas that go beyond their original conceptions. Once these ideas are in a stable public form, they can be revisited, revised, and critiqued through reflection. Viewing an experience from the perspectives of multiple sign systems supports greater complexity of thought and the consideration of new connections and ideas.

One of the ways in which learners can push their understandings and create more complex meanings is through transmediation (Siegel, 1984;

Suhor, 1984). *Transmediation* is the process of taking understandings created in one sign system and moving them into another. Because the meaning potentials in each system differ, this process is not a simple translation of meaning from one system to another. Instead, learners transform their understandings through inventing a connection so that the content of one sign system is mapped onto another's expression plane (Siegel, 1995). Learners search for commonalties in meanings across sign systems, but their search creates anomalies and tension because each system has different meaning potentials and lacks one-to-one correspondence. This tension encourages learners to invent a way to cross the gap as they move to another sign system and, in so doing, to think generatively and reflectively. They create a metaphor that allows them to create new connections, ask their own questions, and open new lines of thinking (Siegel, 1995). Transmediation is thus a generative process in which new meanings are produced and the learner's understandings are enhanced.

For example, Reuben, Matthew, and Tommy transmediated between oral language, music, and art in thinking about *The Barn*. They listened to a piece of music that provided an emotional context to facilitate their talk about death, separation, and fear of the future. However, they could not express all they were feeling through music or language, so they moved to art. They chose pen and ink because it was dark and without color, yet had clean lines, reflecting the tensions they felt.

These understandings about sign systems have led us to extend our definition of *text*. For us, *text* refers to any chunk of meaning that has unity and can be shared with others (Short, 1986; Siegel, 1984). A text, therefore, can be a novel, a picture book, a piece of art, a dance, a song, or a mathematical equation.

INCORPORATING SIGN SYSTEMS INTO THE CLASSROOM

Although these theoretical ideas about sign systems have been discussed for some time, putting them into practice in schools has been difficult because the mandated curriculum and school structures do not support such a perspective. Written language continues to dominate, regardless of the multiple literacies that children bring from their homes and communities. Traditionally, other sign systems are taught as separate subject areas (e.g., art and music) by specialized teachers with no carryover back to the classroom. We wanted to explore approaches that would integrate sign system use into the ongoing daily life of the classroom.

One of our first attempts was to add art, music, movement, mathematics, or drama activities and experience centers to our thematic units. These activities made the units more interesting and gave us a better sense of possible ways to incorporate sign systems into the ongoing curriculum instead of as separate lessons. However, the activity was usually not a natural part of the meaning making within that unit. Children did not need that sign system for what they were trying to think through or investigate. It was an isolated activity, not a tool to use in other situations. We wanted more—we wanted students to use sign systems for exploring, thinking, and communicating their understandings.

Another approach was to study the sign system as a discipline—for example, a unit on photography or on jazz—so students would know how to use that system. We knew so little about sign systems other than language that we needed to look at one sign system and study it with students. While this approach did help us become more familiar with a particular system, we were engaging in the same behaviors that had created problems with language. We had learned that studying language only in isolation, separate from meaning and inquiry, is not effective. Little of that instruction becomes a natural part of how children make meaning and view the world. If learning about language makes sense only when students are engaged in using language for meaningful purposes, then the same is true for other systems.

Still another approach was to encourage greater use of sign systems as students presented their understandings from inquiry projects and literature circles to the class (Kauffman & Yoder, 1990). Instead of assuming that students would write a report or give an oral presentation, we asked them to first think about the ideas that were most significant to their work and then brainstorm ways to share those ideas with others. Their presentations became thoughtful and creative, and their discussions as they prepared their presentations were often characterized by critical dialogue. However, we realized that using sign systems only to present was the same as using writing only to publish. We wanted students to use sign systems as ways to think and explore, not just to share and present to others. Students needed to have multiple sign systems available to them throughout their inquiries, not just at the end of a particular inquiry study.

We also tried bringing experts from these sign systems into the classroom through various artists-in-residence programs. This approach was particularly helpful for those sign systems where we did not know enough about the discipline to figure out how to integrate that system into the classroom. We needed to draw on others' expertise so that children would have demonstrations available from a wider range of systems. The particular programs that came into the school, however, were designed so that the artists taught predetermined lessons. A visual artist, for example, taught children how to make masks. Although the lesson was well presented and children enjoyed making masks, the lesson was separate from their inquiry and did not support their questions. It remained an isolated activity that did not become part of their thinking. The experts tended to teach *about* their sign system rather than actually engaging in the system so children could see them at work. Their focus was on the knowledge of professionals rather than on ways that children could use this system as part of their daily lives. We believe in the potential of artists-in-residence programs, but only when connected to children's inquiry.

In an effort to get away from formal lessons about sign systems, we decided to make the tools of the systems available and give students time to play with these tools. We put out different art materials, math manipulatives, musical recordings, writing utensils and paper, books, musical instruments, puppets, dress-up clothing, and scarves and gave students a studio time when they could use these materials without having to produce a product. Students approached these materials timidly at first but gradually became involved in exploring a wider range of sign systems. While we were pleased with their increased risk taking, we had several concerns. One was that students' play often seemed purposeless. They did not connect their play with sign systems to either personal or class inquiries—it was just a time to "mess around." We knew from research with young children that children use play for purposes that are significant to their thinking about their lives (Rowe, 1998), but these students did not seem to engage in this kind of purposeful play and exploration in the classroom. The heart of the issue appeared to be that they did not know *why* they were being given time to play with these sign systems since the play was not connected to the curriculum or their lives. We also saw many points at which students needed to know more about how the sign system operated. They needed strategy lessons about incorporating dialogue into their dramas or about the technical uses of watercolor. Their play took them only so far and they needed support to more effectively use these sign systems for meaning making.

Each of these approaches offered potential as well as limitations. Although each reflected simplistic answers to a complex issue, nevertheless, each approach gave us a sense of important aspects to incorporate into a curricular framework that would reflect the complexities of sign systems and the roles they play in daily life. Because we were also involved in exploring inquiry-based curriculum, we planned to look at sign systems within an inquiry framework (Short, Schroeder, Laird, Kauffman, Ferguson, & Crawford, 1996).

DEVELOPING A CURRICULAR MODEL OF SIGN SYSTEMS

The field of education has made a major shift from isolated skills and grammar lessons to reading and writing as inquiry (Short & Harste, 1996). We believe that this same shift is possible with sign systems. One of the theorists who influenced our thinking about language was Michael Halliday (1985) who said that in any meaningful language event, learners have the opportunity to learn language, learn about language, and learn through language. Learning language highlights the "doing"—learning by actually engaging in talking, listening, writing, or reading. Learning about language highlights the opportunity to examine language itself and how it operates. Learning through language focuses on using language to learn about the world. These three opportunities are available only within contexts that are meaningful to learners, contexts where they are inquirying into questions significant to their lives.

Initially, we used Halliday's work to examine whether students had language engagements available in the curriculum that highlighted all three aspects—for example, wide independent reading where readers could focus on learning language, literature circles where they could focus on learning through language, and reading strategy lessons where they could focus on learning about language. We found that, while the potential for all three are available in every engagement, each engagement highlighted a particular aspect. For example, when we first began literature circles, we had one discussion group after another without giving time for students to read for enjoyment. Halliday's work helped us search for a dynamic, complex curriculum that cuts across all three aspects instead of engaging in pendulum swings where one aspect is emphasized at the expense of the others.

We decided to take Halliday's theories about language along with our understandings of the significant curricular engagements that support reading and writing in classrooms and use these as the basis for a curricular model of sign systems. In making this connection, we assumed that the other sign systems operate in similar ways as reading and writing, that there is a universal process of meaning making that underlies all of the sign systems. We realized that at some point we might have to reject this assumption, but the only way we could move ahead was to use what we knew about language processes and engagements.

To demonstrate how we use this curricular model in the classroom, we will describe a particular classroom inquiry study. We will then discuss each part of that inquiry to show how the different aspects of the curriculum interrelate and support students in their explorations. The particular classroom experience described in this section occurred in Gloria's primary multiage classroom (ages 6–9). The third-grade students from this classroom then moved on with Gloria the following year to become part of the intermediate multiage classroom (ages 9–11) with which we began this article. The classroom is located at Maldonado Elementary School in the southwestern part of Tucson and serves a diverse working-class community.

A Class Inquiry on the Influence of People on Nature

The primary multiage class began the year by exploring the broad concept of a sense of place. Through various engagements, literature circles, and class discussions, we noticed that the students were asking many questions about how people's actions influence nature, specifically the desert. We planned a number of open-ended engagements so they could explore these interests. Students shared their personal connections and stories of the desert and nature. They browsed a wide range of informational and fiction picture books, examined exploration centers with nature artifacts, and went on desert walks. Children took notes constantly in their literature logs and sketch journals and shared these with each other. They also met in small groups to organize a *web* illustrating what they knew about nature and added their understandings and emerging questions to these webs throughout their experiences.

Through class discussions and written reflections, students indicated a strong interest in patterns in nature and how to live in harmony with nature. Students were particularly intrigued with the picture books and art pieces and wanted to know more about how artists portray nature and the environment. Gloria realized that she needed to understand what they already knew about art and artists in order to support and extend their inquiry. She asked students to meet in small groups to discuss and to web their thoughts (meaning visually display the relationships among their ideas) in response to these questions: "What is art? Who are artists and what do they do? What tools do they use?" (see Figure 3.1). The class also met for large group discussions where Gloria showed a painting and children talked about their understandings of art elements and how these elements are used to create meaning about nature. From these experiences, Gloria gained a better sense of children's understandings and questions about nature and art in order to negotiate the class focus with them.

Children's interest in artists' portrayals of the environment led to literature circles where each group examined and discussed picture books by illustrators who highlight nature in their illustrations, such as Thomas Locker, Peter Parnall, Ed Young, Jeanie Baker, and Lynne Cherry. As students explored their text sets, they recorded their observations in sketch books, literature logs, and graffiti boards. These recording devices supported literature circles on their set of books where they discussed the ways each illustrator used art to convey particular meanings about nature.

FIGURE 3.1. Class Brainstorming Web on Art and Artists

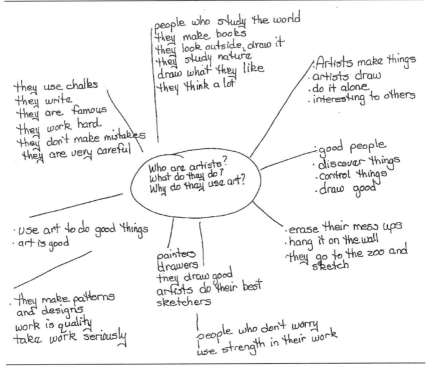

Because of students' questions about how illustrators use particular media, Gloria set up studio experiences where children could play with the media used by those illustrators, such as watercolor, charcoal, pastels, collage, and pen and ink. Students were concerned about technique so Gloria taught several whole-class strategy lessons on contour drawing, line and shape, and revision of art pieces. After the students concluded their illustrator studies and presented them to the class, they met to brainstorm possible new directions for a class focus and decided to move into inquiries around conservation issues.

A Curriculum to Learn, Learn About, and Learn Through Multiple Sign Systems

This class inquiry around the environment and its portrayal in art effectively integrated multiple sign systems. As the class moved to other inquiries, they continued to weave art throughout all of their work. In order to understand why this experience was so generative for them, we returned to Halliday's work to examine the different engagements that were part of this inquiry. His focus on the opportunities for learning available within any meaningful event helped us develop a curricular model for our work (see Figure 3.2).

Engagements That Highlight the Opportunity to Learn

One opportunity for students within meaningful literacy events is to learn sign systems through the process of engaging in the *doing* of that system. Through this doing, children can explore issues related to the class focus, their personal interests, or a particular sign system. The engagements in this circle, such as Studio and Literacy Explorations, are an open choice time for purposeful play.

FIGURE 3.2. Sign Systems within an Inquiry Curriculum

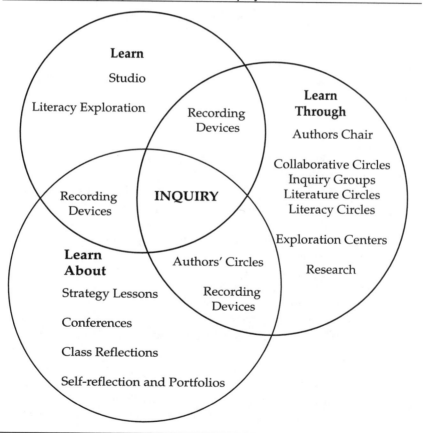

In language, wide uninterrupted reading (Sustained Silent Reading) involves scheduling a time when students can choose books to read for enjoyment without having to write book reports or engage in research. We decided to expand this wide reading time to involve students in "reading" texts from many sign systems—reading a book, listening to music, viewing an art piece, or watching a video of a dance or drama. Students could choose which of these texts they wanted to explore during literacy explorations. During the nature focus, children could listen to musical recordings, spend time with still life displays of nature and desert artifacts, examine art pieces and prints, and read books about artists and nature. Sketch journals played an important role in connecting these experiences because they were the recording device that children kept with them at all times.

Through our experiences with language, we knew that writing workshop supports students in using writing to think as well as to communicate. We decided to explore a studio time where students could compose meaning in a range of sign systems. During the nature focus, the studio included opportunities to use a variety of art materials as music played in the background. The books, displays, art pieces, and so forth were available to them as resources. Children used their sketch journals to prepare for what they wanted to explore during the studio time. Some children explored personal issues, others explored issues of nature, and others played with elements of art.

This art studio later evolved into a Friday morning studio time. Rather than schedule a short studio time on a daily basis, Gloria schedules studio for the entire morning one day a week. Children know they will have a large chunk of time for exploring and creating. During studio, children can use any sign system to create meaning. Areas with tools for the different sign systems have been established—a keyboard with earphones, listening centers with musical recordings, mathematical blocks and geoboards, books, writing paper and utensils, art materials and paper, and dress-up clothing and puppets. On Thursday afternoons, students create a plan for how they will schedule their time the next day, listing what they plan to do and why (see Figure 3.3). They begin Friday morning with a class meeting to talk about their goals for studio and then move to the different areas of the classroom. At various points throughout the morning, children share what they are working on with each other in small groups and the morning ends with whole group sharing. They also write a reflection on what they did and what they learned. Some children have established long-term projects in a particular sign system that they work on every Friday morning while others move across sign systems to explore different possibili-

FIGURE 3.3. Studio Planning Sheet (Alyssa, Age 9)

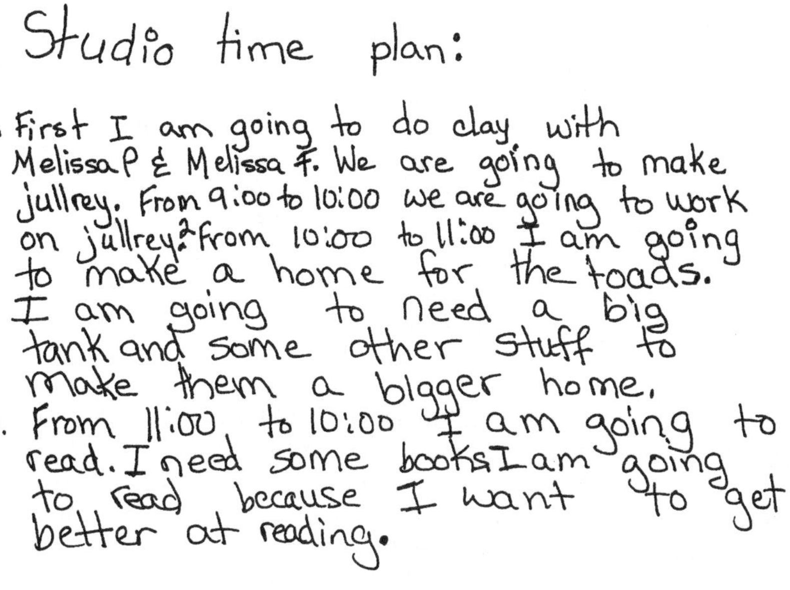

Studio time plan:

1. First I am going to do clay with Melissa P & Melissa F. We are going to make jullrey. From 9:00 to 10:00 we are going to work on jullrey. from 10:00 to 11:00 I am going to make a home for the toads. I am going to need a big tank and some other stuff to make them a bigger home.

3. From 11:00 to 10:00 I am going to read. I need some books I am going to read because I want to get better at reading.

ties. The sign system tools are a permanent part of the classroom environment so students continue to use these tools throughout the week as they work and think together.

Engagements That Highlight the Opportunity to Learn Through

Another opportunity for students within meaningful literacy events is to learn about the world and themselves *through* sign systems. Their focus is on what they are learning, not on the sign system itself. Through engagements such as Authors Chair, Collaborative Circles, Exploration Centers, and Research, students are able to use multiple sign systems to explore and learn about topics and issues that are significant to them.

Authors chair has typically been a place to read aloud to the class from powerful picture books and chapter books in order to build a shared context for the class focus (Short & Harste, 1996). Following the reading aloud, the class talks together about their connections and understandings of that book. For example, Gloria read aloud *The Monument* (Paulson, 1991) because it brought together the art and nature focus that was so significant to children's questions.

Within this model, we expanded authors chair to include texts from a range of sign systems. For example, during the nature focus, a piece of art was often the text shared with the class. The class carefully observed the piece and then offered insights and connections. At other times, the text shared was a piece of music, a graph or model, or a short dance or drama video. As with read-aloud experiences involving books, the text was followed by short class discussions of student connections and questions.

Literature circles, small groups where students read and discuss the same book or a text set of conceptually related books, involve students in conversation and dialogue and encourage them to use literature to make sense of their world and lives (Short, 1997). In the nature focus, students signed up for literature circles on different illustrators of nature books. The picture books in their text sets combined the sign systems of art and language.

One way to expand literature circles is to think about text sets more broadly. For example, when students later explored storytelling across different world cultures, their text sets included a dance video as well as folklore and art prints. In addition, students met in literacy circles to discuss texts from a range of sign systems. Just as students in the past formed groups for in-depth discussions of books, now they gather for a Literacy Circle on a particular painting, sculpture, piece of music, dance, or drama.

As students move into a new inquiry focus, we often use exploration centers so they can connect with what they already know about the topic and begin to make new connections and to generate questions for focused inquiry. In the nature focus, these exploration centers included picture books, poetry, informational books, art prints, musical recordings, tapes of sounds from particular environments, and artifacts, such as bird nests, bones, cactus skeletons, cocoons, and wasp nests. As they explored these centers, students sketched, webbed, and wrote notes about their observations and questions.

Once students find questions for in-depth inquiry, they investigate those questions consulting different resources and recording their research notes with various tools. In the nature focus, they examined the illustrator text sets as part of their inquiry groups. While these groups primarily used picture books and magazine articles about authors, at other times inquiry groups draw upon a wider range of resources for their research. For example, later in the year students engaged in inquiries around consumer issues where they used magazine ads, catalogs, coupons, play money, calculators, computers, and literature. In both sets of inquiries, students recorded their research with a wide range of tools including sketches, webs, graphs, surveys, interviews, written notes, and time lines.

As students finish their inquiries, they present them to the class through multiple sign systems. Portfolios and an art exhibit were the presentations that the class decided they would use to pull together their nature and art inquiries. In other cases, each group makes differing decisions about the presentations. When the intermediate students engaged in mini-inquiries around the topic of learning, the toad group put on a drama about toads eating flies from the fly's perspective, the teenager group created posters and a newspaper about the reasons teenagers use drugs, the mixing color group put together a recipe book of original colors they had created, the Anne Frank group wrote a newspaper on the hardships of living in a concentration camp, and the Mexican culture group made a museum of artifacts on Mexican fiestas. Each group discussed what they wanted others to know about their inquiry and then chose a form of presentation that would communicate their content.

Engagements That Highlight the Opportunity to Learn About

A third opportunity for students within meaningful literacy events is to learn *about* the sign systems and how they operate in meaning making. Learning about sign systems often occurs through short, focused strategy lessons designed to push students' thinking and use of a particular system. Conferences provide time for peers and adults to interact and bounce ideas off each other. Reflection time allows the class to come together to share their choices, processes, and understandings.

A number of strategy lessons were taught as needs arose during the nature focus. When children asked for a strategy lesson on how to use chalk for better blending and shading techniques, Gloria set up an experience where she encouraged everyone to find many ways of using chalk. As students discovered ways to smear, blend, create texture, mix colors, add shadows, or create tension, they shared these concepts with the rest of the class. Students later requested experiences with using line and shape. In addition, Gloria initiated a lesson on contour drawing after students expressed their disappointment that their drawings did not match the images in their heads.

During studio time, Gloria often conferenced with students and suggested new techniques, besides the use of brushes, that they might use in their painting. These techniques included sponges, straws, string, and a toothbrush. Children's interest in these alternative techniques led them to discover other possibilities that they then shared with others. Melissa figured out how to use cotton swabs to make leaves and twigs. She recorded her strategy in her sketch journal and conferenced with other children to show them how they might use this technique.

Authors' circles encourage students to learn about various sign systems as well as to learn through these systems. Authors bring rough drafts of texts they have created to these circles for the purpose of thinking more about those drafts with other authors. The discussions push authors to think about their meaning as well as how they used literacy to create that meaning. These authors' circles are particularly significant to students when they are preparing presentations for an audience. Educators have typically thought about these circles as places where students take written pieces, but students can bring any text they have created for response and critique—an art piece, charts, graphs, dance, drama, music, and so forth.

To highlight revision during composing, Gloria used an experience developed by Molly Bang (1991) during the nature focus. This strategy lesson involved students working as partners with black, white, red, and purple paper to create a scary picture showing tension and fear. Students were given scissors, but no glue. Once students had created their pictures, they were placed on the floor and the class gathered around the pictures and talked about which ones were the scariest and what elements made them seem scary. They were encouraged to think about how their pictures could be made scarier and tested out their ideas by moving parts of the pictures around. Students then took their pictures to their desks, revised them, and returned them to the floor to discuss the revisions and ways to make them even scarier. After this second discussion, students again revised their pictures and then glued on the pieces and displayed them in the classroom. This strategy lesson helped give students a sense of how to use authors' circles with texts other than writing.

Before, during, and after the nature study, students reflected on what they were learning and how they were going about their learning through class meetings and individual reflection journals. The class met for daily oral reflections at the end of the inquiry group time so that they could discuss how their inquiries were proceeding. Students shared the strategies and tools they were using and brainstormed ways to solve problems. Each morning as students entered the classroom, they took out their reflection journals and wrote and sketched connections they were making in their learning at school and at home.

After students had presented their inquiries to each other, the class met for several discussions on what they had learned about nature and art through their inquiries. They also reflected on what they had learned about inquiry processes. They especially focused on the processes and tools that they might use in later learning experiences. They further extended their thinking by pulling together portfolios on themselves as learners. Students looked through their various journals and artifacts to choose the ones they thought reflected the variety of their inquiry explorations as well as the depth of their thinking.

THE COMPLEXITY OF A SIGN SYSTEM CURRICULUM

Through developing this curricular model, we gained a stronger sense of the key issues that need to be addressed if sign systems are to be integrated into classrooms in powerful ways. First, and of foremost importance, the primary focus in the classroom should be on personal and class inquiries. We do not start out by thinking about how to bring a particular sign system into the classroom. We look at the questions that are significant to our students and think about how children can further their inquiry through a wider range of sign systems. This negotiation of topics does create tensions because of district expectations, mandated content, and time restraints. The mandated topics are not ignored but are often approached through children's questions or a short unit focus. These strategies provide the time needed for a negotiated curriculum around topics and issues from children's own lives.

In thinking about possible curricular engagements that highlight different sign systems, we also realized the need for balance across many dimensions. One of these dimensions is that *sign systems are tools for thinking and for communicating*. This double focus highlights sign systems as tools for personal exploration and the creation of ideas as well as for public presentations of ideas. Lucy Calkins (1991) points out that many classrooms overemphasize writing for publication and give children the sense that writing involves a step-by-step sequence of getting an idea, writing a draft, revising it, and publishing. Professional authors, however, often spend long periods of time jotting down observations, quotes, and ideas, which may or may not lead eventually to an initial draft. Calkins urges educators to provide more opportunities for students to use writing as a way to think. We believe that sign systems also have been too frequently viewed as a way to present ideas rather than to generate ideas.

A second dimension is that *sign systems are constructive processes of meaning making that involve both interpreting and composing*. We know that students learn about writing through reading and reading through writing. However, many times we highlight composing and neglect interpreting with other sign systems. For example, students are often asked to sketch and draw, but have few pieces of art available in the classroom. They need to view art as demonstrations to push their own composing, just as writers need to read other authors. On the other hand, students who are asked to listen to music and interpret it also need to have opportunities to play with composing their own music.

The final dimension is *that curricular engagements need to continuously move between learning, learning about, and learning through.* Although we described each circle separately in our examples, within any particular classroom inquiry focus there is a complex interaction between the circles. In the nature focus, art and language were the sign systems that were highlighted. Students interpreted art and language through viewing nature, books, and art prints. They constantly composed through sketch journals, literature logs, and webs. While students did not work directly on their inquiry projects during studio time, their play with art was purposeful because of questions they were raising during their nature inquiries. They came to studio ready to play with art as a system because they needed it for their inquiry into illustrators and nature.

Throughout all of their engagements, students recorded thoughts, images, and ideas in their sketch journals. They used these journals to record observations during outdoor field studies and as they engaged in their illustrator studies. They also carried their sketch journals to studio as a resource and point of reference. Students used their understandings from their illustrator studies and nature studies to explore new connections during studio. They could also record new understandings they were gaining from studio. Through studio and the illustrator text sets, students asked for strategy lessons on art as a sign system. These lessons were not taught in isolation, but were significant to students as they continued in their studio and literacy circle engagements.

This curricular framework recognizes the complexity of the ways in which teachers and students think about an inquiry curriculum. Curriculum cannot be reduced to simple formulas. Teachers need structures that support children in pursuing their own inquiries and that facilitate curriculum negotiation with students. Curriculum is a collaborative process, not a free-for-all where the teacher stands back so as not to impose onto children nor an autocracy where everything is determined in advance by the teacher. The particular engagements found within these circles will vary, of course, based on the inquiry focus and the children's interests and needs. The engagements we listed in the model are not a complete list, but simply the ones we used within this particular experience. Curriculum is always a generative process as students and teachers think together and negotiate engagements that meet their needs and inquiries.

This framework provides a flexible structure that is supportive in our thinking and planning in the classroom. However, we do recognize that it is based on the assumption that there are universal processes of meaning making that underlie all sign systems.

CHILDREN'S REFLECTIONS ON A SIGN SYSTEM CURRICULUM

Because we believe that curriculum is a negotiated process, we shared this sign system framework with the intermediate multiage students. We wanted to know whether the framework made sense to them. We explained the framework and talked about how we were using it to understand what was happening in the classroom.

We first asked students to reflect on their experiences and talk about why and how engaging in "doing" with different sign systems was important for them as learners. Tommy said, "I can do things I thought I could never do." "I can learn things I am interested in," added Michael. "I can learn to do something I've never done before by deciding what would be best for my idea," said Michelle. Melinda agreed, "It is important to express your work and share your feelings."

Second, we asked students why and how they used sign systems to learn about various topics. Adam said, "I learn to listen to others and get new ideas so I can make whatever I am doing better." Ramon noted that he collects ideas, and then "I discuss my ideas I've worked hard on." Cynthia described how ideas and books connected to her, and Juliette added how important it is "to build ideas off of others and what they say."

Finally, we talked about whether students found learning about particular sign systems helpful. Melissa believed that reflections are "a way to look over your life and get new ideas." Camille stated, "You need to know strategies to help yourself solve problems in life and work." Reuben added, "We need strategies so people can help you and you can help them." Michelle agreed, "We can learn how others work. And if you don't know what you think, a discussion helps you get further than when you are alone." These children's reflections make evident the ways in which a sign system perspective values their diverse ways of knowing and increases their ability to make sense of their lives and world.

IF SCHOOLS/SOCIETY SHARED OUR PERSPECTIVE ON LITERACY, HOW MIGHT PEOPLE'S LIVES BE DIFFERENT?

The children's reflections probably give the best indication of how people's lives would be different if schools and society shared our perspective on sign systems. Schools would reflect the diversity of the lives that children bring to the classroom, especially their personal and cultural ways of knowing and thinking about the world. The current verbocentric nature of schools would be challenged along with its labeling of children who need a range of sign systems, not just language, to think and communicate.

By having the opportunity to use multiple sign systems to learn, children would be able to find and share the connections that are important in their lives. Through these connections, they could then critically examine the big issues that they face as people and as learners. They would no longer be restricted to one form of thinking and communicating, but could choose multiple systems that fit their own ways of learning as well as the specific contexts and topics they are exploring.

These choices would give them more flexibility and success as learners and allow them to build more complex understandings because of the availability of meanings from a range of systems. Since each sign system supports a different way of knowing, the use of multiple systems would open up more perspectives on any given topic and give a wider range of ways of thinking about their lives and the world.

Our view of curriculum would challenge the isolated teaching of skills and procedures of any sign system: Learning about the nature and function of a sign system would have to be integrated into actual engagements with that system as students inquired about questions of significance in their lives. The focus of schools would change. The artificial separation between school work and life work would no longer exist because the learning in which children engaged in schools would be part of their ways of thinking and living in the world. Schools would be places where children would connect to and critically examine their lives and come to consider new possibilities for themselves and others.

REFERENCES

Avi. (1994). *The barn*. New York: Orchard.

Bang, M. (1991). *Picture this: Perception and composition*. Boston: Little Brown.

Calkins, L. (1991). *Living between the lines*. Portsmouth, NH: Heinemann.

Eco, U. (1976). *A theory of semiotics*. Bloomington, Indiana University Press.

Eisner, E. (1994). *Cognition and curriculum reconsidered*. New York: Teachers College Press.

Halliday, M. (1985). *Three aspects of children's language development: Learn language, learn about language, learn through language*. Unpublished manuscript, Department of Linguistics, University of Sydney, Australia.

Harste, J. (1994, December). *Curriculum as conversations about knowledge, sign systems, and inquiry*. Presentation at the National Reading Conference, San Diego, CA.

Kauffman, G., & Yoder, K. (1990). Celebrating authorship: A process of collaborating and creating meaning. In K. G. Short & K. M. Pierce (Eds.), *Talking about books* (pp. 135–154). Portsmouth, NH: Heinemann.

Paulson, G. (1991). *The monument*. New York: Dell.

Rowe, D. (1998). The literate potentials of book-related dramatic play. *Reading Research Quarterly, 33*(1), 10–35.

Short, K. (1997). *Literature as a way of knowing*. York, ME: Stenhouse.

Short, K. (1986). *Literacy as a collaborative experience*. Unpublished doctoral dissertation, Indiana University, Bloomington.

Short, K., & Harste, J. (with Burke, C.). (1996). *Creating classrooms for authors and inquirers*. Portsmouth, NH: Heinemann.

Short, K., Schroeder, J., Laird, J., Kauffman, G., Ferguson, M., & Crawford, K. (1996). *Learning together through inquiry*. York, ME: Stenhouse.

Siegel, M. (1984). *Reading as signification*. Unpublished doctoral dissertation, Indiana University, Bloomington.

Siegel, M. (1995). More than words: The generative power of transmediation for learning. *Canadian Journal of Education, 20*(4), 455–475.

Suhor, C. (1984). Towards a semiotic-based curriculum. *Journal of Curriculum Studies, 16*, 247–257.

4

Vision Possible

The Role of Visual Media in Literacy Education

JAMES FLOOD, DIANE LAPP, AND
DEBRA BAYLES-MARTIN

The lights dim and 30 preservice teachers focus on the screen in a "smart" classroom. Through music, narration, and images, students are exposed to a number of concepts regarding the program philosophy, their university instructors, and the public schools in which they will observe. After the presentation, the students log in at computer terminals around the perimeter of the classroom. As they do so, they find an e-mail message from the instructor welcoming them on their first day of class and a menu of activity choices.

Jaime clicks on #1 on his menu: "Respond to the introductory video." He then encounters another series of choices:

(a) Personal impressions
(b) Review introductory video at your own pace
(c) Interact with video narration

He selects (b) and replays the video until an image of a female Latino teacher speaking with a young African American student fills the screen. He copies the image into an electronic file and returns to his e-mail access.

"This is me," he types. "Of course, I'm male, but this is what I want to be like as a teacher. I like the way the teacher looks into the student's eyes. I can tell she is *really* listening and cares about what the child is saying."

Later, Jaime's instructor reads his e-mail message. "How interesting," she muses. "I wonder how long it would have taken me to gain this insight into Jaime without this e-mail? I wonder if anyone else was struck by today's presentation?"

What Counts as Literacy: Challenging the School Standard. Copyright © 2000 by Teachers College, Columbia University. All rights reserved. ISBN 0-8077-3972-3 (paper), ISBN 0-8077-3973-1 (cloth). Prior to photocopying items for classroom use, please contact the Copyright Clearance Center, Customer Service, 222 Rosewood Drive, Danvers, MA 01923, USA, telephone (508) 750-8400.

Jaime's instructor scans other e-mail messages from her students. Sure enough, two other students have mentioned video images, and a third has even noted, "I can't believe this! This student is *me* a few years ago!"

Futuristic? Unrealistic? An expensive and unnecessary curriculum add-on? Such are common words used to describe the role of media, technology, and visual literacy in our classrooms. In this chapter, we will explore the concepts of visual and media literacy and their relative importance to a complete literacy education for our students across all levels of the educational system.

DEFINING VISUAL AND MEDIA LITERACY

Writing in 1991, Carl Kaestle noted that a central challenge in studying literacy is defining the term. As recently as 150 years ago, *literacy* was generally defined (or at least measured) by a person's ability to sign his or her name. Over time, the concept of literacy broadened to include the ability to read longer and more complex texts, to ascertain fact and opinion, and to write persuasive prose. Partly in response to the development of new communication devices and strategies, recent movements in literacy education have again expanded the definition of literacy to include competence in all the communicative arts (e.g., drama, art, film, video, television, and other technological innovations).

Along these lines, Rood (1996) writes:

> We are now in the age of the visual image, students must be able to implement a set of skills in order to interpret the content of these visual images, their social impact, and their ownership. Visual literacy involves three abilities: to visualize internally, to create visual images, and to read visual images (Feinstein, 1993). Within the scholarly debate about the value of visual literacy is the belief that the acquisition of visual literacy bestows the skill of critical viewing. "Learning about visual conventions, gives the viewer a foundation for heightened conscious appreciation of artistry; second, it is a prerequisite for the ability to see through the manipulative uses and ideological implications of visual images" (Messaris, 1994, p. 165). (p. 111)

The term *visual literacy* has been used by communication scholars to refer to the roles of images and media in learning and knowing. Some scholars use this term interchangeably with *media literacy*, while others define media literacy as the understanding and production of messages through physical devices and limit visual literacy to a more passive reception of messages through art, drama, television, and film.

To understand how words and images interact both in the production and comprehension of messages, we have found it helpful to include both word and image in our definition of literacy. In this chapter, we will first discuss ways teachers define literacy and text. Next we will consider the process components of literacy that students must develop to understand and communicate through both symbol systems (alone or in concert); and then we will suggest how broader views of literacy may help us better understand and support the processes involved in literacy development. In the last section, we will address concerns and future directions associated with visual literacy education. Throughout the remainder of this work, we will use the term *visual literacy* to include both production and reception of media communication.

BROADENING DEFINITIONS OF LITERACY AND TEXT

An expanded definition of literacy is not new among educators. Eliot Eisner (1994) has consistently argued for a conceptualization of literacy that includes multiple forms of knowledge representation, especially forms often perceived as more artistic or aesthetic. In many ways, this argument relates to Gardner's (1983) contention that intelligence develops along a number of lines and various cultures differ in the specific forms of intelligence they value. Both Eisner and Gardner contend that school curricula and practices in the United States have consistently rewarded verbal and logical-mathematical intelligence over other forms. They hold that valuing word and number knowledge over all others offers unfair advantages to students who conform with system expectations but negatively affects students with strengths in other areas. Such concerns have led many educators to expand both their definition of literacy and that of the texts involved in that literacy instruction.

Extending the Notion of Text: Four Levels

As educators broaden their personal conceptions of literacy, they seem to follow a progression, often extending the notion of *text* from any written material to include the classics and eventually challenging the very idea of what a text is. We have found it instructive to consider the steps toward broadening the definition of text as progressing through four levels.

Level One: Exposure to the Classics

To broaden students' exposure to text and thereby encourage greater literacy development, some teachers select classic works of literature as reading material for students, believing that contemporary works lack the value of older pieces. Typical of this view is California's *English Language Framework* (1986), which states that "classic literature speaks most eloquently to readers and writers" (p. 7). Advocates of this view seek to help students develop the "cultural capital" that results from understanding literature frequently quoted by liberally educated members of American society. Ideally, such exposure allows students to become insiders to the references and idioms which permeate Western communication (Bloom, 1987; E. D. Hirsch, 1987).

Unfortunately, teachers working from this view often dismiss texts from underrepresented cultures and/or current television programs. (The latter seems a little ironic, given that many classic literature pieces began as popular works designed for mass audiences [Beach, 1992].) Another danger in this practice is disenfranchisement, when teacher-identified classic texts are too removed from students' personal experiences or when students rarely "see themselves" in their reading. In contrast, current prime-time television programs and contemporary films often arise out of issues pertinent to modern life and thus connect immediately with students. Many current programs and movies also make use of intertextuality, a practice which can provide links between media developed for the present and literature of the past. Perhaps educators who desire to enhance literacy study with the classics should center on how modern-day expression parallels and builds upon classic themes. To reach their students better, teachers should work from the present to the past, rather than in the opposite direction.

Level Two: Beyond the Classics

In many classrooms, reading and language arts educators successfully extend the notion of text to works beyond the classics. Such educators argue cogently for using picture books, short stories, poems, plays, and pieces of nonfiction with students to motivate learning. Teachers reflecting this view cite animated discussions and thoughtful reader responses as indicators of greater student involvement in literacy instruction.

We applaud the extension of literacy instruction to include a number of print sources. Including primary information sources, such as personal diaries, newspapers, and letters, in instruction allows students to develop a greater feel for the concepts and concerns of a particular time period or curriculum concept. However, the question remains of whether it is desirable to limit students' literacy experiences to printed text, even including that on computer screens. This question is often addressed in a third level of text expansion which includes visual media in literacy instruction.

Level Three: Teaching with Visual Media

In addition to bringing classic literature into the classroom and extending literacy experiences to include numerous print sources, many teachers embrace a third method of extending text in their courses by teaching with media. For example, students may read a printed text and then view a film version and compare the two. In other cases, a film may be used as an introduction to the print copy of a text in an effort to motivate students to read the original. Classrooms where such texts are extended in this way offer students the opportunity to consider decisions media producers make, such as when to depart from the original text and what to highlight. Still, the exercises may be relatively passive for the students, relying more upon analysis rather than on active personal production and communication.

Teachers who expand their literacy curricula to embrace video and film help move the educational endeavor beyond an exclusive focus on the printed word. We support such steps, for while written language skills are important in today's world, language is only one symbol system that humans use to express and share meaning. As our understanding of the communicative arts expands, we view communication as a social, cultural, and contextual phenomenon that involves relationships with many forms of symbolic expression. These forms include visual images, sounds, music, dance, and others associated with electronic technology.

As educators embrace television, video, and other visual media in their classrooms, the chance of connecting with students' personal lives is enhanced. As Hobbs (1997) points out, we live in a society where media viewing has become the central leisure activity for most people and the predominant source of information about people and events in the universe. Instruction where visual media is used to extend understanding of print may help students link viewing abilities developed outside of school to forms of communication common in school contexts.

While teaching with media offers many advantages, some educators argue that there exists an important difference between using television, computers, video, and film to teach *with* versus teaching *about* visual media. These educators advocate achievement of a fourth level of redefining literacy texts.

Level Four: Visual Media and Alternative Texts

A fourth and even greater extension of the concept of text involves the production and use of supplementary and alternative texts. Many educators have created and continue to produce excellent media presentations (often in the form of videotapes) for various educational organizations (such as IRA, ASCD, NRRC, NCTE, and CSR). Such materials are widely used in university classes to demonstrate verbally and visually a variety of aspects of teaching literacy. Other educators have produced materials designed to support specific coursework in K–12 classrooms. Additionally, numerous authors have focused on greater use of visual images in predominantly print-based media. In fact, pictures in professional journals, books, and teaching manuals have proliferated in recent years.

For educators at the fourth level of literacy expansion, however, the real key in visual media use lies in helping students create alternative texts. Students encouraged to explore how visual images can be collected and presented in order to communicate an idea or feeling become authors of a new sort and, in so doing, grapple with the inner workings of communication and creation. Educators who engage students in this kind of authoring encourage deep and personal processing, not only of students' ideas, but of how idea presentation affects author and audience. Once a student has faced the challenge of defining a concept for others, he or she is likely to bring greater sensitivity to viewing or reading the messages of others.

Extending Definitions of Literacy and Text: Shortcomings

While useful and important, current efforts to extend notions of literacy and text generally suffer from two major shortcomings. First, curriculum changes and extensions tend to be made most often by teachers rather than by students. As a result, students continue to function largely as receivers and interpreters of messages rather than as producers and communicators of ideas. Second, changes center more often on video, film, and print sources than on dance, electronic imaging, and other media forms. If communicating is the heart of literacy, perhaps students should be encouraged to formulate, express, and communicate ideas through a variety of means. Before making wholesale curriculum changes, however, it is prudent to examine the question of whether instruction in visual literacy enhances students' facility with the communicative arts and under what conditions that enhancement might occur.

ENHANCING LITERACY PROCESSES THROUGH EXPERIENCES WITH VISUAL MEDIA

Literacy involves at least six process components: the ability to access, analyze, synthesize, interpret, evaluate, and communicate messages. These six components provide a useful framework for understanding the ways in which people develop communication skills. They also suggest areas for educators to consider in expanding literacy curricula.

Access

The first process component, the ability to access messages, occurs at both internal and external levels (Bransford, Sherwood, Hasselbring, Kinzer, & Williams, 1990). At the internal level, *access* is the ability to retrieve information that has been stored in long-term memory. Ideally, when students encounter information, they store it so that it is available through a number of alternate routes. If they cannot recall one connection, they can select a different link to retrieve the concept.

Instructional approaches can affect the facility with which students learn flexible storage and access strategies. For example, rather than memorizing a specific problem-solving rubric, students who are taught with access in mind generate their own problem-solving approaches. They reflect on the utility of their processes, consider improvements, and refine their access and storage skills as they work.

In addition to flexible storage (and thus enhanced retrieval) of information, literacy access also includes skills of decoding and comprehending, as well as the ability to locate and retrieve information from external sources. While much of curriculum focuses on teaching students to decode and comprehend printed material, helping students decode and comprehend other texts (e.g., films or advertisements) is less common. Yet, such texts are abundantly available to students.

Issues of external access are critical in other ways as well. Just as students who are read to at home and have access to their own reading and writing materials from an early age are more likely to succeed in print-related achievement at school, so it is that students who are given the opportunity to experiment with electronic communication systems are more likely to succeed than their less-advantaged peers. The same is true of access to other forms of print and visual communication (e.g., art, dance, and film). Barriers to external access are problematic and occur on political, economic, and social levels. For example, Scott (1995) reports that the national average of computers to students is 1 to 12. However, in disadvantaged school districts, it is 1 to 23. He concludes that "access to computers is seriously affected by the relative wealth of the school's student population" (p. 7).

The benefits of access are also determined by the kind of access available. Obviously, real technological access cannot be achieved by providing a single computer terminal and keyboard for each classroom. As Carey (1997) maintains, a low computer-to-student ratio in classrooms creates an environment in which the computer is essentially a display device for teachers; a moderate computer-to-student ratio provides a time-shared work station; and only when there is a high ratio can computers become a personal enabling tool for each student to explore and extend his or her communication facility. Additionally, technological access also includes software selection and electronic networking options.

If experience with and access to visual media is indeed an important part of literacy development, ways to provide all students the opportunity to experiment and gain facility with various communication media must be found. Until there are larger numbers of computers in classrooms, for example, it is doubtful that all students will have such opportunities with electronic technology. The same is true of access to film, dance, and other visual representations.

Fortunately, although increasing external access opportunities may require more time and money (especially in the case of classroom technology), experiences with movement and other visual forms can be easily included in more lesson plans in the form of mime, role-playing, even simple dance. We can also plan lessons that help students increase internal access facility. Structuring learning experiences to encourage students to access regularly their own personal knowledge and that of their peers is something that can be done immediately in all classrooms and at limited cost.

Acting on Information

Once access is achieved, the next four process components of literacy are the ability to *analyze, synthesize, interpret,* and *evaluate* messages. Most reading programs provide numerous activities designed to help students practice these skills with printed texts. Additionally, many teachers extend their instruction to address these action components in visual media, often by implementing a unit of study focused on advertising techniques. In such units, students identify and evaluate particular techniques (e.g., the bandwagon approach or celebrity testimonials) common in commercial advertising. While such curriculum extension represents an attempt to link classroom experiences with students' daily lives, it generally provides at best a limited foray into the wide variety of media techniques and purposes to which students are exposed each day. As information proliferates in geometric proportions in our society, the ability to analyze information, synthesize numerous bits into useful wholes, and interpret and evaluate their usefulness will likely grow ever more important. With all kinds of texts, developing the ability to access and act on information enhances the sixth process component: communication.

Communicating Messages

The process component *communication* lies at the very heart of literacy. Efforts to enhance students' ability to communicate include traditional notions such as understanding one's audience, using symbols effectively, and organizing and sequencing material for effective presentation. Often, these ideas are addressed in formal writing curricula, where students produce written products to communicate information about a particular topic. The classic book report and research paper represent well-known efforts to help students practice effective communication. Speech classes also focus on these areas, encouraging students to adopt various public speaking techniques to better share their ideas with others.

While students have many opportunities to write papers or give presentations and speeches throughout their formal educational experience, they have far less opportunity to explore newer notions about communication, such as how media can be produced to both communicate and obliterate particular concepts, and what communication conventions attain within dance, drama, film, and other presentational media. When opportunities do occur, they are often relatively passive analysis activities, rather than more active experiences. Providing opportunities for students to be creators and senders of media messages allows them to access different knowledge representation sources and explore communication strategies often unaddressed in more traditional curriculum. Curricula designed to extend students' ability to communicate through the visual arts often focuses on specific production skills, such as learning how to make effective choices about framing, point of view, and style; learning how to use visual and auditory symbolism; and learning how to manipulate time and space through editing.

While each of these areas provides a wealth of avenues for students to consider in communicating information they have accessed and acted upon, the question of whether such activities actually enhance other literacy development remains crucial, especially given the limited time students are involved in formal schooling.

TEACHING VISUAL MEDIA FOR LITERACY DEVELOPMENT

While admittedly in its infancy, research about how instruction in visual literacy affects students' overall literacy growth is encouraging. Desmond (1997) maintains that there is ample evidence that teaching students to be critical consumers who recognize visual manipulation and stereotyping has beneficial effects on many aspects of literacy, from cognitive growth to aesthetic awareness. As we address the question of the efficacy of teaching visual media (as opposed to teaching with visual media), we will address four key questions:

Are there background requirements for understanding visual media?
Does visual media education result in cognitive development?
Does visual media education enhance aesthetic appreciation?
Does visual media education enhance general literacy development?

Background Requirements

The ability to interpret visual images has often been taken for granted among literacy educators. Indeed, adult-literacy educators have long relied upon printed images as a bridge for other literacy learning (e.g., materials used by Laubach Literacy International), believing that an adult nonreader will recognize the visual image of a bird (or other common concrete object) and be able to use that recognition to recall letters and words in printed form.

However, the idea that visual images can be interpreted without prior experience in two-dimensional representation is not accepted by all. Some researchers have argued that the ability to recognize (and thus comprehend) the content of still or moving images requires prior familiarity with a set of representational conventions (Cohen, 1987; Gumpert & Cathcart, 1985). Schiffman (1996) holds that visual messages are not inherently self-explanatory, nor are they necessarily "cross-culturally appropriate" (p. 68). She points out that visual images can combine a number of symbols, each of which may enhance or confuse a viewer's comprehension of an idea.

Challenging this view, Hochberg (1984) and Messaris (1994) argue that visual conventions require little or no previous experience on the part of the interpreting viewer, even in the case of some conventions that might appear to be highly unrealistic or removed from the experience of novice viewers. According to Messaris, people use particular cues in perceiving their physical and social realities, and these cues are the same ones required for inferring what is represented in a still or moving image. If Messaris is correct, visual images may serve as helpful introductions for curriculum concepts, allowing students to access information and develop a basic understanding through the same abilities they use to make sense of visual cues in everyday life. Still, there are many questions to be addressed in this area. For example, how do viewers come to understand devices like the movement of a clock or the shedding of a calendar to show the passage of time? Are such devices intuitively understood by all viewers? What other concepts or visual conventions might require preteaching? Are such concepts culturally bound?

While intriguing, the question of whether viewers require background experience with some conventions of visual media is less important than the question of whether experience with visual media enhances general cognitive growth or other literacy development. Obviously, there is little to be gained in introducing various visual media conventions to students if their experience with visual media offers little or no change in their facility with the communicative arts.

Cognitive Development

Some educators argue that experiences with visual media enhance general cognitive abilities, especially those with a spatial component (Chideya, 1991; Greenfield, 1984). Gardner's (1983) work with multiple intelligences also argues for experience with still and moving images related to his spatial intelligence category. Gardner describes *spatial intelligence* as the ability to envision relationships among objects in three-dimensional space. He holds that this ability is important in art (e.g., painting, sculpting, and dance), geometric thinking (in the design and construction of solid objects such as bridges or furniture), and interacting with the physical environment. While Gardner's system includes no pictorial intelligence category, which would map directly to the concept of two-dimensional images such as film and video viewing, he does suggest that visual images are involved in three-dimensional skills. Thus, experience with both two- and three-dimensional images may enhance a child's spatial intelligence.

In another vein, some educators believe that students who come to school speaking a language other than the mother tongue of the country benefit from the use of visual media in their classrooms. B. Hirsch (1989) and others support the use of drama, music, and other visual experiences to convey meaning and content to second-language learners. Second-language instructors often supplement course textbooks with newspapers, television programs, commercials, children's books, and a variety of printed discourse forms (photo essays, on-line journals, and e-mail) in their efforts to design authentic tasks and materials for their students. Regarding the efficacy of these efforts, Rice (1984) found that the visual elements of television often help teach vocabulary by providing easily interpreted and redundant information visually along with the verbal message.

Many second-language instructors maintain that language cannot be separated from culture and that students learn a great deal both about a culture and its language through television viewing. Thus, there has been a great increase in the use of authentic TV materials in English-language instruction. In many parts of the United States, foreign-language TV stations provide news reports, commercials, and dramatic entertainment programming that can be used for in-class exercises (Willmorth, 1997).

News reports offer timely and relevant content and a predictable format, which helps students comprehend a new language. Newscasters often repeat a limited number of vocabulary words, which can help students acquire important general informational and cultural knowledge. Additionally, television commercials contain native speech with idiomatic constructions and, like news stories, reflect cultural assumptions. As teaching materials, television commercials often have the virtues of short duration and humorous tone. Willmorth (1997) stresses that using authentic materials increases student motivation, provides sustained exposure to a limited set of topics, improves retention of vocabulary items, and builds an awareness of cultural concepts.

Unfortunately, the picture is less positive where current computer programs intended to support EFL instruction are concerned. Xiao and Jones (1996) describe materials as overly sequential and not very interactive. However, they note that the future of computer language-learning materials is bright, because the medium lends itself to a focus on audio work with the phonetic elements of language, animation of motion words, and, like television newscasts, familiarization with cultural aspects of a particular country.

Aesthetic Appreciation

Exposure to the arts is an esteemed component of liberal education. Along these lines, recent work with student book clubs has done much to support the development of students' literary appreciation. However, aesthetic appreciation goes well beyond response to printed literature; it also includes response to visual art forms. According to Kaelin (1989), *aesthetics* "may be thought of as the discipline concerning itself with artistic communication—with the description of creativity of works of art" (p. 71).

Because the aesthetic aspects of film, video, and television viewing have been ably treated in other reviews (Dondis, 1973; Messaris, 1994), we will limit our discussion of aesthetics to children's picture books. In Roser and Martinez' volume on classroom literature discussion, Barbara Keifer (1995) notes that the children's picture book has often been overlooked as a separate and unique art form appropriate for aesthetic response activities. Bader (1976) maintains that the art form of the picture book hinges on the interdependence of pictures and words, and Marantz (1992) argues that picture books are a form of visual art that enhances children's overall literacy growth.

To explain how picture-book exposure supports children's aesthetic development, Keifer (1995) first notes that the verbal and visual arts have a great deal in common. Both have similar syntactic and semantic properties. Composition, whether undertaken by a writer or an artist, requires the conscious selection and organization of several elements to communicate a style and a meaning. Keifer argues that teachers help children develop their aesthetic response to picture books when they analyze ways that illustrators communicate messages as well as how illustrations support or enhance the meaning of a story. By the introduction of principles of art into a literature discussion, Keifer cogently argues, children's aesthetic responses can be significantly broadened.

Along similar lines, Goldstone (1989) writes about the need for visual literacy skills to aid "the scaffolding of images for the reader and [to] help the reader to climb into the story" (p. 592). Goldstone advocates the use of pictures in books to expand students' vocabulary and comprehension and maintains that "being able to interpret visual images provides children with skills and the confidence to interpret the more symbolic form of the printed page" (p. 595). Extending this notion to encompass other uses of visual images, Koskinen, Wilson, Gambrell, and Neuman (1993) found in their work with captioned videos that students "want to watch captioned television, feel confident processing information from a familiar medium, and seem to attend to the semantically rich and multisensory context" (as quoted in Bazeli & Olle, 1996, p. 373).

Because effective vocabulary instruction depends upon the amount of practice and breadth of training in the use of words as well as in active processing, Bazeli and Olle (1996) suggest that teachers might fruitfully build on the work of Koskinen et al. and have students produce their own captioned videos. Early products might include single vocabulary word captions at key points, while later works could involve more complex captioning.

Other Literacy Development

Studies linking visual media education and literacy development are relatively new. However, across a number of settings, early reports suggest that experiences with visual media can and do favorably support other literacy development.

Supporting Writing Skills

Finding little in the professional literature about the role of visual images in the writing process, Bailey, O'Grady-Jones, and McGown (1996) studied 25 second graders to determine the effects of technology on student writing. Students had been working in a writing workshop throughout the academic year, so when the study began in April, they were familiar with basic writing processes. Over a period of 4 weeks, the students brainstormed, webbed (pasted clip art and words to a web), storyboarded, drafted, edited, published, and presented (electronically) a "word and picture story" of their own. Bailey et al. found that students exhibited one of four general patterns in using clip art to support their writing. Some students looked over the available clip art for relationships among images and then wrote about a relationship. Others used visuals and no words on their story webs. A third group used the clip art to trigger a writing memory, but then relied on personal recollection for related images. A fourth group followed a process of trial and error finding a clip art item, writing about it, abandoning the piece, finding a new clip art item, and so on.

While students were "distracted" at times by the color graphics and opportunity to use the technology, they were also excited by the possibilities. In the final analysis, Bailey et al. (1996) found that the length and quality of students' compositions increased when technology was made available to support the writing process. Students also took "greater risks" with "vocabulary, dialogue, and sentence structure" (p. 143).

Experimenting with Visual Media and Teacher Preparation

Brigham, Hendricks, Kutcka, and Schuette (1994) observe that recent developments in multimedia and hypermedia simplify the creation of instructional presentations, allowing teachers and students to experiment with media-supported communication. Using HyperCard, HyperStudio, and SemNet Academic (produces semantic maps), Brigham et al. trained education majors to develop or adapt instructional materials for students with learning disabilities. Although one semester was too limited a time for preservice teachers to master fully the three programs, Brigham et al. reported that actually working with the technology encourages one to think more critically about its use in teaching and learning.

In a similar approach, Taylor and Stuhlmann (1995) teamed beginning education students with fourth graders to create three separate projects: a slide show book report with KidPix 2, a newsletter with The Writing Center and the QuickTake camera to digitize pictures, and a multimedia presentation using Kid Works 2. Taylor and Stuhlmann reported that involving students (both preservice and elementary) in using such technology helped them view it as a "normal part" of a classroom environment.

Motivating and Engaging Students

Like Bailey et al. (1996), many educators have discovered that the analysis and use of contemporary media products and programs motivates and engages students as they build literacy skills that transfer to and enhance reading and writing abilities. In one study, Sultan and Jones (1996) taught one group of fourth graders about Newton's laws of motion using posters with printed images (two-dimensional). A second group was taught the same concepts using animated computer graphics (including the same information as on the posters). Given free-time choice, students overwhelmingly chose to return to the computer animated graphics, suggesting an inherent engagement with the technology.

Additionally, analysis of a variety of texts (books, films, television) helps students gain interest in writing and speaking and nurtures their natural curiosity and motivation toward learning. Nehamas (1992) contends that helping students approach visual media with informed, analytic, and evaluative attitudes helps them overcome potential media manipulation. Couch (1996) suggests that parents and teachers can help students gain facility with critical viewing by asking children to control their viewing time, make choices on program quality, analyze what they see and hear, and share their judgments with others, thereby engaging children in talking about media with significant adults and peers in their lives.

Cortes (1991) also notes that expanding curricula to include media can help connect the classroom with the larger community, making education more enjoyable and meaningful for those involved. He believes that the use of media in classrooms helps to stimulate students to consider multiple perspectives on current and historical multicultural dilemmas. The ability to understand numerous viewpoints is certainly critical for complete literacy development.

Authentic Learning Through Integrated Curriculum

Mass media products can be connected to all areas of the curriculum and provide opportunities for synergy among large groups of people. In several communities, educators have designed curriculum projects that fully integrate media literacy concepts and traditional curriculum concepts. For example, in Billerica, Massachusetts, teachers collaborated on a districtwide program to analyze critcially tobacco advertising as part of the health curriculum. Students were asked to explore historical, political, and economic dimensions of tobacco advertising. They began by reviewing and analyzing volumes of persuasive material designed to make smoking look attractive. They then created their own community public service messages designed to challenge smoking behaviors. More than two thousand students in grades K–12 developed slogans; wrote newspaper editorials; designed billboards, bumper stickers, and posters; wrote and recorded radio ads; and videotaped public service announcements. Making classroom and community connections even more tangible, a local billboard company agreed to display a student's design on the major highway of Billerica, giving thousands of citizens an opportunity to read a child's message. Such experiences provided a powerful learning experience for students as they explored links between their own research, interpretation, and communication of ideas.

Working in a different direction, Gibbs and Cheng (1996) developed the notion of *Document Maps* in an effort to guide students in using the World Wide Web. Noting that users often become disoriented in cyberspace, Gibbs and Cheng helped their students arrive at key information nodes on the net, after which they were able to direct their own personal inquiries. Providing Document Maps for students (and teachers) may help decrease anxiety and increase success in navigating the information superhighway.

A third example involves a project in a local elementary school where the graduating sixth graders were putting a yearbook together. As the children considered ways to capture the life of the school in photographs, they decided to do a feature on a Day in the Life in their school. In preparation for shooting the photos, students studied the Day in the Life photography-book series by analyzing the content and form of the books. As students discussed what was most typical about a day at their school, they selected activities, people, and places at the school that best represented the school's character. Mike Franklin, a photographer from the *San Diego Union Tribune* who had one of his photographs published in *A Day in the Life of California*, was invited to the school. He discussed his experiences with the Day in the Life series and brainstormed photography ideas with the students. He helped the students recognize the plethora of choices inherent in photography, especially issues of framing, angle shots, and light tone. After students took and developed the designated photos, they wrote the story of their project. Mike Franklin then took the photo essay to the newspaper, where the feature editor selected six photos to include in the May 1993 Currents Section of the newspaper. This was a powerful learning experience for both school and community members. Adults from the school and the community observed a routine school day from a child's perspective. The children, in turn, came to recognize the power of newspaper words and pictures in a new and personal way.

Regardless of its source, it is likely that the success of using visual media to support literacy development will depend greatly upon the teachers who use it. Although referring to computer use, Green's (1995) point can be extended to any visual media experience: "For example, in schools across the country, children go to computer labs. Any laboratory can be a place to create and discover or it can be boring and routine. It is the responsibility of teachers to set the stage for the discovery to happen. Using computer technology and all it can offer, teachers can excite and inspire children" (p. 3).

ADDRESSING CONCERNS ABOUT
VISUAL LITERACY EDUCATION

Although many advocate increased attention to visual media in our schools, it is important to note that research in this area is relatively limited, and thus the number of unresolved issues is great. While some may find this discouraging or disappointing, we believe it signals the same hopefulness as any new frontier, providing the opportunity to ask new questions and think in creative ways. However, as we experiment with visual media in education, it is important to keep parental and instructional concerns in mind.

Parental Concerns

While many parents have taken an active role in the education of their children, there are still some parents who are disenfranchised from schools. Because of their absence from the school setting, such parents may have little voice in instructional decisions. As educators expand notions of literacy, they would do well to expand also their invitations for more parents to become involved in their children's schooling, perhaps in new ways. The inclusion of the visual arts as a part of the literacy curriculum can help us broaden and redefine roles for parents, teachers, and students. Yet such broadening will not occur without conscious effort on the part of instructional planners to include all potential contributors.

At the same time, parents who have expressed concerns about the role of visual media in education must also be acknowledged, and their questions addressed. Bianculli (1993) addresses five major areas of concern expressed by parents about visual media, both in school and out:

- Violence in film and television desensitizes children and alters their conception of the social world.
- Television damages the process of elections.
- Mass media organizations disrupt the private lives of individuals.
- Values of sensationalism that are created by mass media have reshaped culture and the arts.
- Television will displace reading.

Other studies question how much instruction should center on help-ing students become media literate (savvy about processes and protocols) versus helping students become literate through media (Carstarphen, 1995; Strech, 1995). In considering such questions, parents and teachers can create viable plans for exploring existing research and conducting pilot programs suited to the educational needs of their communities. As parents, educa-tors, and other interested individuals discuss concerns about television and related visual media, it is important to realize that there are many differ-ent kinds of television shows and media opportunities. Just as parents and teachers have learned to discern among types and purposes of particular books children read, so too will criteria be needed to evaluate the media with which our children interact. One promising format for developing such criteria has its roots in an article in *TV Guide* (1994), "The Best New Kids' Show on TV," where several TV shows were recommended to par-ents and children as "Best Bets." As parents and educators generate their own criteria for useful visual media, they may also want to create Best Bets lists for widespread distribution.

Instructional Concerns

While many teachers have experimented with various forms of visual media in an add-on fashion, Shephard (1993) suggests that add-ons are a weak and ineffective use of technology in supporting full literacy devel-opment. If the definition of literacy is expanded to place students at the cen-ter of their learning, the means for them to access, act upon, and communi-cate information that they value must be made available to them. Using media as a supplement to a lesson, or as an add-on, generally maintains the teacher as the center of instructional decision making, offering students little opportunity to voice additions or challenges to the curriculum.

Naturally, teachers have a large range of attitudes about the value and consequences of broadening the conceptualization of literacy, especially if it means widespread television and film viewing in their classrooms, or if it means providing numerous hours for students to explore and experiment with computers. Along with many parents, educators worry about the ef-fects of media on children. They worry about managing time, teaching "the basics," and meeting ever more stringent standards. Thus, before commit-ting time and energy to its use, educators want to be sure that mass media will play a helpful role in the educational process. Even though they real-ize that many students have a tremendous amount of knowledge about and interest in media, they are still reluctant to embrace media without seri-ous research that unequivocally demonstrates its efficacy in enhancing lit-eracy. Such concerns are valid and important. Answering them will not be an easy task, but by working together as teachers, researchers, parents, and students, we can design inquiry projects to help us understand how visual media supports or hinders literacy development.

Future Directions

The questions about how to teach with media and about media are complex. As schools and communities explore the role of media in literacy education, no doubt exciting experiences await us and our students. Throughout the process, it is essential that classroom teachers be actively involved in any and all decision-making processes from start to finish (Green, 1995). This step is critical, given the teacher's central role in orchestrating classroom instruction and technology use. As questions are raised in community meetings, we can design inquiry projects and analyze our findings. While our questions and concerns will be compelling, doubtless we will need to be patient, realizing that it will take time and experimentation to find out what will really help our students' literacy growth. Even so, we welcome the opportunity to explore a new curriculum frontier, creating possible visions of the future.

IF SCHOOLS/SOCIETY SHARED OUR PERSPECTIVE ON LITERACY, HOW MIGHT PEOPLE'S LIVES BE DIFFERENT?

Last Saturday evening we saw a production of Moss Hart's *Light Up the Night* at the La Jolla Playhouse. It was fun to see a well-acted and familiar play that we had enjoyed reading. Most of the characters in the play were caricatures of self-absorbed theater people, and the actors hammed it up to the delight of the audience. But the part of the young playwright was confusing to us. When we last read the play, we thought the young playwright was supposed to be shy and introspective, but the actor portrayed him as an idealistic activist who was rather self-assured. This unsettled us and made us wonder if the actor's interpretation, which had been presented to us in a dramatic production, was perhaps closer to what the author had intended. This same phenomenon has probably happened to all of us as we have viewed a production of *Romeo and Juliet* or *Othello*. We may have said things like the following to ourselves: "Is that the real reason why Desdemona had to die?" or "This interpretation is way off base—Othello was a classic narcissist."

We couldn't help ourselves—we needed to discuss our feelings about *Light Up the Night* with friends who had read the play and seen the same production that we had. The discussion always led back to issues of personal interpretation. The actor played the role as he understood it, and we, the audience, had the opportunity to compare and contrast his visual portrayal with our own reading of the play. His performance was so riveting that we also had the opportunity to expand our interpretation of the play. Whether we ultimately agreed with his interpretation or not, we had *seen* it and it had made a deep impression upon us. The acting out of the play had changed our understanding of the play and had broadened our overall understanding of it.

This event led us to think again about the role of visual literacy in the general literacy curriculum. In our paper, we argue that the visual arts and the communicative arts should be a seamless curriculum that enables students, teachers, parents, and community members to meet every child's needs. When children are free to interpret authors' messages in their own ways, as the actor did in his portrayal of the young playwright, they learn to wrestle with their own comprehension as well as to listen to the interpretations of others. The actor in this play did not write an analytical essay about the character he was portraying; children too need opportunities other than writing to create an interpretation that they can share with others. Interpretations can be demonstrated in many different forms from drama to art to music to sports to film to video to computer.

A new and broader literacy curriculum is needed to ensure that students' attempts at making meaning will be valued in our classrooms. Students' lives will be enhanced when we can think of literacy as an everyday tool that flows directly to and from children's multiple intelligences. In the past, we have tended to value spatial and verbal intelligence to the exclusion of all other forms of intelligence. This actor's bold and innovative interpretation of the young playwright enabled us to see the play more deeply and thoroughly than when we had read and discussed it. All of his actions—his swagger, his strut—as well as his delivery of his lines helped us to construct a new broader meaning of the play. Drama helped us see things that we had not seen before.

Children's lives will be better when we embrace the reality that they live in a visual world in which images are ubiquitous and meaningful to them. Not only do we have to acknowledge that the visual arts and the communicative arts are part of each other, but we also need to design curricula that will help children to comprehend messages and to send messages that show their understanding of the ways in which the visual and communicative arts help each other. We need to build on children's abilities and interest in art, music, drama, physical education, video, film, and computers to let them know that each of them has a right to be part of the action of the classroom. Children with intelligences and subsequent literacies in areas other than spatial and verbal intelligences will be well served with a broadened interpretation of literacy that includes the opportunity to demonstrate understanding of both oral and written texts. They will also be well served by instruction in the construction of new kinds of text that integrate the visual and the communicative arts.

REFERENCES

Bader, B. (1976). *American picturebooks from Noah's ark to the Beast within.* New York: Macmillan.

Bailey, M., O'Grady-Jones, M., & McGown, L. (1996). The impact of integrating visuals in an elementary creative writing process. In R. E. Griffin, D. G. Beauchamp, J. M. Hunter, & C. B. Schiffman (Eds.), *Eyes on the future: Converging images, ideas, and instruction. Selected readings from the Annual Conference of the International Visual Literacy Association* (pp. 135–144). Chicago: International Visual Literacy Association.

Bazeli, M. J., & Olle, R. E. (1996). Using visuals to develop reading vocabulary. In R. E. Griffin, D. G. Beauchamp, J. M. Hunter, & C. B. Schiffman (Eds.), *Eyes on the future: Converging images, ideas, and instruction. Selected readings from the Annual Conference of the International Visual Literacy Association* (pp. 371–377). Chicago: International Visual Literacy Association.

Beach, J. A. (1992, November). New trends in perspective: Literature's place in language arts education. *Language Arts, 69,* 550–556.

The best new kids' shows on TV. (1994, October 27–November 4). *TV GUIDE,* 3–11.

Bianculli, D. (1993). *Teleliteracy.* New York: Pantheon.

Bloom, A. (1987). *The closing of the American mind.* New York: Simon & Schuster.

Bransford, J. D., Sherwood, R. D., Hasselbring, T. S., Kinzer, C. K., & Williams, S. M. (1990). Anchored instruction: Why we need it and how technology can help. In D. Nix & R. Spiro (Eds.), *Cognition, education and multimedia: Exploring ideas in high technology* (pp. 115–141). Hillsdale, NJ: Erlbaum.

Brigham, F. J., Hendricks, P. L., Kutcka, S. M., & Schuette, E. E. (1994, February). *Hypermedia supports for student learning.* Paper presented at the Annual Meeting of the Indiana Federation, Council for Exceptional Children, Indianapolis, IN.

California. State Board of Education. (1986). *English language framework for California public schools, K–12.* Sacramento: California State Board of Education.

Carey, J. (1997). Exploring future media. In J. Flood, S. B. Heath, & D. Lapp (Eds.), *Handbook of research on teaching literacy through the communicative and visual arts* (pp. 62–67). New York: Macmillan.

Carstarphen, M. G. (1995, March). *New media literacy: From classroom to community.* Paper presented at the 46th Annual Meeting of the Conference on College Composition and Communication, Washington, DC.

Chideya, F. (1991, December 2). Surely for the spirit, but also for the mind. *Newsweek,* 61.

Cohen, J. (1987, May). *The television generation, television literacy, and television trends.* Paper presented to the Eastern Communication Association, Syracuse, NY.

Cortes, C. (1991). Empowerment through media literacy. In C. Sleeter (Ed.), *Empowerment through multicultural education* (pp. 143–157). Albany: State University of New York Press.

Couch, R. A. (1996). Challenging popular media's control by teaching critical viewing. In R. E. Griffin, D. G. Beauchamp, J. M. Hunter, & C. B. Schiffman (Eds.), *Eyes on the future: Converging images, ideas, and instruction. Selected readings from the Annual Conference of the International Visual Literacy Association* (pp. 217–222). Chicago: International Visual Literacy Association.

Desmond, R. (1997). TV viewing, reading and media literacy. In J. Flood, S. B. Heath, & D. Lapp (Eds.), *Handbook of research on teaching literacy through the communicative and visual arts* (pp. 23–30). New York: Macmillan.

Dondis, D. (1973). *A primer of visual literacy.* Cambridge, MA: MIT Press.

Eisner, E. (1994). *Cognition and curriculum reconsidered* (2nd ed.). New York: Teachers College Press.

Gardner, H. (1983). *Frames of mind: The theory of multiple intelligences.* New York: Basic Books.

Gibbs, W. J., & Cheng, H. P. (1996). Formative evaluation and world-wide-web hypermedia. In R. E. Griffin, D. G. Beauchamp, J. M. Hunter, & C. B. Schiffman (Eds.), *Eyes on the future: Converging images, ideas, and instruction. Selected readings from the Annual Conference of the International Visual Literacy Association* (pp. 259–265). Chicago: International Visual Literacy Association.

Goldstone, B. (1989). Visual interpretations of children's books. *The Reading Teacher, 48*(8), 592–595.

Green, L. C. (1995). Teachers and instructional technology: Wise or foolish choices. *IDRA Newsletter, 22*(10). (Published by Intercultural Development Research Association, San Antonio, TX).

Greenfield (1984). *Mind and media: The effects of television, video games, and computers.* Cambridge, MA: Harvard University Press.

Gumpert, G., & Cathcart, R. (1985). Media grammars, generations, and media gaps. *Critical Studies in Mass Communications, 2*(1), 23–35.

Hirsch, B. (1989). *Languages of thought: Thinking, reading and foreign languages.* New York: College Entrance Examination Board.

Hirsch, E. D., Jr. (1987). *Cultural literacy: What every American needs to know.* New York: Houghton Mifflin.

Hobbs, R. (1997). Visual literacy. In J. Flood, S. B. Heath, & D. Lapp (Eds.), *Handbook of research on teaching literacy through the communicative and visual arts* (pp. 7–14). New York: Macmillan.

Hochberg, J. (1984). The perception of pictorial representations. *Social Research, 51*(4), 841–862.

Kaelin, E. F. (1989). *An aesthetics for art education.* New York: Teachers College Press.

Kaestle, C. (1991). *Literacy in the United States.* New Haven, CT: Yale University Press.

Keifer, B. (1995). Responding to literature as art. In N. Roser & M. Martinez (Eds.), *Book talk and beyond* (pp. 191–201). Newark, DE: International Reading Association.

Marantz, S. (1992). *Picture books for looking and learning: Awakening visual perceptions through the art of children's books.* Phoenix, AZ: Onyx Press.

Messaris, P. (1994). *Visual literacy: Image, mind and reality.* Boulder, CO: Westview Press.

Nehamas, A. (1992). Serious watching. In D. J. Gless & B. H. Smith (Eds.), *The politics of liberal education* (pp. 163–186). Durham, NC: Duke University Press.

Rice, M. (1984). Cognitive aspects of communicative competence. In R. L. Schiefelbusch & J. Pickar (Eds.), *The acquisition of communicative competence* (pp. 141–189). Baltimore, MD: University Park Press.

Rood, C. (1996). Critical viewing and the significance of the emotional response. In R. E. Griffin, D. G. Beauchamp, J. M. Hunter, & C. B. Schiffman (Eds.), *Eyes on the future: Converging images, ideas, and instruction. Selected readings from the Annual Conference of the International Visual Literacy Association* (pp. 111–117). Chicago: International Visual Literacy Association.

Schiffman, C. B. (1996). Visually translating educational materials for ethnic populations. In R. E. Griffin, D. G. Beauchamp, J. M. Hunter, & C. B. Schiffman (Eds.), *Eyes on the future: Converging images, ideas, and instruction. Selected readings from the Annual Conference of the International Visual Literacy Association* (pp. 67–78). Chicago: International Visual Literacy Association.

Scott, B. (1995). Access to educational technology: What's going on? *IDRA Newsletter, 22*(10). (Published by Intercultural Development Research Association, San Antonio, TX.)

Shephard, R. (1993). Elementary media education: The perfect curriculum. *English Quarterly, 25,* 35.

Strech, L. L. (1995). Technology use in language arts instruction. (Eric Document Reproduction Service No. ED 382 183).

Sultan, A., & Jones, M. (1996). The effects of computer visual appeal on learners' motivation. In R. E. Griffin, D. G. Beauchamp, J. M. Hunter, & C. B. Schiffman (Eds.), *Eyes on the future: Converging images, ideas, and instruction. Selected readings from the Annual Conference of the International Visual Literacy Association* (pp. 95–100). Chicago: International Visual Literacy Association.

Taylor, H. G., & Stuhlmann, J. M. (1995). Project KITES: Kids interacting with technology and education students. *Emerging Technologies, Lifelong Learning,* NECC. (Eric Document Reproduction Service No. ED 392 430).

Willmorth, M. (1997). Television and language learning. In J. Flood, S. B. Heath, & D. Lapp (Eds.), *Handbook of research on teaching literacy through the communicative and visual arts* (pp. 31–39). New York: Macmillan.

Xiao, X., & Jones, M. G. (1996). Computer animation for EFL learning environments. *Eyes on the future: Converging images, ideas, and instruction. Selected readings from the Annual Conference of the International Visual Literacy Association* (pp. 361–369). Chicago: International Visual Literacy Association.

5

Connecting, Exploring, and Exposing the Self in Hypermedia Projects

JAMIE MYERS, ROBERTA HAMMETT,
AND ANN MARGARET McKILLOP

Multiple literacies suggest multiple forms of communication beyond the printed word. However, because every text is constructed and interpreted within a cultural purpose, multiple literacies also suggest the use of forms of communication within multiple social practices. Critical literacy practices are often contrasted to school literacy practices and argued as important contexts for literate actions to achieve democratic purposes. Within such a critical practice, literacies communicate meanings and, perhaps more importantly, construct possible identities and relationships between community members. The work we share in this chapter explores our attempts to use the tools of technology to expand the definition of literacy beyond the printed word to include sound, image, and video and to support a pedagogy that aims at the social construction of a literacy practice with collaborative and democratic identities and relationships. We emphasize at the beginning our belief that the technology alone is not inherently liberating, but hope to show how its particular ability to hold in place and juxtapose texts allows for the exploration of the self across the texts of our culture and provides the basis for democratic community.

The common sense understanding of literacy as the ability to establish a meaning for a collection of alphabetic signs is broadened by the idea that things like a wink of the eye, a photograph, a song, or a film are *texts* that can be authored and interpreted because they are based upon organized sets of socially negotiated signs. But what is most important to keep in mind when thinking about the process of constructing meaning in any one of these multiple media is the impossibility of constructing meaning in isolation from the other media. Simply put, the meaning we generate in

What Counts as Literacy: Challenging the School Standard. Copyright © 2000 by Teachers College, Columbia University. All rights reserved. ISBN 0-8077-3972-3 (paper), ISBN 0-8077-3973-1 (cloth). Prior to photocopying items for classroom use, please contact the Copyright Clearance Center, Customer Service, 222 Rosewood Drive, Danvers, MA 01923, USA, telephone (508) 750-8400.

the experience of a song heard on the radio is shaped in possibility by all of our prior experiences with all texts of all media. This intertextuality is so seamless that we often are given over to discussing the specific meanings embedded in a single text as if the author's creation and our interpretation could exist independently from all the texts of all cultures and time. Thus, although the idea of multiple literacies in different forms of media may help us argue for the valid inclusion in school of multiple ways to represent and communicate ideas, to speak of *literacy* in the first place is to refer to the continual act of using signs to socially construct action and a meaningful identity in relation to others through texts which inherently depend on all forms of media.

Vygotsky (1986) echoes our sense of literacy: "The relation between thought and word is a living process; thought is born through words. A word devoid of thought is a dead thing" (p. 255). However, we would like to expand this definition of literacy beyond the continual use of words to author thought, to a reflective position in which the thinker considers the possible meanings for multimedia "words" within possible social identities and relationships. Such reflection might be understood as a critical consciousness that, without, leaves the individual within an experience in which texts control the person rather than the person using texts to socially negotiate a sense of the self, others, and the world. We believe that an individual can intend the potential meanings of a text, yet have no control over the interpretations by others. Texts are cultural constructions. "A word is a microcosm of human consciousness" (Vygotsky, p. 256). A word is a trace that moves out in all directions through the texts of all time and space. So, we think about literacy as an emerging knowledge of how intertextuality can be consciously used to shape identities and relationships within each textual interaction. It remains a challenge for schools to structure experiences which would support the development of such a critical literacy.

Any literate action, critical or not, is embedded in a particular socially constructed practice(s) in which texts serve specific purposes as they constitute social relationships and define the nature of knowledge about the self and the world. The common school classroom tends to involve a social practice in which print texts are privileged, the midwestern dialect as "standard" English is primary, knowledge already constructed by experts lies beyond the first-hand experience of students, and the teacher has the responsibility to pass along all the skills and ideas—the correct discourse— for the good of the student. Social relationships in this literacy practice are competitive and hierarchical, with those who reproduce more of the target text garnering more human value; student identity absorbs or resists the judgments made on what seem to be every single action and word. Many students who miss points on this assignment or that quiz quickly divest themselves of any intellectual involvement in the world of ideas in which the teacher hopes to motivate interest (Myers, 1992). In response to this social literacy practice, motivation techniques, classroom management, and low self-concept become popular concerns in educational psychology.

Multiple literacy practices do however coexist with school literacy. Hopefully, it is easy to see how the notes students might subversively pass among themselves and the articles scholars might seek to publish in a professional journal are two examples of different literacy practices with very different social contexts from many classrooms. In these events, personal experience is being shared, ideas are being negotiated, the self is being exposed, and the result is not an authoritative "right" or "wrong" verdict, but a conversation or debate about matters of shared value. When these communities of literacy work best, in our judgment, the social relationships are democratic as members believe they can risk exposing their thoughts, consider their opinions among equals, and negotiate their representations of the world through the community response. The meanings at both the center and circumference in these communities extend beyond any single life time/space in the texts produced, but the literacy activities have more to do with how the social practice authorizes voice and knowledge than with any particular form of textualizing the word (Street, 1984). It is not impossible to support such communities of critical inquiry in the school classroom, but it is a literacy practice which is seldom experienced, or pedagogically intended, within that cultural context.

Multiple literacies as different social practices (Heath, 1986; Fishman, 1991) in which texts are used to construct personal identity and social relationships focuses classroom pedagogy on the establishment of structures which at least invite—if not advocate openly for the space needed—students to socially construct what we have defined above as a critical literacy. In such a literacy practice the self is constructed reflectively in collaboration with others as the community of students explore shared issues and diverse meanings through texts of multiple media (Myers, 1995). As they connect different texts about an experience, explore the potential meanings made visible by juxtaposing different texts and readers, and expose their own interpretive value-laden positions, they construct and deconstruct the underlying intertextual meanings that form their individual and cultural subjectivities. We seek to construct such a critical literacy practice through the use of computer technology within a pedagogical context which we call *hypermedia authoring.*

Hypermedia documents allow for nonsequential reading and writing that integrates multiple media. Thus, electronic text, graphics, sounds, and video excerpts are organized to enable a reader to follow links which connect and display sequences of the texts. Multimedia encyclopedias and other CD-ROMs are common examples of hypermedia when the reader can click on words to hear an illustrative sound or a voice-over explanation, watch a short movie on the topic of interest, or read more elaborating text. However, we believe that these types of hypermedia products position learners as consumers and are based upon the old assumptions of the banking concept of learning (Freire & Macedo, 1987), where the goal of learners is to accumulate what they are given by the authorized teacher or text. Although we do believe that learners can, often subversively as members of another inquiry community, construct meaningful personal representations as consumers of hypermedia products, we believe that learners benefit most when they negotiate representations of the ideas being studied by collaboratively constructing a hypermedia artifact (Jonassen, Myers, & McKillop, 1996; Landow, 1992; Lanham, 1990).

A LITERACY PRACTICE IS MORE THAN
THE REPRESENTATIONAL TOOL

Here we report on the work of seventh-grade students and undergraduates in English teacher education who, in small authoring groups, used several software tools to construct hypermedia documents. The central tool is StorySpace®, which allows the author to create spaces that will hold any media type and then to make as many links as desired between specific instances of media in different spaces. With several supporting software tools, the authors can also digitize sounds (SoundEdit Pro®), scan and manipulate images (Ofoto®, Adobe Photoshop®), digitize video and create original quicktime movies (Adobe Premiere®), and word process (Microsoft Word®). Generally speaking, the process of constructing a hypermedia document requires the small group to build a collection of media texts as electronic files, to generate spaces in StorySpace to hold texts, and then to construct relevant links between texts to create hypertextual pathways through the entire project.

Although both seventh graders and undergraduates used the same representational tool, the literacy practices they constructed were not identical. The seventh graders' poetry projects bore a striking resemblance to electronic texts that seek to transmit authoritative knowledge. Literary conventions about poetry were defined and exemplified by multimedia texts. There were some interesting exceptions in which students created aesthetic experiences by juxtaposing original poems and images. But for the most part, the students authored a typical expository school text; they did not question the purpose of knowing literary conventions to experience poetry. In contrast, the undergraduates demonstrated over and over again in their hypermedia authoring an ability to critically appropriate texts by layering intertextual and oppositional meanings through the juxtaposition and linking of multiple media. The hypermedia tool supports this literate practice by providing the representational devices and the convenient unified space needed to manipulate the presentation of texts in time and space. However, we firmly believe that the technology underlying this tool is not a deterministic cause for any critical literacy practice that emerges.

Past experience of school literacy practices, together with the classroom pedagogy that framed the hypermedia projects, explains most of the difference between the critical literacy practices that developed (a fuller description of the studies can be found in McKillop & Myers, 1999). Small groups of three or four students worked on a single hypermedia project. But what students were asked to do with hypermedia differed vastly. The seventh grade poetry groups were given the following scenario to direct their hypermedia project:

POETRY UNIT PROPOSAL

You live in State College. The year is 2021, two years after a nuclear holocaust has decimated your community, your country, life as it was. Although many aspects of your life are still disrupted, your community feels the need for some sort of continuity and beauty. Your computer consulting firm (you do still have a few computers left that work) has been assigned the task of bringing the knowledge of poetry to school-age children. Areas that you will need to concentrate on include the following: how a poem looks; how a poem sounds; how a poem expresses an idea; how a poem uses language in a special way. While some poetry still exists from before the attack, you may need to write new poems of different types to provide students with the foundation they need. You may need to integrate or create film, sound, images, or original movies to complete your task. You will be working as a group for some sections of the project and as individuals for other sections. . . . Good luck.

Thus, within the context of composing their own original poetry, the students were asked to relate the knowledge that they were constructing to other—hypothetical—students. The traditional social relationship between expert teacher and ignorant student was maintained, and the purpose for literacy was to pass on knowledge. The resulting hypermedia projects closely followed the four part menu suggested in the above scenario by using multimedia to illustrate poems that explain how poetry looks, sounds, expresses ideas, and uses figurative language.

Even though we believe that the pedagogical context did not support the type of critical literacy practice in which students consciously explore meanings to critique their own socially constructed subjectivities, we believe the seventh graders collaboratively created a different literacy practice more valuable than the traditional school literacy. Within this literacy practice, when the students connected word, sound, image, and video by creating hyperlinks and juxtaposing multimedia, they constructed ideas which cut across all texts.

> If I read it over before this I'd think . . . that poem rhymes and then once I learned all these other different things I could read over the same poem and say well that poem has a bunch of other things in it too. Maybe I would say something else first instead of saying it rhymes 'cause that was the only thing I knew then. And I'd say well that poem could be different by putting these words in it but the way it is there is, it's exciting because the words are better used or something. (Cynthia, interview, June 5, 1995)

Without the hypermedia authoring, Cynthia, one of the seventh-grade students, would have continued to think of poems as representing one thing—metaphor, rhyme, sound—because the classroom pedagogical context in which many of the poems were originally written prior to the hypermedia project directed students to write a poem using metaphor, then rhyme, and so on. As a result of collaborating in a small group to author hypermedia spaces about poetry, the students found the poetic devices in many poems and became much more sensitive to the way words can be used to create a desired meaningful effect.

During their work at the computer, the seventh-grade groups authoring poetry hypermedia experienced "sharing the ownership of knowing" (Oldfather, 1992, p. 1). They negotiated meaning about each text when they debated how, when, where, what, and why to bring together multiple texts. They made suggestions on each other's work when they revised texts to fit the whole sense of the group project. They, not the teacher, made decisions about "correctness" and effective communication of ideas. "Sharing the ownership of knowing is a dynamic of classroom interaction in which a teacher's constructivist epistemological stance facilitates students' sense of their own construction of meaning, and the integrity of their own thinking. Within such a context students may experience epistemological empowerment, and high levels of motivation for literacy learning" (Oldfather, p. 1). Perhaps a major role of the technology was its ability to reflect back almost immediately on the computer monitor the representations being constructed by the group and to bring together in simultaneous "windows" the multiple texts the group saw as important to manipulate in time and space in order to construct socially meaningful knowledge. Even if the seventh graders did not make visible in their projects multiple, or contrasting, meanings about the world through poetry, they did connect, expose, and explore the self through their own poetry as examples of community knowledge about the world of poetry. This context of collaborative inquiry that framed their social relationships may be enough to claim that a form of critical literacy practice emerged.

IMPLICIT AND EXPLICIT CRITIQUE IN HYPERMEDIA

The undergraduate students built hypermedia documents on a central text, such as Silko's novel *Ceremony*, or a theme, such as hate and propaganda in novels and society. The small groups constructed their documents by juxtaposing sections of a central text, other print texts, and popular culture texts like songs, music videos, movie clips, pictures, and magazine ads in order to construct reinterpretations and interrelated readings of the text (Rosenblatt, 1978). The composers of hypermedia, like readers of literature, (1) made personal connections between the self and the text, (2) explored the self through the juxtapositions of texts, and (3) in a social context of the classroom, exposed the self in the positions taken. They negotiated meaning through resistant readings; their self-explorations supported a critique of society and possible subjectivities; and the exposure of self promoted a sense of personal agency or a political project. Figure 5.1 displays how a small group of undergraduates (calling themselves *das grup*) made personal connections, explored possible subjectivities, and exposed their values in four interlinked spaces which touched upon their readings of three novels—*Ceremony* by Silko (1977), *The Dollmaker* by Arnow (1954), and *To Kill a Mockingbird* by Lee (1960)—a speech by Franklin D. Roosevelt during World War II, and a picture of a barefoot boy.

The entire *das grup* project had 45 spaces that included 21 quotations from the novels or other texts, 20 comments by the group members, 12 sounds which were songs and voice-overs, and 16 images. The 4 spaces displayed in Figure 5.1 were connected by three links allowing the reader to move between them in different sequences depending upon where the reader began. Only 1 space appeared at a time, disappearing when the reader followed a highlighted link. Within the flow of the entire project, most readers first encounter the *roosevelt* space which is located in a group of spaces about the novel *Ceremony*. As you open this space to read the

FIGURE 5.1. *das grup* computer based literature responses

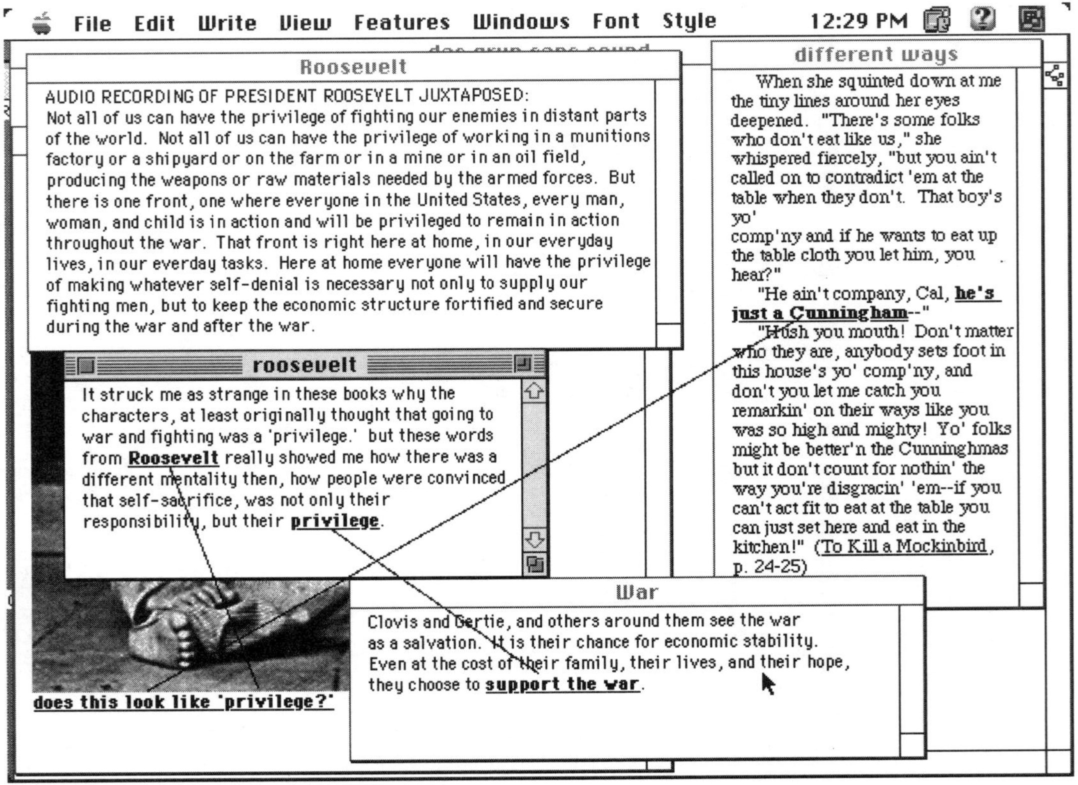

Roosevelt

AUDIO RECORDING OF PRESIDENT ROOSEVELT JUXTAPOSED:
Not all of us can have the privilege of fighting our enemies in distant parts of the world. Not all of us can have the privilege of working in a munitions factory or a shipyard or on the farm or in a mine or in an oil field, producing the weapons or raw materials needed by the armed forces. But there is one front, one where everyone in the United States, every man, woman, and child is in action and will be privileged to remain in action throughout the war. That front is right here at home, in our everyday lives, in our everyday tasks. Here at home everyone will have the privilege of making whatever self-denial is necessary not only to supply our fighting men, but to keep the economic structure fortified and secure during the war and after the war.

roosevelt

It struck me as strange in these books why the characters, at least originally thought that going to war and fighting was a 'privilege.' but these words from **Roosevelt** really showed me how there was a different mentality then, how people were convinced that self-sacrifice, was not only their responsibility, but their **privilege**.

different ways

When she squinted down at me the tiny lines around her eyes deepened. "There's some folks who don't eat like us," she whispered fiercely, "but you ain't called on to contradict 'em at the table when they don't. That boy's yo' comp'ny and if he wants to eat up the table cloth you let him, you hear?"

"He ain't company, Cal, he's **just a Cunningham—**"

"**Hush you mouth! Don't matter who they are, anybody sets foot in this house's yo' comp'ny, and don't you let me catch you remarkin' on their ways like you was so high and mighty! Yo' folks might be better'n the Cunninghams but it don't count for nothin' the wey you're disgracin' 'em—if you can't act fit to eat at the table you can just set here and eat in the kitchen!" (To Kill a Mockinbird, p. 24-25)**

War

Clovis and Bertie, and others around them see the war as a salvation. It is their chance for economic stability. Even at the cost of their family, their lives, and their hope, they choose to **support the war**.

does this look like 'privilege?'

contents, an audio recording of Roosevelt's speech is juxtaposed with the printed commentary. The words of the audio recording are typed into a window; only the window with the student's commentary was visible in the original project. The students explore the subjectivity of people who believed that fighting in a war "was not only their responsibility, but their privilege." In sharing their response that it seemed strange for Tayo, Rocky, and other Native Americans, who were convinced that they would gain the rights of citizenship by fighting for the American nation, to want to go to war, the students expose their value positions and begin to explore the underlying beliefs that would support different values.

From the *roosevelt* space, the reader can follow two links to the spaces *cassie* or *war*. Technically this is accomplished in one of two ways: by making the hyperlink buttons active, then selecting a link button to follow, or by choosing an option to follow a link from this space. With the second option, if the space has multiple links, then a menu of choices is presented for the reader to select a link to follow. The *cassie* and *war* spaces reinterpret Roosevelt's speech about working on the home front to provide the economic security through self-denial in everyday tasks. The students' commentary on Gertie's and Clovis's decisions to use the war as a chance for personal economic gain without regard to their family, lives, or hope, makes the idea of self-denial problematic. And Roosevelt's words about "privilege" are made more directly problematic by the image of a young barefoot boy with the subtitled question: "does this look like privilege?" From this question the reader can follow two links. One link returns to the *roosevelt* space, which a reader might not have heard yet if they entered this space from the *war* space, which resides in a group of spaces about *The Dollmaker*. The second destination is to the space *different ways*, which layers the issue of privilege onto a quote from *To Kill a Mockingbird* in which Calpurnia is scolding Scout when she says, "and don't you let me catch you remarkin' on their ways like you was so high and mighty!"

In linking these ideas across the three novels, the students explicitly explore how the motivations of people who go into war are intertwined with class issues in all three novels. The students expose their own underlying values in questioning Roosevelt's use of the word *privilege*—first juxtaposed with the experience of Native Americans and poor Appalachians who looked to the war to gain acceptance in the dominant culture, then linked to a picture of a poor child and to the "high and mighty" attitude Scout takes towards the town's lower class families. Trend (1994), in defining critical literacy as the construction of resistant or oppositional readings, explains that "the key for an emancipatory use of media materials in the classroom lies in helping students to locate oppositional readings to those offered . . . [I]t is important to stress that culture isn't limited to what is legitimated in books and other instructional materials" (p. 234). In this critical literacy practice, students select and create texts that challenge what they see as erroneous and harmful in situations, themes, and readings. Nearly twenty small groups of undergraduates over the past two years have created projects that are full of examples of how hypermedia supports the critical literacy practice of exposing intertextual values by juxtaposing texts.

The Incredible Themes small group also selected the experience of Native Americans after the war as a site for critique by juxtaposing an excerpt from a popular song by Live (1991) titled "The Beauty of Gray." The music, along with the lyrics, is powerful when set beside this quotation from *Ceremony*:

> I'm half-breed. I'll be the first to say it. I'll speak for both sides. First time you walked down the street in Gallup or Albuquerque, you knew. Don't lie. You knew right away the war was over, the uniform was gone. All of a sudden that man at the store waits on you last, makes you wait until all the white people bought what they wanted. And the white lady at the bus depot, she's real careful now not to touch your hand when she counts out your change. You watch it slide across the counter at you, and you know. Goddamn it! You stupid sonofabitches! You know! (p. 42).

In this juxtaposition, we believe the students assert their position against the oppression experienced by the Native Americans from the whites, by suggesting with the song lyrics that "full" breeds exist only in a "lie," as the music tempo and instruments bring home the refrain, "This is not a black and white world . . . maybe today we will all get to appreciate the Beauty of Gray." Still, Tayo's experience of prejudice presented in the quote makes the song lyrics equally problematic.

Pagano (1990) believes that "to teach is to bring others to look at things in new ways, to orient them to the horizon of their world, . . . [to] shift . . . authority from the text to the interpretation of the text" (p. xiii-xiv). Hypermedia provides students the tool to set one text beside another text with a similar or contrasting perspective, thus presenting one's own view of the world through the decision of how to connect multiple texts. This activity decenters any one text and pushes meaning into the intertextual life of all cultures' texts. In our own work with hypermedia, we experience the same examining of texts in new ways that we see happening in our students. We are constantly alert for texts surrounding us that might help express the complexities of our readings of other texts, that will illuminate important themes, or that will offer surprises and new insights. In the process of constructing their hypermedia projects, the students demonstrate this same excitement and interest as they share their discoveries across groups, talk about all the ways they can connect texts as they digitize the new gem, and discuss, comment and build on, and extend each other's interpretations. The following excerpt from class discussion after the Incredible Themes group shared their project illustrates the social construction of this critical literacy practice.

> *Mike:* I felt with this that they emphasized struggle, especially with the songs, that what they were talking about was everything from the struggle for human rights whatever to the struggle to just say hello to someone, you know what I mean.
>
> *Ron:* I thought that this organization of the space was good, in that [class laughter] it led to better connections between them because it kind of broke down the, where the finer lines were in all the novels good, and I thought some of the more powerful spaces were the ones that had actually no text in connection to any of the novels, especially the, I don't know, the ones where everything seems so unconnected, like they say hello and the film and gum and I was like, "What the hell is that?" [class laughter] and that's Boo Radley and you go "Oh, my God." (Sharing Incredible Themes StorySpace, class transcript, April 24, 1995)

Ron's description of the hypermedia space with the image of half a stick of gum juxtaposed by lyrics from the song "Hello in There" by John Prine (1971), without any text at all to explain any connection, illustrates how the juxtaposed song and image create an intertext that brings to a very personal level the life experience of Boo Radley in *To Kill a Mockingbird*.

One power of these hypermedia spaces seems to be the ability of students to construct meanings without an explicit explanation that a particular text stands for a specific idea. Instead, texts from life experience outside school brought together with school texts engage the students in the negotiation of meanings rather than the reception of an authorized meaning. The representations students then create are not meant to reproduce an authorized text, but to present "knowledge as mutable, relative to context and as subject to multiple perspectives" (Oldfather, 1992, p. 2). In using the hypermedia tool, the students socially construct a literacy practice that involves synthesizing ideas, making judgments, developing opinions, and discovering the self to become "epistemologically empowered" (p. 2). Meaning shifts from the text as a vessel that transmits certain truths across time and space, to the continual negotiation of meaning by connecting, exploring, and exposing the underlying cultural values and assumptions within our responses to the cultural texts juxtaposed in the hypermedia experience.

The hypermedia projects demonstrate a critical literacy as "the process through which students learn to critically appropriate knowledge existing outside their immediate experience in order to broaden their understanding of themselves, the world, and the possibilities for transforming the taken-for-granted assumptions about the way we live" (McLaren, 1989, p. 52).

A PEDAGOGICAL CONTEXT FOR
HYPERMEDIA CRITICAL LITERACY

The pedagogical context in the undergraduate classes with the three novels was much more deliberate about creating a literacy practice in which meanings for texts are constructed and contested in social interaction as members connect, explore, and expose the history of prior texts that continually coalesce in and from their identity. Instructional activity moved between whole-class discussion of the novels, which were being read simultaneously, demonstrations of the computer software for constructing hypermedia, and small group work on the novels and the hypermedia project. For literature discussions, tables and chairs in the room were generally positioned in a circle so the 17 students could face each other, and individual tables were used for small group work. Multimedia construction took place at seven computer workstations which were against the walls around the perimeter of the room, in an adjoining resource room, and on a cart stationed either in the classroom or in the adjoining office of the teacher.

Instructional activities focused upon supporting the construction of a hypermedia interpretation of some significant idea(s) in, between, and beyond the three novels. The six small groups were encouraged to organize the media texts to support the construction of multiple meanings about ideas, thus authoring a hypermedia cultural critique. Key discussions about the novels in class framed a purpose for thinking and a direction for representing responses in the hypermedia projects. In one class, the teacher, Jamie (one of the authors of this chapter), prompted a literature discussion by using one quote from each of the three novels. The students first responded in writing to a quote from *The Dollmaker*, then discussed life experiences in which they were controlled by others' expectations. Quotes, one each from *To Kill a Mockingbird* and *Ceremony*, were introduced over the next hour as each connected to the ideas being discussed:

> *Jamie:* Let me introduce another episode from a different book. This is on page 41 of *To Kill a Mockingbird*. "Dill was in hearty agree-

ment with this plan of action. Dill was becoming something of a trial anyway, following Jem about. He had asked me earlier in the summer to marry him, then he promptly forgot about it. He staked me out, marked me as his property, said I was the only girl he would ever love, then he neglected me. I beat him up twice but it did no good, he only grew closer to Jem," et cetera, et cetera, et cetera, what do you think? [long pause] Is that common, . . .

Peg: O yea!

Jamie: for girls to just woop on them a little bit when they are neglected? [class laughter and agreement]

Jamie: Maybe there's different ways of wooping.

Peg: I think everyone, I think guys are the same way. I know my boyfriend when he feels neglected, it's sarcasm—O well, if you could make time for me in your busy schedule—I mean everybody does that instead of physically beating each other . . .

Jamie: Is there just a subtle connection between this and the expectations that Gertie's living under, or has for herself? Or is it more obvious? Would Scout have said nothing to Uncle John and Grandma and said, "Sure, I'll go to Detroit?"

Class: No, no, no

Kelly: She would have said, "Damn this."

Mike: Pass the damn peas! Yes!

Jamie: But, is Scout also experiencing some of the same gendered expectations?

Class: Yes, yes

Mike: Yes, but I think the difference is Scout's only role model is her father, not only role model, but major role model, and so she's not, she's not constantly engendered with the father being superior and the mother being subservient.

John: It's kinda funny how the one part she says "Dill asked her to marry him, then promptly forgot," and from our discussion that seems like what happened between Gertie and Clovis, in some way they got married then they forgot.

[discussion turns to marking women as property] (class transcript, February 17, 1995)

At the end of the literature discussion, students were given the following suggestion by the teacher for their hypermedia projects:

Think back on our conversation today when you're searching for a purpose for what we might be trying to do with these three novels . . . the experiences in these three novels and the ideas in these three novels are beyond the novels, reaching far beyond the novels into the comments that we overhear on the street as Rick has said in terms of "I got a girl," into movies as Matt has implied, into music, everywhere these ideas show up. And what these ideas do . . . is they build this representation of what it means to be a spouse, or to have expectations, or to be frustrated, things like that. . . . Before I close with a poem I should try to explain that we think that the computer program StorySpace might provide a space in which you could explore ideas, one idea that finds itself being represented in these novels and beyond these novels, because it allows you to put those representations into some relationship to each other to try to explore that idea. (class transcript, February 17, 1995)

The teacher's pedagogy pushed the connections between the three novels into the life experience of the students and framed the hypermedia project as a location in which such life ideas could be represented. It was likely significant that the pedagogy also included the simultaneous reading of the three novels rather than a sequential reading of the stories. For each class, students completed another chunk of each novel, so the juxtaposed stories were constantly in relief to each other over the month of the reading experience. The class conversation continually generated many links to life beyond the novels as identified by the students, and small groups worked on their hypermedia projects based on three questions the teacher wrote on the chalkboard: (1) What ideas or themes might your group represent in StorySpace? (2) What texts do you need to build these representations? and (3) What narrative frame is appropriate for organizing a pathway or story through the texts?

Even though the classroom pedagogy framed the purpose for representing ideas in the hypermedia, the teacher believed the class lacked any experience of critique of cultural values embedded in their responses to the novels. The media and texts that were juxtaposed seemed only to focus one perspective on an issue and not construct the possibility of oppositional readings. A week later the teacher (Jamie) sought to make such a critical literacy practice visible by having groups locate three or four significant events from a novel, explain how these events are connected, and explore how these connections represent the personal and cultural values of themselves as readers of the text.

Dan: The unifying theme was basically on the change like I think the beauty, I mean, I personally love the Gallup scene so much even though it is just really short. It's describing, you know, how the Native Americans, or how the Laguna people have sold out you know, and they're putting on these festivals. I just think that's so vivid to show how Laguna culture and Native American culture has distorted itself to adapt to a capitalistic society so they can survive, you know. I think that shows the need for the definition to create a stronger Laguna society that can survive with its own values in American white society.

Jamie: So you folks feel that you were drawn to this idea of change because it's important today or I mean it's been important in terms of our own culture?

Dan: Well, I think, ha, go ahead . . .

Ann: I think the fact you go through such a powerful process, and in today's society, but I guess in the past it's similar, many people are unwilling to experience the change or to attempt to change because it can be painful and it's not going to be simple, just the fact that many people in today's society or whatever are afraid of the kind of change that Tayo's searching for.

John: I think that's a line that runs through all three of these books, change. And Tayo is changing from day to day. Gertie, I don't know if she's unwilling to change, or she could change, or she changes a little bit but doesn't change the bigger things in her life. And in *To Kill a Mockingbird*, it's like Aunt Alexandria wants Scout to change, and if she made this change it wouldn't be the same book, it wouldn't be the same person, we wouldn't be as excited as you know we are to pick up *To Kill a Mocking-bird* and to go through the pages . . .

Jamie: Having you locate these significant events while you read and then even respond to those in terms of why you find them to be significant, I think is a very basic and important way to get into the interpretation of novels through the collective group rather than through an expert authority in terms of what a novel means. And then really critical is to try to examine why you find those incidents significant. What is it about your own life and your own beliefs that you're bringing into these books, and because those beliefs that you hold are really shaping the interpretations that you're making. So it's important to try to focus not just on the events in the text, but the events that you have experienced that are shaping your interpretations of the text. And, I think that today came out real clear that there are differences of opinion, or there's different meanings for family, and for what change might mean, and for strength, especially

when you start talking about gender . . . so there's a whole lot
of, what's the word . . . well, difference, but maybe even
debate, or ahum . . . challenging, I guess, of what ideas or of
what things mean to us. And what I would like to challenge
you to do in the next classes in which you're going to work just
with your small group—your StorySpace group—and whatever it is you need to do to try to create that representation of an
idea in these novels, is I'd like to challenge you in terms of
whether or not your representation also questions the meaning
of that idea that might be held differently across the culture . . .
whether or not you can bring in different beliefs on those ideas
through the images and music and video clips and text, excerpts
from other books you've read, from plays, poetry, et cetera, and
read those in as well. (class transcript, March 1, 1995)

In the classroom discussions of the novels presented briefly above, the
teacher posed questions first to connect themes between and beyond the
novels and then to make problematic those ideas readers found to be significant. The teacher sought a new critical literacy practice. The hypermedia
project was framed as the place where the students could explore ideas in
the novels and challenge these ideas by connecting other texts from personal experience beyond the three novels. We believe that there is both an
empowering and an emancipatory aspect to this literacy practice. As Freire
(1994) writes,

literacy is an act of knowing, a creative act that should view learners as subjects in the reading process and not as objects of the educator's action. To
view learners as subjects and to engage in critical dialogue with learners leads
to "conscientization," the process of becoming critically conscious of the sociohistorical world in which one intervenes or pretends to intervene politically.
The same is true of the text: It requires the reader's intervention, even though
the reader must also respect the work produced. (p. xii)

CRITICAL LITERACY PRACTICES AS SOCIAL ACTION

The literacy practices constructed by the students who have worked with
hypermedia technology share aspects in common with all literacy practices.
The seventh graders constructed a practice in which knowledge was negotiated among members of the authoring community. In socially constructing this knowledge, however, they did not move into the explicit critical
examination of their own subjectivities and how self-identity is constructed
through and by texts. We believe that this is a direct result of the assign-

ment and not suggestive of an inability of these students to examine texts and subjectivities critically. The undergraduates went beyond the social construction of knowledge to explore the cultural values underlying their responses to texts and to expose their value positions on several issues of importance in their lives. We believe that sufficient evidence has been presented to conclude that the literacy practice constructed provided "a space in which a new subjectivity can begin to articulate itself" and in which the "process of reflection creates a degree of autonomy for the subject" (Janmohamed, 1994, p. 245). In our enthusiasm for this critical literacy practice, we want to caution the reader, as we remind ourselves, that literacy practices are socially constructed cultural ways of being and using texts that are unique to the members of the particular community. The students who worked in the hypermedia communities also participated in many more communities beyond the classroom in which texts are used to construct social relationships and identities. Literacy practices are multiple, and even if common patterns can be abstracted across communities of experience, no classroom pedagogy or representational technology can alone determine the shape of a culturally constructed literacy practice within any group of students.

We would like to close this exploration of critical literacy practices involving hypermedia representational tools with a brief discussion of what we find missing generally in all of these hypermedia projects: a political project for transformation and critical emancipation. In its more complex sense, many proponents of critical literacy argue that critical empowerment demands reflection and action to change power structures, to challenge race, class, and gender inequities, and to transform culture at the school and in other social institutions. Students are empowered to and through action or agency—doing something in response to "conscientization" (Pagano, 1990). The hypermedia projects displayed demonstrate how students organized multiple texts to explore possible subjectivities and, implicitly or explicitly, to expose their own cultural values.

Our question remains, is this public assertion of value, the exposure of self-identity in the form of deeply held beliefs, a critical action in response to reflection that will lead to different interactions and a transformation of culture in the lives of the students (Simon, 1987) beyond the classroom community? Is it enough that their lives together in the classroom community transformed past roles and expectations for students in relationship to teachers and knowledge? Shor (1992) suggests that "the more involved the student, the more he or she wrestles with the meaning in the study, exercises his or her critical voice in debate with peers, and expresses his or her values in a public arena, the more empowering is the experience" (p. 22). For the large part, we believe that the critical literacy practice constructed through the use of hypermedia has the potential to generate a social practice of collaboration, critique, and agency. We believe that such a social practice must be experienced in school because it is increasingly the last place for public debate in which diverse groups of citizens are represented, even though within the larger context of society, "students" are marginalized citizens. We advocate a classroom pedagogy in which the exploration and critique of cultural values and subjectivities is framed by the democratic social relationships essential to the everyday negotiation of difference as we use multiple signs to represent thought, voice intertextuality, expose the self, and construct community. Hypermedia tools of representation within a critical pedagogy have the potential to support the social construction of such a critical literacy practice.

IF SCHOOLS/SOCIETY SHARED OUR PERSPECTIVE ON LITERACY, HOW MIGHT PEOPLE'S LIVES BE DIFFERENT?

Literacy is often narrowly considered as simply acts of communication through the use of the written and read word, and sometimes includes speaking and listening. Thus literacy "skills" and instruction focus on the description of these skills and school activities to deliver their intentional development. But literacy is far more, and to examine its nature and consequences within technologies of communication requires a broader, cultural perspective.

Our acts of literacy do at least two other things beyond communication. They serve as representations of our possible identities, and they construct our social relationships. When we write a letter to a family member, phone a colleague, or frame a photo in our camera view finder, we implicitly represent who we are at that moment and, in the act of producing an utterance or artifact, establish our relationship with the others involved in the literacy event. Likewise, the meanings we construct with the words or images we receive in print, in voice, and in gesture bear the marks of our identity and relationships with others.

One of the most common and pervasive examples of school literacy is any artifact given to the teacher for evaluation; in fact, almost all of the words in school instruction are bound up in this evaluative context. The literacy act establishes the social relationships not only between the student and teacher, but between student and student (usually in a competitive way although many are working to frame shared meanings within a collaborative context). And through the interaction, students are deeply involved in constructing their identity through the responses to the words and actions they offer others. Critical forms of literacy may exist more within the contexts of clubs, sports, and hallways in school in which peers coconstruct identity and relationships.

The question of how lives might be different if we intentionally sought to support a critical literacy perspective similar to the one we advocate is mitigated by the more practical concern if technology will be used to accomplish the same ends as current school instruction in which the teacher transfers knowledge to the student whose identity and social relationships are constructed through the classroom evaluative response. Given this common school perspective on literacy, technology has probably remained fairly neutral in its impact on cultural practices involving literacy. However, newer computer technologies in particular (which may in fact be spilling into school through the students themselves—they always seem to be teaching the teachers how to use the stuff) promise ways in which human interactions might structure more equitable, collaborative relationships and support a valuing of difference and life-long growth rather than conformity and reification in the construction of identity.

At the center of such a move is a shift within our commonsense understanding of meaning from a dyadic to a triadic definition. In practice, we assume that a word or act stands for a single meaning. Yet, we know that words and actions can have multiple meanings depending upon the point of view or reference of the interpreter. When we take into consideration this point of reference for a meaning, then the act of literacy becomes triadic: (1) the word or act, (2) the meaning attributed, and (3) the reference or layer of context. School instruction, or any conversation between an expert and a novice, boss and worker, even husband and wife, tends toward a dyadic definition of meaning in which one and only one thing is meant. Activities using technology can be based in this same dyadic frame of knowledge transfer.

Using technology to support activities in which meaning is negotiated or examined for the purpose of constructing shared meanings in a democratic community is a form of critical literacy that may support more equitable decision making, more thoughtful consuming, or more embracing of difference through the creation of a sense of belonging. At this time, we believe that new technologies offer particular communication and representation tools which may support such a triadic experience of literacy in at least three areas of our lives. In e-mail and netnews networks, participants share personal experiences, offer alternative points of view, ask questions, and question answers. Meanings are negotiated across cultures and the webs of meaning and belonging across the world are drawn tighter together in our personal lives. In the World Wide Web, ordinary citizens have the power to publish ideas in multimedia format and, in linking to connected ideas, create communities of interest world wide that could enhance our democratic lives. It remains a middle-class revolution to date, but ultimately the cost of knowledge production—historically a social activity requiring communication and multiple forms of representation—will be far less electronic space than in the bookstore, and for this reason alone, the transition is a forgone conclusion. In the power of desktop multimedia software, users can create their own multimedia documents, taking the "consumer" further inside the intent of visual representations and motivations in our commercial lives. At least these three activities of knowledge production should be at the heart of critical uses of classroom technology.

By bringing closer together in time and space both the producers of words and images and also the artifacts of their interactions, certain uses of technology promise to support the critical literacies required for community-belonging in a multicultural world. Students already have, or quickly learn, the skills to work the machines; as educators we must provide a vision and an experience of the democratic and human purposes that can be served in our uses of the machines.

REFERENCES

Arnow, H. (1954). *The dollmaker*. New York: Avon Books.

Fishman, A. (1991). *Amish literacy*. Portsmouth, NH: Heinemann.

Freire, P. (1994). *Education for critical consciousness*. New York: Continuum.

Freire, P., & Macedo, D. (1987). *Literacy: Reading the word and the world*. South Hadley, MA: Bergin and Garvey.

Heath, S. B. (1986). The functions and uses of literacy. In S. de Castell, A. Luke, & D. MacLennan (Eds.), *Literacy, society, and schooling* (pp. 15–26). New York: Cambridge University Press.

Janmohamed, A. (1994). Some implications of Paulo Freire's border pedagogy. In H. Giroux & P. McLaren (Eds.), *Between borders: Pedagogy and politics of cultural studies* (pp. 242–252). New York: Routledge.

Jonassen, D. H., Myers, J., McKillop, A. M. (1996). From constructivism to constructionism: Learning *with* hypermedia/multimedia rather than *from* it. In B. Wilson (Ed.), *Constructivist learning environments* (pp. 93–106). Englewood Cliffs, NJ: Educational Technology Publications.

Landow, G. P. (1992). *Hypertext: The convergence of contemporary critical theory and technology*. Baltimore, MD: Johns Hopkins University Press.

Lanham, R. A. (1990). The extraordinary convergence: Democracy, technology, theory and the university curriculum. *South Atlantic Quarterly, 89*(1), 27–50.

Lee, H. (1960). *To kill a mockingbird*. New York: Warner Books.

Live (1991). The Beauty of Gray. On *Mental jewelry* [record]. Radioactive Records.

McKillop, A. M., & Myers, J. (1999). The pedagogical and electronic contexts of composing in hypermedia. In S. L. DeWitt & K. Strasma (Eds.), *Contexts, intertexts, and hypertexts.* Cresskill, NJ: Hampton Press.

McLaren, P. (1989). *Life in schools: An introduction to critical pedagogy in the foundations of education.* New York: Longman.

Myers, J. (1992). The social contexts of school and personal literacy. *Reading Research Quarterly, 27,* 297–333.

Myers, J. (1995 May/June). Moving readers response into cultural critique. *Teaching and Learning Literature,* 3–7.

Oldfather, P. (1992). *Sharing the ownership of knowing: A constructivist concept of motivation for literacy learning.* Paper presented at the annual meeting of the National Reading Conference, San Antonio, TX.

Pagano, J. A. (1990). *Exiles and communities: Teaching in the patriarchal wilderness.* Albany: State University of New York Press.

Prine, J. (1971). Hello in there. On *John Prine* [record]. New York: Atlantic Recording Corporation.

Rosenblatt, L. (1978). *The reader, the text, and the poem: The transactional theory of the literary work.* Carbondale, IL: Southern Illinois University Press.

Shor, I. (1992). *Empowering education: Critical teaching for social change.* Chicago: University of Chicago Press.

Silko, L. (1977). *Ceremony.* New York: Penguin Books.

Simon, R. I. (1987). Empowerment as a pedagogy of possibility. *Language Arts, 64*(4), 370–383.

Street, B. (1984). *Literacy in theory and practice.* New York: Cambridge University Press.

Trend, D. (1994). Nationalities, pedagogies, and media. In H. Giroux & P. McLaren (Eds.), *Between borders: Pedagogy and politics of cultural studies* (pp. 225–241). New York: Routledge.

Vygotsky, L. S. (1986). *Thought and language* (A. Kozulin, Trans.). Cambridge, MA: MIT Press.

6

Multiple Ways of Knowing

Lessons from a Blue Guitar

CHRISTINE H. LELAND, JEROME C. HARSTE,
AND CHRISTINA HELT

> They said, "You have a blue guitar,
> You do not play things as they are.
> The man replied, "Things as they are
> Are changed upon the blue guitar."
> —Wallace Stevens, 1954.

Dennis, Teresa, and James were fourth graders whom we observed as part of an ongoing investigation into how a holistic, inquiry-based, *multiple ways of knowing* approach to instruction supports literacy learning among "severely labeled" children. These three children acquired the label *learning disabled* early in their schooling. Along with this label, they shared the common fate of struggling with the traditional school curriculum, which equated *literacy* with written language. Defining literacy this narrowly, we felt, served to make children vulnerable. We wished to trouble (Lather, 1997) current definitions of both literacy and learning disabilities, showing, in fact, how one definition feeds the other. In this project, we studied literacy as the use of sign systems and in relationship to instruction and learning. We saw *sign systems* (art, music, drama, language, movement, math, and so forth) as representing the various ways humans have developed to mean. We assumed that each sign system made a unique contribution to a person's overall meaning potential and that any instance of literacy was in fact a multimodal event (Harste, Woodward, & Burke, 1984).

What Counts as Literacy: Challenging the School Standard. Copyright © 2000 by Teachers College, Columbia University. All rights reserved. ISBN 0-8077-3972-3 (paper), ISBN 0-8077-3973-1 (cloth). Prior to photocopying items for classroom use, please contact the Copyright Clearance Center, Customer Service, 222 Rosewood Drive, Danvers, MA 01923, USA, telephone (508) 750-8400.

CURRICULUM IN A NEW KEY

Dennis sat staring at his response journal. He had just finished reading *The Dead Man in Indian Creek* (Hahn, 1990). To support him in responding to his reading, we suggested that he might wish to draw rather than write. He picked up his pencil and made a line that divided the page into two sections. He began to draw, stopping every now and then to put his pencil down and reread sections of the text. He ended up with two pictures (see Figure 6.1), which he described as follows: "In the first picture, Otis the dog is chasing a van down the street. Evans was heading toward the highway. [In the second picture] Otis guards Flynn by their fort. Flynn was down in the hole, so Otis was waiting for him to come out so he could bite his leg." Dennis consulted the book again, thought for a moment, and said, "Wait a minute. I drew the pictures in the wrong order. The second one really happened first, and the first one happened second."

On another day in the same classroom, Teresa sat sucking her thumb while the class explored carbon dioxide, nitrogen, and oxygen. It was hard to tell whether she was paying attention. Toward the end of the lesson, the students were asked to show what they had learned from the experiment through either a written explanation or a drawing. Teresa's picture (Figure 6.2) may initially leave a viewer unimpressed. It is easy to glance at it and decide that she had learned very little. Teresa surprised everyone, however, by standing up in front of the class and explaining that her picture was that of a fireman who was attempting to put out a fire, but was having a lot of trouble. When asked why the fireman was experiencing so

FIGURE 6.1. Dennis's Response to a Chapter from *The Dead Man in Indian Creek*

FIGURE 6.2. Teresa's Response to a Science Lesson

much difficulty, Teresa answered, "There is a lot of oxygen inside the dome and this makes the fire stronger and harder to put out."

James did a great job of reading aloud *The Gold Cadillac* (Taylor, 1987) with his partner, but when it came time to write about the story in his literature log, he seemed to lose interest. To pass the time, he started to be disruptive, poking the boy sitting next to him with his pencil. Just before the close of this activity, James copied a sentence directly from the text into his log: "We got us a cadillac." Later, when asked to share his response, he prefaced his remarks with the thought that his sentence was "dumb." With questioning, however, he gave an oral rendition of the story. As he talked, Chris Helt, a researcher who was seen by the class as another teacher, wrote what he said into his literature log. James read what Chris had written and agreed that this was what he wanted to say about the story. The contrast between the copied single statement and the story he dictated was striking. Under one condition, James reflected his special education label—*learning disabled*. Under another condition, he looked like the best reader in the class.

RECOMPOSING CURRICULUM

Researchers have noted that students with learning disabilities have difficulty managing their learning (Hallahan, Kauffman, & Lloyd, 1985), evaluating and monitoring their own performance (Reid, 1988; Reid & Stone,

1991; Swanson, 1990), changing strategies (Derry, 1990; Torgeson, 1979), memorizing (Ceci, 1987; Mastropieri & Scruggs, 1987; C. R. Smith, 1983; Swanson, 1987), acquiring basic skills (Reid, 1988), drawing generalizations (Borkowski, Carr, & Pressley, 1987; Keogh & Hall, 1983), and approaching a task positively (Brown, 1978; Hallahan, Kauffman, & Lloyd, 1985; Weins, 1983). The argument we make in this paper is that these characteristics are context-dependent. Like MacInnis and Hemming (1995), we wish to explore how more supportive curricular environments affect the real performance as well as our perceptions of children labeled as learning disabled.

Farnan, Flood, and Lapp (1994) make the case that "writing is not a 'friendly' process for every student, and, for several reasons, it may be particularly difficult for students identified as having learning disabilities" (p. 292). When asked to write, learning disabled students usually react in a predictable manner, withdrawing from the stressful situation in different ways. While Dennis typically would sit at his desk and stare into space, Teresa would curl herself into a fetal position in some less trafficked area of the classroom and suck her thumb. James would act out in some way, causing a disruption in the classroom. It would have been easy for teachers to assume that these fourth graders either did not read or could not read well enough to engage in writing a reflection on the story.

Myers (1996) argues that the definition of literacy is once again changing. The demands of the twenty-first century will require students who can create multivocal as well as multimodal texts. This is the essence of a multiple ways of knowing approach to learning, which builds from the idea that different sign systems offer different potentials for individuals to make meaning. While education has traditionally given special privilege to language as the preferred sign system for learning (Moffett, 1992; Eisner, 1990), a multiple ways of knowing focus encourages children to make use of other sign systems as well. Gardner (1995) advocates "multiple windows leading to the same room" (p. 205), and suggests that this is achieved by looking at a topic from different perspectives.

Using a multiple ways of knowing approach with children who have been labeled as learning disabled represents a considerable departure from the norm. Research on the instruction provided for students in remedial programs reveals that these students usually receive large amounts of practice on individual skills (Arlington, 1983; Moll & Diaz, 1987). Teachers perceive that these students are weak in basic skill areas and therefore concentrate on eradicating or fixing these weaknesses. The tendency to reduce learning tasks to isolated skills has been particularly strong among "special" educators. "We have held the assumption that learning disabled youngsters are best taught when we break the product of process of learning into smaller and smaller pieces. . . . In fact, our faith in reducing the learning task is so great that our first response to the failure of a child to learn a behavior is to break the task down even further" (Poplin, 1988, p. 395). Testimonials from teachers support this claim.

> As a *reading specialist* and resource room teacher of learning disabled children, I have struggled through years of setting behavioral goals and objectives, trying to teach mastery of isolated skills in a sequence of ascending difficulty. . . . However, the degree of proficiency attained in reading and written language was often disappointing; in addition, the children remained turned off to books, and often to school as well. (Brand, p. 306; emphasis in original)

Some researchers have suggested that the teaching methods routinely used with problem learners might be responsible for causing the perceived learning problems. Lyons (1988) conducted a study of children who were identified early as being learning disabled, but were later mainstreamed (and unlabeled) after completing a reading recovery program. She questioned whether these children were ever really learning disabled or if they were, in fact, instructionally disabled. Poplin (1988) supports the idea that instruction can cause children to look disabled.

> Learning a skill one day and forgetting it the next is often implied as a characteristic of the learning disabled student. I propose, however, that this characteristic is more a result of the reductionistic methods we employ than characteristic of the students we serve. (p. 394)

A critique offered by Sawyer (1991) reinforces the notion that what is thought to be a cure often exacerbates the problem:

> The practice of immersing poor readers in programs designed to boost decoding skills is probably responsible for retarding growth in vocabulary and syntax due to limited exposure to more advanced vocabulary and sentence structure. Poor readers read less, and they read less complex material. (p. 11)

We see a multiple ways of knowing curriculum as an advocacy curriculum for children, as well as for society. If Myers (1996) is right, multiple literacies is the way of the future. Rather than exclude children as traditional curricula have been prone to do, a multiple ways of knowing curriculum is *inclusive*, building from the strengths the learner brings. When Dennis used art and oral expression to tell what he knew about the book he had read, he came out looking and feeling like a reader. No one questioned his comprehension. It could be assumed. Similarly, when Teresa used art and oral expression to show her understanding of a science lesson, she too looked different. She not only understood but could apply what she had learned to new, imagined settings. James merely copied a sentence out of the book he was reading when asked to give a written response to the story. Yet, when given an opportunity to tell the story, he grew, as did our understanding of what he had read. Under multiple ways of knowing conditions these children, their classmates, and their teachers' understanding of them grew.

READING A NEW SCORE

In no instance was this growth more evident than when drama was introduced into their classroom. Wolf (1993) suggests that "one possible solution to the problems of labeled children is the confluence of reading with drama" (p. 541). While labels focus on the things that children cannot do, drama, on the other hand, focuses on what they can do. Earlier observations of the whole class participating in various drama activities (Harste, Leland, & Smith, 1994) indicated that these children had positive feelings about this sign system. As a result, the classroom teacher began to offer dramatization as a way for students to respond to assigned readings. All three students participated with various peers in a number of different drama experiences.

In one instance, the students did 30 minutes of uninterrupted silent reading, then formed groups of three to act out a scene from the day's reading of *The Dead Man in Indian Creek*. Groups had ample time to plan and practice before sharing their scene with the rest of the class. Although we had never seen Dennis offer to read aloud in class, he volunteered to play the character of Flynn, a bad guy who was smuggling drugs. During the dramatization of the scene, Dennis paraphrased what Flynn said in the story. The three students in the group were such convincing actors that their classmates had no trouble recognizing the scene they were portraying.

In another instance, Teresa and Dennis were in the same group with two other classmates. They had been asked to read and discuss the poem "Some People" by Rachel Field (1952) with their group and then act it out for the rest of the class. After the initial reading and discussion, the group decided that it would be useful to have a narrator who would read the poem aloud while the others acted it out. During the rehearsal time, Teresa read aloud while the group used drama to convey words and phrases like "tired," "shrivel up," "fireflies," and "shiny in your mind." When it was time to perform for the class, Teresa decided that she would rather act than read in front of the class. These examples suggest that drama can reduce anxiety for students with learning disabilities when they are asked to express themselves before an audience. While Teresa and Dennis were not ready to risk reading aloud to the class, they were willing to share their dramatizations.

Participation in a drama activity might not sound important, but for Teresa it was a milestone. A shy and withdrawn child, she had spent most of her kindergarten year curled up in a box in the play area, sucking her thumb and ignoring her teacher's attempts to communicate with her. During the succeeding years, Teresa gradually began to join the group more frequently, but it was not until teacher Joe Turner introduced drama in fourth grade that she came into her own. She loved drama and volunteered often. It was interesting to note that when the class was engaged in drama, she did not suck her thumb, and on rare occasions, she even sounded quite authoritarian, taking charge of situations and directing others in relation to her intent. A good example is Teresa's interaction with a social worker who came to school to make arrangements for a home visit with one of the students. Teresa stepped up and told the social worker that she did not think she had the right to "barge into people's homes." Her teachers, Chris Collier and Joe Turner, were stunned. They attributed Teresa's willingness to speak up to her work in drama. According to Joe, "Teresa took on a role and in that role was someone quite different than she normally was."

WRITING A NEW SCORE

Another form of drama served to coax these reluctant writers to put words on paper. In a written conversation (Short, Harste, & Burke, 1995), two or more participants assume the voices of characters from literature and write to each other in the voice of the character selected. This is a low-risk activity because they are invited to step out of their own role and pretend that they are someone else. They can always say that it is the other person talking if there is any criticism of what has been written. Although James, Dennis, and Teresa often found ways to avoid doing assigned writing, they all participated willingly in written conversations as they played different characters from *The Dead Man in Indian Creek*. James's participation in a written conversation was considered a breakthrough, especially since his partner had expected to be doing the writing for both of them. James surprised him by saying, "No, I can do it." Teresa, playing the role of Pam, wrote back and forth with a classmate who played the role of Evans (see Figure 6.3). The conversations of all three children were compatible with the story line and even extended the characters by generating what they might have said in these situations.

FIGURE 6.3. Teresa's Written Conversation

Teresa   (playing the role of Pam)
Tawanna   (playing the role of Evans)

Teresa: Hi Evans.

Tawanna: What you doing today.?

Teresa: Nothing why?

Tawanna: I just want to ra Well do you now where Porker and matt is?

Teresa: Yes They went trick or treating.

Tawanna: Thats right I forgot Is that the Phone?

Teresa: yes you did. forget or plan

Tawanna: What plan.

Teresa: To go out to eat

Tawanna: Where?

Teresa: Who Said eniything about going out to eat

Tawanna: I just said. Let's go to the creek to look at the moon light and the stars.

Teresa: Oky

By these examples we do not intend to imply that drama is a prompt, and writing is the real end goal of writing instruction. Nor do we wish to suggest that drama is somehow more important than writing. Rather, both drama and writing are vehicles for making and sharing meaning. More broadly, a good language arts program ought to help children explore and expand all of their communication potential.

CHANGING THE TUNE

Students with learning disabilities are frequently described as non-systematic learners who are easily distracted. While this description may or may not be true, depending on the child and the situation, it does nothing to move the field in the direction of helping children like Dennis, Teresa, and James to achieve success in school. The advice offered by Echevarria and McDonough (1995) is more helpful: "These students need to be involved in instructional settings that provide opportunities for active learning" (p. 108). Movement among the sign systems provided this opportunity for Dennis, Teresa, and James. It gave them a chance to enter the conversations of their classroom and to have their voices be heard.

We have learned (the hard way) that deficit models do not work. All we end up with is a list of all the things that students cannot do. When we invite students to use sign systems flexibly in their efforts to make sense of the world, we end up with a list of all the things they can do. There is a relationship between the environment we create and the semiotic or meaning potential of learners. What we can mean is dependent upon the tools we have available. Culture makes multiple sign systems available, but for them to be useful for instruction, we must recognize the opportunities they provide for literacy and learning (Harste, 1996).

We also end up with an expanded idea of what literacy is. Since literacy events are multimodal, we need to look beyond the evidence of written expression. Encouraging our students to use oral language, art, and drama together allows them access to the discourse community and provides them with the tools to be literate in the twenty-first century. Perhaps more than any other children, those who carry the label *learning disabled* need to be convinced that they can indeed become members of what Frank Smith (1985) has called "the Literacy Club." One of the things we have learned from our work in literacy is that before learners become literate, they must *believe* themselves to be literate. In this insight there is a lesson for all of us. It is easy to intimidate learners, regardless of labels; much harder to support them. There is a yin and yang here. James recently did a drawing showing what the book *Faithful Elephants* (Tsuchiya, 1988) meant to him. In his picture (Figure 6.4), there is a dark side and a light side. While the dark side portrays little hope, the bright side shows a rose blooming and a world arising to the beginning of a new day. For us, a multiple ways of knowing curriculum carries this same hopeful message. We, like new literates everywhere, must first imagine a new instructional world before we can create it. It is this interplay between theory and practice that rightfully drives curriculum. In some ways it is all art—a matter of seeing; in other ways it is all drama—living the life we want to live, being the people we want to be.

IF SCHOOLS/SOCIETY SHARED OUR PERSPECTIVE ON LITERACY, HOW MIGHT PEOPLE'S LIVES BE DIFFERENT?

Our goal in this chapter was to describe a *practical theory* of literacy that evolves through *theoretical practice*. As part of this goal, we want to explore the possibilities that children can develop theories of themselves as literate individuals and that teachers can develop theories of themselves as agents of change.

FIGURE 6.4. James's Response to *Faithful Elephants*

If teachers were to position themselves vulnerably and engage in ongoing reflection about their own stances in regard to struggling learners, they would become aware of the relationship between what children can do and the constraints that are presented by the environment in which they operate. Teachers could then begin to create a different reality where these students do not look so "special." By pushing the boundaries of a traditional verbocentric curriculum, they could provide access to literacy for many more students. They would realize that curriculum has to explore new possibilities and give both teachers and students new opportunities to imagine what could be. Without this opportunity to imagine new possibilities, there is literally no place to go and no chance of outgrowing our former selves.

If schools and society valued multiple ways of knowing, there would be much less labeling of children. Children who were formerly thought to be deficient because they were unwilling or unable to generate the standard language-based responses that teachers traditionally look for would now be encouraged to access many different ways of making and sharing meaning. Dennis, Teresa, and James would take their places as valued members of the learning community; their voices would be heard. We think that the term *learning disability* would cease to exist once educators realized that all students have the ability to learn when their strengths (rather than their weaknesses) are seen as the starting point for building curriculum.

Note: This research was supported in part by grants from the Faculty Development Undergraduate Mentorship Program at Indiana University-Purdue University at Indianapolis, and the RITE (Research in Teacher Education) Program at Indiana University.

REFERENCES

Arlington, R. (1983). The reading instruction provided readers of differing ability. *Elementary School Journal, 83,* 255–265.

Borkowski, J., Carr, M., & Pressley, M. (1987). "Spontaneous" strategy use: Perspectives from metacognitive theory. *Intelligence, 11,* 61–75.

Brand, S. (1989). Learning through meaning. *Academic Therapy, 24*(3), 305–314.

Brown, A. (1978). Knowing when, where, and how to remember: A problem of metacognition. In R. Glaser (Ed.), *Advances in instructional psychology* (pp. 55–113). Hillsdale, NJ: Erlbaum.

Ceci, S. (1987). *Handbook of cognitive, social, and neurological aspects of learning disabilities,* Vol. 2. Hillsdale, NJ: Erlbaum.

Derry, S. (1990). Remediating academic difficulties through strategy training: The acquisition of useful knowledge. *Remedial and Special Education, 11*(6), 19–31.

Echevarria, J., & McDonough, R. (1995). An alternative reading approach: Instructional conversations in a bilingual special education setting. *Learning Disabilities Research & Practice, 10*(2), 108–119.

Eisner, E. (1990). Implications of artistic intelligences for education. In W. J. Moody (Ed.), *Artistic intelligences: Implications for education* (pp. 31–42). New York: Teachers College Press.

Farnan, N., Flood, J., & Lapp, D. (1994). Motivating high-risk learners to think and act as writers. In K. D. Wood & R. Algozzine (Eds.), *Teaching reading to high-risk learners* (pp. 291–314). Needham Heights, MA: Allyn and Bacon.

Field, R. (1952). *Poems.* New York: MacMillan.

Gardner, H. (1995). Reflections on multiple intelligences: Myths and messages. *Phi Delta Kappan, 77*(3), 200–209.

Hahn, M. D. (1990). *The dead man in Indian Creek.* New York: Avon Camelot Books.

Hallahan, D., Kauffman, J., & Lloyd, J. (1985). *Introduction to learning disabilities.* Englewood Cliffs, NJ: Prentice Hall.

Harste, J. (1996). *Cultures and classrooms.* Keynote address at the United Kingdom Reading Association Conference, Newcastle, U.K.

Harste, J., Leland, C., & Smith, K. (1994). *Curriculum as drama: Drama as curriculum.* Paper presented at the National Reading Conference, San Diego, CA.

Harste, J., Woodward, V., & Burke, C. (1984). *Language stories and literacy lessons.* Portsmouth, NH: Heinemann.

Keogh, B., & Hall, R. (1983). Cognitive training with learning disabled pupils. In A. Myer & W. Craighead (Eds.), *Cognitive behavior therapy with children* (pp. 163–191). New York: Plenum Press.

Lather, P. (1997). *Troubling the angels: Women living with HIV/AIDS*. Boulder, CO: Westview Press.

Lyons, C. A. (1988, December). *Patterns of oral reading behavior in learning disabled students in reading recovery: Is a child's learning disability environmentally produced?* Paper presented at the National Reading Conference, Tucson, AZ.

MacInnis, C., & Hemming, H. (1995). Linking the needs of students with learning disabilities to a whole language curriculum. *Journal of Learning Disabilities, 28*(9), 535–544.

Mastropieri, M., & Scruggs, T. (1987). *Effective instruction for special education.* Austin, TX: PRO-ED.

Moffett, J. (1992). *Harmonic learning: Keynoting school reform.* Portsmouth, NH: Boynton/Cook.

Moll, L., & Diaz, S. (1987). Change as the goal of educational research. *Anthropology and Education Quarterly, 18*, 300–311.

Myers, M. (1996). *Changing our minds: Negotiating English and literacy.* Urbana, IL: National Council of Teachers of English.

Poplin, M. (1988). The reductionistic fallacy in learning disabilities: Replicating the past by reducing the present. *Journal of Learning Disabilities, 21*(7), 389–400.

Reid, D. (1988). *Teaching the learning disabled.* Boston: Allyn & Bacon.

Reid, D., & Stone, C. (1991). Why is cognitive instruction effective? Understanding learning mechanisms. *Remedial and Special Education, 12*(3), 8–19.

Sawyer, D. J. (1991). Whole language in context: Insights into the current great debate. *Topics in Language Disorders, 11*(3), 1–131.

Short, K., Harste, J., & Burke, C. (1995). *Creatina classrooms for authors and inquirers.* Portsmouth, NH: Heinemann.

Smith, C. R. (1983). *Learning disabilities: The interaction of learner, task, and setting.* Boston: Little, Brown.

Smith, F. (1985). *Reading without nonsense.* New York: Teachers College Press.

Stevens, Wallace. (1954). *Collected poems.* New York: Knopf.

Swanson, H. (1987). What learning disabled readers fail to retrieve: A problem of encoding, interference or sharing of resources? *Journal of Abnormal Child Psychology, 15*, 339–351.

Swanson, H. (1990). Instruction derived from the strategy deficit model: Overview of principles and procedures. In T. Scruggs & B. Wong (Eds.), *Intervention research in learning disabilities* (pp. 34–65). New York: Springer-Verlag.

Taylor, M. (1987). *The gold Cadillac.* New York: Bantam Skylark.

Torgesen, J. (1979). Factors related to poor performance in reading disabled children. *Learning Disability Quarterly, 2*(3), 17–23.

Tsuchiya, Y. (1988). *Faithful elephants.* Boston: Houghton Mifflin.

Weins, J. (1983). Metacognition and the adolescent passive learner. *Journal of Learning Disabilities, 16*, 144–149.

Wolf, S. A. (1993). What's in a name? Labels and literacy in readers theatre. *The Reading Teacher, 46*(7), 540–545.

7

An African American Child's Science Talk

Co-construction of Meaning from the
Perspectives of Multiple Discourses

JAMES PAUL GEE
AND KATE CLINTON

Though this paper grew out of a general interest about language in science education, we focus here on our interactions with one low-socioeconomic-level African American fourth-grade girl ("Kim," a pseudonym) in a hands-on science discussion. How we construed what was going on in this child's language, we argue, has important implications not only for us but also for her. In this chapter, we will first sketch our general approach to language and literacy, then turn to our specific analyses, and finally draw conclusions about language and literacy from our analyses.

Every language is composed of many different "social languages" (Bakhtin, 1986). Each different social language gives us different verbal resources with which to display and recognize different socially situated identities. But language never does this by itself. It is always part and parcel of something bigger, what we will call *Discourses*, with a capital *D*. Discourses (Gee, 1996) are ways of talking, listening, reading, and writing—that is, using social languages—together with ways of acting, interacting, believing, valuing, and using tools and objects, in particular settings at specific times, so as to display and recognize particular socially situated identities, such as being (different kinds of) lawyers or doctors; policemen or street gang members; Anglo-Americans or African Americans; bench chemists, theoretical physicists, or elementary school science students.

There are many different uses of written and spoken language coordinated in different ways with talk, tools, beliefs, values, action and interaction within different Discourses. Thus, there are *multiple literacies*, that

What Counts as Literacy: Challenging the School Standard. Copyright © 2000 by Teachers College, Columbia University. All rights reserved. ISBN 0-8077-3972-3 (paper), ISBN 0-8077-3973-1 (cloth). Prior to photocopying items for classroom use, please contact the Copyright Clearance Center, Customer Service, 222 Rosewood Drive, Danvers, MA 01923, USA, telephone (508) 750-8400.

is, different Discourses that involve, along with much else, different ways of reading and/or writing. In our view, then, it is better to focus on multiple Discourses than on *literacy*.

As Discourses gain power and status in a society, they often attempt to efface all traces of multiplicity in the social languages they use. For example, the "hard sciences" arose historically out of a rich variety of social languages and different genres (e.g., narrative and dramatic dialogues played a large role in seventeenth and eighteenth century science). But contemporary science and science classrooms tend to value a narrow range of expression (Montgomery, 1996). Thanks to the dominant view of science in our society, we as teachers and researchers may often be listening on too narrow a bandwidth for what will count as valued talk, thinking, or writing in science or other academic areas.

BACKGROUND TO THIS STUDY

In working with elementary school classrooms devoted to hands-on collaborative science activities, we had come to wonder whether some nonmainstream children were learning less "science content" than other "better prepared" children (Delpit, 1995). To begin to study the matter we set up one-on-one discussions with individual children and a graduate student researcher (hereafter "Leslie"), centered around a light box and variously configured plastic shapes that refracted and reflected light in distinct ways.

The children we interviewed had already done an in-class set of activities on light, without much overt instruction. Leslie asked one child at a time to demonstrate how the light box worked, giving them very little overt guidance and "scaffolding" and letting the children proceed pretty much as they wished in interaction with the materials. We were interested in seeing what forms of talk we would get from different children and how school-like it would or would not be in this open-ended setting.

To help the reader visualize the setting, here is the sort of thing the children saw: A beam of white light came out of the light box, entered one of the translucent plastic shapes placed in front of it, and came out of the shape as lines of white light radiating along the tabletop in several different directions. In the case of a plastic prism, in addition to other radiating lines of white light, one line hit a white piece of paper and made a "rainbow" of colors.

Our initial hypothesis was that nonmainstream children would not produce school-based (and science-based) talk. Kim quickly seemed to confirm this hypothesis. On an initial viewing of the videotape, Kim's language seemed, at many points, to be wandering, confused, and "strange." However, after intensive discourse analysis, the story became a good deal more complex. It became the story of Kim and the researchers who interacted with her, just as her school story is often the story of herself and the teachers and peers who interact with her. Many of these teachers and peers may well make some of the same initial assumptions we did, but they do not have the luxury of engaging in hours of discourse analysis.

FIRST IMPRESSIONS

Our first impressions of Kim's initial session were deeply influenced by what we saw as its narrative-like quality. We say "narrative-like" because, while Kim engaged in an extended range of speech activities that had narrative-like elements, that is, concrete details and events, it was not always clear how to categorize these. Indeed, that was part of our problem. Kim's approach contrasted with that of the other children interviewed, who did not have these sorts of speech activities. For ease of reference, we will simply use the term *narrative* for the segments we are interested in.

Kim's narratives start at the very outset of her interview. Prior to demonstrating the light box, Leslie asks Kim what she already knows about light. This request generates four short segments from Kim, the last of which is about what she has learned about dinosaurs in school.

DINOSAUR NARRATIVE (NARRATIVE 4)

1. *Leslie:* Where does the light come from when it's outside?
2. *Kim:* Sun.
3. *Leslie:* From the sun. Hum.
4. *Kim:* Cause the sun comes up really early.
5. *Leslie:* Um and that's when we get light.
6. *Kim:* Me and my class is talkin' about dinosaurs and how they died and we found out some things about how they died.
7. *Leslie: Oh really. Does that have to do with light?*
8. *Kim:* One of them is that dinosaurs need light to live and they need food that the light grows the food the trees . . .
9. *Leslie:* Ooh.
10. *Kim:* And when we looked in our book on it and on one page it was how that there was this dinosaur, see the size of this [points to a plastic shape].
11. *Leslie:* Uh huh.
12. *Kim:* But a little bigger than that and wider [motions with hands].

13. *Leslie:* Uh huh.
14. *Kim:* Well it's like that one [points to a larger plastic object].
15. *Leslie:* Uh huh.
16. *Kim:* But like that wide and say this one right here [points to another plastic object].
17. And this [points to the same plastic shape] is the dinosaur.
18. Say this [points to another plastic shape] was the pond of water like a footprint full of water.
19. And this [points to previous plastic shape] is the dinosaur drinkin' out of the water.
20. But the dinosaur probably woulda never found this puddle.
21. *Leslie:* If it was way over here and there was no light the dinosaur would have still been looking.

This excerpt displays many of the features that made us hear Kim's language as not school-based. First, Kim starts abruptly, at line 6, talking about dinosaurs with no apparent link to the overall topic of light. This causes Leslie in line 7 (italicized) to think that Kim has gone off topic. Second, Kim's use of the plastic shapes to stand for dinosaurs and ponds, rather than abstract properties like shapes and angles, made the narrative sound to us like a play narrative. It sounded as if Kim were going to enact a story about a dinosaur looking for water. This use of the plastic objects was a pervasive feature of Kim's narratives in the first tape.

As we reanalyzed Kim's responses, we decided that it was likely that Kim had read that a meteor had blocked out the sun, leading to the demise of the dinosaurs. In any case, her argument is that without light the dinosaurs would have been unable to find food and water, and furthermore, food sources would have died off. That Kim knows her overall theme or point and that, indeed, she has one, is clear in line 8 when she states a clear generalization in response to Leslie's question as to what dinosaurs have to do with light: ". . . dinosaurs need light to live and they need food that the light grows."

Our initial response to this narrative and to Kim's other narratives was that she did not understand the science content. Our assumptions about what we expected to hear in school-based talk about science activities led us to conclude that Kim's narratives were not in the service of generalizations (useful to the study of science). Rather, Kim's narratives sounded as if they were too rooted in concrete events. In other words, Kim assigned concrete values (dinosaur, pond) to the plastic objects, while we expected the objects would stand for more abstract values such as geometrical shapes and certain configurations of angles. Kim violated our expectations for how narrative-like details would function in this kind of task, not because she failed to do what we had expected (she clearly stated a generalization to Leslie under questioning in line 8), but rather because the form of her language failed to be what we expected and were listening for. As we realized later, however, Kim was correct, and we erred in our initial analysis.

INITIAL OVERVIEW

The dinosaur narrative shows a part of the initial framework in which we viewed Kim's videotape. To continue to track our initial construals, we explain here how we first understood the overall structure of Kim's interview. What follows is our first outline of the whole interview. It has four parts, each of which is measured in terms of the number of pages in the transcript it takes up:

> Part I. What do you know about light? [4 pages]
>> Narrative 1: Mom says Kim needs more light.
>> Narrative 2: A book Kim read on light.
>> Narrative 3: Adjusting light in the research room.
>> Narrative 4: Dinosaur narrative
> Part II. Leslie and Kim interact over materials. [not transcribed]
> Part III. Evaporation Narratives [6½ pages]
>> Narrative 5: Tunnel narrative
>> Narrative 6: Bedroom narrative
>> Narrative 7: Round road narrative
>> Narrative 8: Adjusting light in the research room.
>> Narrative 9: The sun
> Part IV. Leslie and Kim interact over materials. [16 pages]
>> Narrative 10: Rainbow text [½ page]

Part I is start-up talk about what Kim already knows about light. In Part II, Leslie demonstrates the light box for Kim, showing her what happens when the light beam is shined through various plastic shapes. Leslie then begins a discussion in which Kim actively manipulates and discusses the materials, using descriptive and expository talk. In Part III, Kim tells a whole series of narratives about sound evaporating in various spaces— *evaporating* is her word. It is our changing views of the narratives in Part III that are the heart of the story we have to tell. But before we discuss those narratives, we want to make clear, by discussing the context within which we viewed them, why we initially viewed them as we did. What we named the "dinosaur narrative" was part of the preceding context. What is referred to as the "rainbow text" (whose genre is quite unclear, as we will show) ends Kim's string of narratives. These two end points, the dinosaur narrative and the rainbow text, shaped how we first saw what Kim was doing in what we called the "evaporation narratives."

We turn now to the rainbow text in Part IV. Here, Kim does something that many viewers have found strange. The text has given rise to endless speculation on the part of all who have seen it, with little consensus. For ease of reference in this paper, we will number the lines of our excerpts from the transcript consecutively, though, of course, most of the interview intervenes between the preceding dinosaur narrative and this text.

Rainbow Text (Narrative 10)

22. *Leslie:* And can I ask you another question . . . So it comes out, it's a regular light; it's a regular light coming out from a light bulb. What's here? What's here, Kim?
23. *Kim:* Like a rainbow.
24. *Leslie:* Like a rainbow.
25. *Kim:* I think that . . .
26. *Leslie:* How does that happen?
27. *Kim:* [Picks up prism (triangle); stares at it for a while, then removes her gaze from it.] Because (pause) the um, what makes a . . .
28. Water and sun always makes a rainbow [said musingly, while looking up and away].
29. *Leslie:* Water and sun always makes a rainbow, and why is that?
30. *Kim:* Because [puts down prism] . . .
31. Say this was the water [picks up a big square for the water, then puts it in front of light box] . . .
32. And this [picks up an oblong object, intending it to be the sun, puts it in front of light box, and then moves it away] . . .
33. And this was the sun [picking up a rectangular object and puts it front of light box, making it the sun] . . .
34. And this is the water [places her hand on the rectangular object and moves it up and down, making it now the water] . . .
35. If you put these two right together [moves the oblong and the rectangular object for the sun together into light beam] . . .
36. It'd make a rainbow [pause, takes hands off objects]
37. which [pause, adjusts rectangular object used to try to make a rainbow; long pause while manipulating object. Then moves this object out of the way and picks up the prism, places the prism close to the light box, then places the oblong right behind the prism]. . . .

38. It kinda, if you put those two together, see right here, it's a rainbow,
39. but when it, right here it's just regular light, but now it's not, 'cause
40. it's blue and yellow, but . . .
41. *Leslie:* And how does that happen? Even if we take this one away [Leslie moves away the oblong object].
42. *Kim:* It's green, yellow, and red.
43. *Leslie:* And look at this, yeah, and blue. It looks like there's some blue there.

There are several things that may seem odd about this text. First, Kim again assigns the shapes concrete values (water and sun), and she readily switches their values (lines 31–34). Second, she lets a plastic shape play the role of the sun, when the light box would seem, perhaps, to have been a better candidate, since it is supposed to be representing light in this whole enterprise. Third, Kim is not bothered when Leslie removes one of her objects at the end of the interaction (line 41). She goes right on discussing the color effects caused by the light beam and the remaining plastic shape.

However, once again it is clear that Kim intends her language and action to support a generalization, a generalization she clearly states at the outset: "Because . . . water and sun always makes a rainbow" (line 28). Clearly, this generalization is supposed to answer Leslie's question of how the prism makes a rainbow of colors when the light from the light box goes through it (line 26). The problem is that it is not at all clear how a generalization about real world objects like sun and water can explain why the prism causes the light beam to break into a rainbow of colors. What was needed, we assumed, was a focus on the abstract and geometrical properties of the plastic shapes themselves, not on objects they might stand for in the world of Kim's experience.

Initially, the rainbow text seemed to us to be the end product of Kim's series of evaporation narratives in Part III (which we will discuss in a moment) and, in turn, influenced how we saw the narratives. In light of the rainbow text and the dinosaur narrative, we initially saw the evaporation narratives as play, overly concrete, confused, and moving rather randomly from topic to topic. As we came to understand them better, however, our assumptions changed. We eventually also changed our view of the rainbow text itself. We came to see that text as a co-construction between Leslie and Kim. Furthermore, while the rainbow text had seemed important and central to us at the outset, we later came to see it as not very significant within the interaction as a whole. The rainbow text turns out, in fact, to be quite atypical of what Kim is doing in her narratives and in the rest of her nonnarrative interaction in the interview. It becomes more a story of the researchers and less a story of Kim.

CHANGING VIEWS

Now we turn to the evaporation narratives in Part III. Soon after Kim had been asked to describe what was happening when the light beam interacted with the various plastic shapes, she hit on the idea that there are mirrors on the inside edges of the shapes. In the transcript that follows we attempt to clarify what we take to be her meaning by placing explanatory material in brackets: (Later we will discuss a model of what Kim has in mind that makes what she is talking about a good deal clearer.)

44. *Kim:* Inside of here [holding a plastic shape] there's these [mirrors].
45. And then the mirror, they [the light beams inside the plastic shape] *evaporate*, like the voice, they *evaporate*.
46. And they go through all of 'em [the plastic shapes] when you stick it [the main light beam] over.
47. And, but they [the light beams inside the plastic shape] still go out [of the plastic shape] because of the way you stick it in.

Though Kim's word *evaporate* (italicized above in line 45) is unorthodox, Leslie does not interrupt her. After a page and half more of the transcript, however, Kim uses the word again (italicized in line 51 below):

48. *Kim:* But if I turned it [the plastic shape] around like that . . .
49. Everywhere I turned it, it's [the radiating lines of light] going to go a different way, because of how . . .
50. It's either how I'm turnin' it . . .
51. And the way it *evaporates* on the, um, on the shape . . .

Now Leslie does interrupt Kim and asks a question that sets off the series of evaporation narratives: "Can you tell me what you mean by evaporating on the shape?" We print here the first two of these narratives, according to our initial outline of the interview. (The numbered subtitles refer to our revised view of the structure, which we will discuss next.)

TUNNEL NARRATIVE (NARRATIVE 5)

1. A Really Quiet Place

52. *Kim:* You know like if you was in a really quiet place . . .
53. And there was one hole like—this, these two . . .
54. You're in one hole side . . .

55. And um—you, yeah like a straw . . .
56. And there was one hole quiet side . . .
57. And there was a topping of it . . .
58. The straw is the top . . .
59. Cause I don't have a top.
60. And there's one hole on one side . . .
61. And one hole's on the other side . . .
62. And—the, we'll use—
63. And if there was a really tiny person that could slip in there and started talkin . . .
64. Like to his friend or somethin'.
65. If he had a friend . . .
66. And he started talking . . .

2. A Real Tunnel

67. Well . . . well in a bus tunnel, a tunnel, a real tunnel . . .
68. Like what a train goes over, with water, underneath the tunnel . . .
69. You, that would be like, somethin' like that high . . .
70. And then it'd go—
71. And every noise you make would—
72. Every noise you make it'd evaporate and go all over the tunnel.

BEDROOM NARRATIVE (NARRATIVE 6)

3. Mom's Bedroom

73. And it doesn't just have to be with a tunnel . . .
74. Cause that happens in—
75. here we used to live, that was happenin' in my Mom's bedroom.
76. Every time—the room—
77. Sometimes tunnels can be fl—
78. Like um, say this was a tunnel . . .
79. Even though it's shaped like a [word can't be heard].
80. And I had, I had this thing . . .
81. And we stuck it in there to make it—from here to there with a whole bunch of shluff [stuff] to fill it up all the—
82. To fill the tunnel or the room up to here.
83. And then you start, you—
84. Say this straw is the bed.
85. You climb up on the bed and you start yelling.

86. It won't evaporate on the bottom, because of the way all the stuff is . . .
87. It's covering all of the space that you have.
88. And—well when you take out the space . . .
89. All the stuff that was covering the space . . .
90. And you put more stuff.
91. You put in new stuff that like um like the straw.
92. *Leslie:* So if you take out all—
93. So if you take out all the stuff . . .
94. And you're sittin' on the bed.
95. And you're yellin' . . .
96. *Kim:* Yeah . . .
97. *Leslie:* Then it—
98. *Kim:* It'd go all . . .
99. *Leslie:* will evaporate everywhere, because there's no stuff to soak it up.
100. And it just keeps going.
101. *Kim:* Yeah . . .
102. And it even go under the bed.
103. Cause under the bed—
104. If you took all your stuff out and put it back in under the bed, it wouldn't evaporate.
105. Um, only if the bed is the size of the tunnel.

While delivering this text, Kim is manipulating the plastic shapes in front of her, as well as a straw that was on the table. Our first impression of these two evaporation narratives, and the three that follow, was that Kim was simply moving from topic to topic—from a person in a quiet space to tunnels to bedrooms—using playlike narratives. She seemed too caught up with concrete details and too little concerned with the general topic of light and patterns of refraction and reflection. (If you do not see the text this way, keep in mind that you are reading it as a transcript, not hearing it as live speech.)

We now view this whole section of the transcript (Part III, Evaporation Narratives) as one long argument, not separate narratives. Therefore, we now break the text above into three tightly integrated subsections— labeled with numbered subtitles. We can offer a hypothesis as to one (but not the only) reason we were initially confused by Kim's language here. At the outset of the above text (lines 52–66), Kim may be thinking out loud. Thinking out loud is a socially recognizable activity that, like other such activities, is enacted in language in specific ways. Kim, however, enacted this activity in a way we did not initially recognize as thinking out loud: She used no overt linguistic markers of thinking out loud (e.g., "let's see" or "let me try this") and no macrostructure markers of where she was going. We heard her as directly making claims and answering questions, rather than preparing to make claims and answer questions.

It is pretty clear, on reflection, that in lines 52–66, Kim is using the objects and straw to set up a tunnel and work out how she wants to state her claims. This is apparent in line 67 when Kim utters two "well's" and restates her claims in terms of "a real tunnel." In line 72 Kim makes her major claim ("Every noise you make it'd evaporate and go all over the tunnel"), answering the question she was originally asked ("Can you tell me what you mean by evaporating on the shape?"). After stating her major claim, Kim says, in line 73, "And it doesn't just have to be with a tunnel," making it clear that the tunnel is meant to exemplify a general claim. That she intends to be making a general claim is apparent also in line 82 where she says "to fill the tunnel *or* the room up to here," indicating that she is aware that what is important here is the notion of an enclosed, hollow space, not whether it is specifically a tunnel or a room.

Now we see that Kim is using concrete language in the service of a generalization, as she did in the dinosaur narrative and the rainbow text, although initially we were not aware that she did so. In fact, she is using evaporation to set up an analogy between light and sound. During the actual interview, Leslie did not hear Kim as speaking to an on-the-topic generalization, but rather thought Kim had moved off topic and gotten immersed in details. After line 105, Leslie stops Kim and asks another question:

106. *Leslie:* Now I have a question, what does that have to do with light?
107. *Kim:* Evaporating? [High rising intonation/surprise/looks away and then back]
108. *Leslie:* Um hum
109. *Kim:* [long pause] Um, it could do with light.
110. *Leslie:* It could do with light?
111. How could it do with light?

Compare Leslie's question in line 106 above to her question in line 7 of the dinosaur narrative ("Does that have to do with light?"). Remember, this was Leslie's on-line response, triggered by her own expectations, based on the social language she expected to hear, not her leisurely view after a close and repeated perusal of the tapes and transcripts. Since this sort of thing happens several times in the interview, there is something about how Leslie's expectations interact with Kim's language that causes a mismatch.

At this point we might hypothesize that there are several things that together cause this mismatch. First, Kim does not overtly announce either her main point or how her current language ties back to her earlier language (locally or globally). Second, Leslie does not understand why Kim is using narrative rather than scientific detail in this context since she herself would probably not have done so. Finally, and, perhaps, most important, it turns out that Leslie, when she was listening on line (i.e., during the actual interview), and we ourselves, when we were initially listening to the tapes, made a crucial mistake: We heard Kim as if she were still trying to engage in the main task—a discussion about what the materials can tell us about light—when she was not, in fact, doing this. She had switched activities and also speech genres and social languages.

Leslie had originally interrupted Kim's attempts to describe and explain the workings of the light box and the shapes with a question about what Kim meant by the word *evaporate*. Leslie had essentially asked Kim for a definition. In order to give it, Kim had to exit the main line of her talk (about patterns of light, carried out in descriptive and expository language) and rise to a *meta*-level to talk about language itself. However, Kim accomplishes this task by working out narrative-like examples of how and where the word would apply. This does not sound to Leslie like an attempt at definition.

As Kim goes on with her evaporation narratives, Leslie (and we later) lost track of what she was doing and thought that she was attempting anew to give her views on light based on the light box materials. That is, we believed that she was simply continuing the mainline task. Heard this way, Kim seemed not only to have changed modes radically, but to have left behind the main topic, turning to sound in enclosed spaces. What we are saying, then, is that we misunderstood the activity in which Kim was involved (specifying word meaning), despite the fact that Leslie had asked for it and Kim had, in fact, done it.

CO-CONSTRUCTING PROBLEMS

One of the major procedures in any discourse analysis is to attempt to find a *model* that makes the whole (or large parts) of what someone has said or written coherent and meaningful (Clark, 1996). Only when we fail at this after intensive analysis can we (tentatively) conclude that someone has failed to make sense. Finding such a model on line, when it does not match the one we ourselves would have used in a given setting, is exceedingly difficult. And, of course, people (in any social group) often fail to indicate what their overall model is if they assume it is shared with their interlocutors.

After detailed analysis of all of Kim's talk in the first interview, we have hypothesized that she is using the following model: Kim believes the plastic shapes (which are translucent in such a way that one can see the light inside them) to be hollow. She assumes there is a "mirror" on the inside of each wall of a shape (though by *mirror* here she just means a reflecting surface). The light enters the hollow shape and bounces off the mirrors (walls) inside the shape, eventually coming out of the shape. How the light comes out depends on where the light entered on the surface of the shape and also on the particular shape involved. Most of the light exits the shapes as radiating beams of white light, but some of the exiting light forms a rainbow of colors either because some of the mirrors are colored or because of particular properties of how the light either bounces around in the shape or leaves it. This model makes a good deal of sense of Kim's talk about mirrors.

Kim's crucial uses of the word *evaporate* involves for her an analogy between light and sound: both are rays or beams that reflect off surfaces and can echo inside a hollow enclosed space. In the act of defining the word through narrative instances of its use she is making clear, as far as she is concerned, the way her analogy helps contribute to her earlier discussion about light.

If this analysis is correct, two things become clear. First, Kim must believe that she is answering Leslie's question about what she means by *evaporate* and that this meaning has a lot to do with her model of how light is working in the light box materials. Thus, it must be quite disorienting when Leslie asks her in line 106, "What does that have to do with light?" This disorientation ought to (and, we believe, does) have effects on Kim's subsequent communication with Leslie, which includes the "rainbow text."

Second, Kim, in offering her definition of *evaporate*, has expressed an analogy between sound and light, one that relates the action of light inside the plastic shape to the action of sound inside a room or tunnel. This analogy is, of course, very useful. However, Kim (like Leslie and ourselves) does not know exactly why, at a material level, there are such detailed analogies between light and sound. She does not know the underlying material connections between sound and light. She is not a physicist; nor are we. For example, it is one thing to say that light, water, and sound are all waves; it is quite another to know what this means at a material level when light travels through no medium, but water and sound do.

In fact, concrete analogies allow us to relate two phenomena in just such cases where we cannot fully specify all the connections. The history of science itself is replete with analogies used in this way prior to the development of more detailed knowledge (Holyoak & Thagard, 1995; Margolis, 1993; Matthews, 1994). We can predict, then, that Kim will be disoriented (as we would be) when she is pushed not to talk and think with her analogy, as she was attempting to do when she first used the word *evaporate*, but to actually specify the material connections between light and sound.

These two points—being asked what the definition of *evaporate* has to do with light and being asked to specify the material connections between light and sound—relate closely. The question in line 106 ("What does that have to do with light?") can also be interpreted by Kim as a request for the material connections between light and sound, even though Leslie meant it only in the sense of asking for clarification as to where she and Kim were in their overall discussion ("Are we still on the topic of light?"). Given that Kim does know where she is in the conversation (i.e., specifying the meaning of her word), thinks she has specified what *evaporate* means, and has, thus, clarified her core analogy, this interpretation of Leslie's question—from Kim's perspective—is plausible.

And, as we will see, there is evidence that Kim has, indeed, interpreted Leslie's question in just this way (perhaps, as an alternative to having to interpret it as implying she is not talking about anything relevant). Leslie's question ("What does that have to do with light?"), as well as the ongoing mismatch between her expectations and Kim's actual talk, eventually leads, we argue, to the sort of co-construction in which Kim is having to talk out of a growing sense of disorientation caused by her conversational interaction with Leslie.

Leslie's question sets off three more narratives (7–9). In these, Kim eventually takes up the idea that sound and light may actually physically interact with each other in some way. For example, Kim says at one point: "But sometimes I think that when somebody says somethin' in a tunnel and there's light where the tunnel is, a whole bunch of light, I think that the light has somethin' to do with it, because of the way they're sayin' it." She also discusses sound going all the way to the sun and coming back. Here Kim seems to be pushed beyond the bounds of how she originally intended to use her analogy. Unfortunately, analogies are useful precisely because they allow us to avoid such boundaries.

Leslie abruptly stops this line of discussion, saying "Well I wanted to ask you about this one," while getting one of the plastic shapes (a prism) to make a rainbow. Leslie then says, "Is there anything special about that light?" She eventually elicits the rainbow text from Kim. Far from being the end of her evaporation narratives, this text actually serves as a transition back to the mainline task of discussing the light box materials.

We now see the rainbow text as very much a co-construction between Leslie and Kim. Kim is answering the question about the rainbow in a setting where she can plausibly believe, as we have just seen, that Leslie is interested in the material connections between things (like light and sound), though, in fact, Leslie is not. Further, Kim has seen that her use of the word *evaporate* and its concomitant analogy fails with Leslie. Thus Kim, knowing that in the real world a material interaction between water and sun makes a rainbow, offers this as an answer. This, too, may well be another instance of Kim's thinking out loud—her line "water and sun always makes a rainbow" (line 28) is certainly said with just that sort of intonational contour. Kim's manipulation of the shapes may simply be an attempt to exemplify what she means, namely, that materially juxtaposing two things gets you a certain result.

It may also be the case that at this point Kim is trying to figure out the rules of this game with the plastic shapes. After all, her model and its core analogy centered around *evaporate* has not been heard, explored, or directly commented on. Rather, it has been said to be irrelevant to light in the absence of further specifications and connections, which Kim cannot fully make, anymore than we could.

Whatever the case may be with the rainbow text (and we argue that by the time it occurs, the mismatch between Kim and Leslie is so complex that no one is going to know definitively what the case is), when Leslie removes one of Kim's shapes (line 41), Kim goes on for 16 more pages of the transcript discussing the light box materials. She now uses only descriptive and expository language. There are no more narratives, which in this context Kim has recruited to specify the meaning of a word. In fact, our colleague Sarah Michaels has suggested (personal communication) that Kim seems to use her narrative-like texts when talking about what she already knows about (for example, her description of light in the case of the dinosaur narrative) and she uses descriptive and expository language to explore areas she does not already know about (for example, the rainbow text).

LANGUAGE AND LITERACY

As Kim enters her evaporation narratives she uses a particular social language to give the meaning and import of a word. Leslie (and we) would have used a different social language at this point. Kim's social language is undoubtedly rooted, in part, in her home- and community-based Discourses, which value rich narrative detail, figurative language, and performance (Foster, 1989; Heath, 1983; Hecht, Collier, & Ribeau, 1993;

Smitherman, 1977), as well as in her apprentice-level construals of school-base Discourses. Thus, her social language in these narratives is a hybrid, as social languages very often are.

We can look at Kim's evaporation narratives in two ways. In one way, we can see the "interference" of her home- and community-based Discourses and the absence of control over school-based Discourses, including school science. In another way, we can realize that science—real science, not just school science—uses analogies (like waves of light, sound, and water) to think through new areas and discover new connections. We can realize, too, that giving a concrete instance of how a word is used in context is one important way to specify word meaning in a variety of Discourses, including academic ones. Thus, we can see Kim as engaged in academic talk and thinking.

The point is not that either of these is uniquely true. The point is, rather, that how we see Kim's talk and interaction (e.g., how schooled or literate it is or isn't) is not a matter of what is in her mind or her language. It is a matter of what is made in and of the interaction between Kim, Leslie, and us. What Kim did, which was undoubtedly linked to her home- and community-based Discourses and identities, was also perfectly recruitable as an entry point into school-based and science-linked thinking and talk. That it was not so recruited has less to do with the lack of overt instruction than it does with the mismatch between Kim, on the one hand, and Leslie and us, on the other. This mismatch, we have argued, is more deeply rooted in language than it is in thought, though, of course, the two are interconnected. Further, it is this mismatch that makes Leslie unable to recruit Kim's thinking and talk into her academic Discourse, and Kim unable to recruit Leslie's more expert assistance as a scaffold.

We pointed out at the outset of this paper that there are multiple ways of talking and thinking connected to literate Discourses like science and school science, however much schooling and science itself may work to efface this multiplicity. Our point here, then, is that these literacies are not rooted in people's private minds, but in their social interactions, the construals we make of each other, and the assistance we (can) offer or not.

If children like Kim are to succeed in school, both they and we must change. Teachers and researchers must understand these children's language within the context of the multiplicity and "hybridity" of social languages and Discourses. They must be able to recruit these children's talking and thinking as a way into school-based and academic Discourses.

On the other hand, Kim, like all children, must come to understand the perspectives and expectations of her school-based interlocutors— indeed, we all must, in a pluralistic society, come to understand many diverse perspectives and expectations rooted in diverse Discourses. Furthermore, she must come to be able to control those aspects of academic language that signal perspective, intent, connections, and overall argumentative structure. Such aspects are not as necessary when two people who share a great deal communicate with each other. Thus, they are not emphasized in anyone's home- and community-based Discourses, except where families have purposely incorporated them into such Discourses as a way of accelerating their children's school success. They are, however, important in the public sphere and crucial in a pluralistic society.

Discourses, as we said at the beginning of this paper, are about the construction of multiple kinds of people. Our initial construals of Kim's talk, rooted in our own Discourses, made her the kind of person who does not think and talk in literate and school-based ways. As such, she becomes ripe for clinical diagnosis as "learning disabled" or "special" in some other way. We believe, to the contrary, that a close analysis of her talk shows that she is prepared for (and engaged in) creative thinking in school-based and science-linked Discourses, awaiting appropriate recruitment and scaffolding.

IF SCHOOLS/SOCIETY SHARED OUR PERSPECTIVE ON LITERACY, HOW MIGHT PEOPLE'S LIVES BE DIFFERENT?

Leslie is attempting to scaffold Kim in the early stages of her acquisition of a school-based science Discourse, but she cannot find significant "handles" in Kim's language, handles of sense onto which she can grab in order to incorporate Kim's sense into her own. Worse, in attempting to impose an interpretation on what Kim is saying, Leslie at times co-constructs with Kim confusion and a lack of sense that, in turn, gets attributed not to their interaction, but to Kim herself (by Leslie and initially by ourselves as researchers listening to the tape).

Our perspective argues that we as teachers and researchers must reflect on and change our interactions with children like Kim. We must learn to hear them and see their sense. We must learn not to attribute to them a lack of sense we have co-constructed with them. We must give them more overt guidance, though within interaction, about the forms of language that a specific Discourse uses, forms of language for which we are, however unconsciously, listening.

But, in the end, this is not enough. Kim's problem is not primarily literacy or science, or even school. Just as we came to understand her, she was moved, once again, to another, even poorer, town and school as part of the "social services" her mother received. Kim's problem is poverty, racism, and massive social dislocation. Removing these problems would do more to render people like Kim and Leslie recognizable to each other than all the educational reforms in the world put together. We should never let educational research blind us to this fact.

REFERENCES

Bakhtin, M. (1986). *Speech genres and other late essays.* Austin: University of Texas Press.

Clark, H. H. (1996). *Using language.* Cambridge, U.K.: Cambridge University Press.

Delpit, L. (1995). *Other people's children: Cultural conflict in the classroom.* New York: New Press.

Foster, M. (1989). "It's cooking' now": A performance analysis of the speech events of a black teacher in an urban community college. *Language in Society, 18,* 1–29.

Gee, J. P. (1996). *Social linguistics and literacies: Ideology in discourses* (2nd ed.). London: Taylor & Francis.

Heath, S. B. (1983). *Ways with words: Language, life, and work in communities and classrooms.* Cambridge, U.K.: Cambridge University Press.

Hecht, M. L., Collier, M. J., & Ribeau, S. A. (1993). *African American communication.* Newbury Park, CA: Sage.

Holyoak, K. J., & Thagard, P. (1995). *Mental leaps: Analogy in creative thought.* Cambridge, MA: MIT Press.

Margolis, H. (1993). *Paradigms and barriers: How habits of mind govern scientific beliefs.* Chicago: University of Chicago Press.

Matthews, M. R. (1994). *Science teaching: The role of history and philosophy of science.* New York: Routledge.

Montgomery, S. (1996). *The scientific voice.* New York: Guilford.

Smitherman, G. (1977). *Talkin' and testifyin': The language of black America.* Boston: Houghton Mifflin.

PART II

Community Literacies

We defined *community literacies* as:

> the appreciation, understanding, and/or use of interpretive and communicative traditions of culture and community, which sometimes stand as critiques of school literacies.

Gloria Ladson-Billings' classic article, "Reading Between the Lines and Beyond the Pages: A Culturally Relevant Approach to Literacy Teaching," opens Part II. This article shows us that it is the teachers' instructional skill which helps students from nonmainstream cultures bridge the gap between their community literacies and school literacy. Other authors in Part II help extend the idea of "community literacies" with a variety of examples of how students and adults may be legitimately literate in community literacies apart from the standard form of literacy taught in school.

8

Reading Between the Lines and Beyond the Pages

A Culturally Relevant Approach to Literacy Teaching

GLORIA LADSON-BILLINGS

The current demographic shifts in the public school student population (particularly in urban areas and large states such as California, Texas, and New York) have forced educators to examine more closely the academic performance of students from various cultural, ethnic, and linguistic backgrounds. With the exception of some youngsters of Asian descent, students of color are not performing on par with their white counterparts on literacy measures or other indicators of school success (Irvine, 1990; Quality Education for Minorities Project, 1990).

The seriousness of this disparity in academic performance and literate competence is exacerbated by a range of social and economic problems facing African American students. For example, the dropout rate for inner-city youth is 36 percent and rising (Whitaker, 1988); at the same time, African American youngsters are twice as likely to be suspended from school as white youngsters (Edelman, 1987). African American students comprise 17 percent of the nation's public school population, but 41 percent of the special education population (Kunjufu, 1984). In addition, one-third of all African American families live below the poverty level of $10,989 per year for a family of four (Whitaker, 1988).

The stark contrast between the academic performance of students of color—African American students in particular—and the general white population has been highlighted in several studies on literacy (e.g., NAEP, 1986) and has been at the center of discussion in reading and writing research and practice. Much of the recent discourse has focused on cultural

Chapter 8, Reading Between the Lines and Beyond the Pages: A Culturally Relevant Approach to Literacy Teaching, by Gloria Ladson-Billings was originally published in *Theory into Practice, 31*, 312–320. (Theme issue on "Literacy and the African American Learner.") Copyright © 1992, College of Education, The Ohio State University. Reprinted with permission.

and ethnic conditions of children and the relationship between these conditions and the structure of appropriate contexts for literacy learning.
However, comparatively less research has discussed how teachers frame
culturally relevant approaches to literacy teaching or how they, despite the
dismal realities described in the previous paragraphs, dedicate their lives
to teaching African American students.

Much of the discussion about cultural frameworks for teaching African American children has focused on exemplary teachers (e.g., Foster,
1991) of African descent; identified the interpersonal skills and pedagogical approaches of these teachers; and located the issues facing teachers of
African American children within a framework of commitment and belief
that the students are capable of overcoming very long educational odds.
This article builds on the ongoing discussion in this area by describing
two such teachers, in this case one African American and the other Italian
American. In discussing their different approaches to teaching literacy, the
article describes the common threads that make their pedagogy appropriate for teaching African American students successfully.

While the literacy debate is discussed in the next section, the discussion
throughout the article is not restricted to current perspectives, which have
ranged from social and cultural contexts for literacy to appropriate reading
approaches. Rather than becoming embroiled in debates about literacy, the
article focuses on a primary mediator of learning in classrooms—the teacher—
and describes how two professionals translate their vested interest in the
children and families they serve into expertise in teaching. In doing so, these
teachers read between the lines and beyond the pages of both discourse
in the field and the apparent experiences and stories of their students.

THE LITERACY DEBATE

In February 1990, the president of the United States and the nation's gov-
ernors proposed six goals for education (Cuban, 1990). One of these goals
was, "By the year 2000, every adult American will be literate and will possess the skills necessary to compete in a global economy and to exercise
the rights and responsibilities of citizenship" (Mikulecky, 1990, p. 304).
While there may be general support for this goal, the way to achieve it has
been the subject of ongoing debate.

Thirty years ago, this debate was between the use of phonics versus
sight words as the most effective way to teach reading (Larrick, 1987). Some
time later the linguistic approach was introduced (Carbo, 1987). Currently,
the debate has shifted so that the aforementioned approaches constitute
what have been labeled *traditional* approaches, standing juxtaposed to what
is referred to as *whole language* (Edelsky, 1990; Goodman, 1989).

At the international level, the literacy debate has been less about instructional method than the social and political purposes of literacy. Thus the notion of a literacy "campaign" in countries such as China, Brazil, Tanzania, Cuba, and Nicaragua connotes the idea of literacy for human liberation and social empowerment (Arnove & Graff, 1987). Often these campaigns occur during periods of social unrest and revolution and are built on the notion that literacy happens in social, historical, and political contexts, which help provide the motivation for those seeking literacy. A basic assumption is that *what* people are taught to read is as significant as the fact that they read.

Neither the debate over methodology nor the sociopolitical struggle for human liberation and power have directed attention to the literacy needs of African American students. Teachers of African American students who have a commitment to improving the students' literacy find themselves left out of the literacy debate (Delpit, 1986). No matter how attractive and "humanizing" the whole language approach may seem, these teachers are confronted with students who lack certain literacy skills. At the same time, they recognize that stacks of worksheets and pages of workbook exercises do not necessarily result in functional and advanced literacy.

Despite the importance of this argument in literacy discussions, the whole language versus traditional literacy debate, as described in this article, assumes a less critical role in efforts to promote literacy for African American students. Rather, the compelling issue is the development of a culturally relevant approach to teaching in general that fosters and sustains the students' desire to *choose* academic success in the face of so many competing options.

DEFINING CULTURAL RELEVANCE

The anthropological literature of the past 10 years has presented us with an assortment of terms to describe classroom attempts at more closely matching school culture with student culture to promote academic success. The terms *culturally appropriate* (Au & Jordan, 1981), *culturally congruent* (Mohatt & Erickson, 1981), *culturally responsive* (Cazden & Leggett, 1981; Erickson & Mohatt, 1982), and *culturally compatible* (Jordan, 1985; Vogt, Jordan, & Tharp, 1987) have been used to describe these efforts. However, the research undergirding these concepts has not been widely applied to instruction for African American learners. One hypothesis for this lack of application is the persistent denial of the existence of a distinct African American culture, one that is not merely linked to poverty and the legacy of slavery. This view suggests that African American students only reflect an adaptation of the dominant white culture.

A variety of concepts and terminology has been used to try to describe the relationship of culture to teaching. A recent term, *cultural synchronization* (Irvine, 1990), has been used to describe specifically the necessary interpersonal context that must exist between the teacher and African American students to maximize learning. *Culturally relevant teaching* (Ladson-Billings, 1990a, 1990b, 1991, 1992) is a term I have used to describe the kind of teaching that is designed not merely to *fit* the school culture to the students' culture but also to *use* student culture as the basis for helping students understand themselves and others, structure social interactions, and conceptualize knowledge. Thus, culturally relevant teaching requires the recognition of African American culture as an important strength upon which to construct the schooling experience.

Culturally relevant teaching is a pedagogy of opposition that recognizes and celebrates African and African American culture. It is contrasted with an assimilationist approach to teaching that sees fitting students into the existing social and economic order as its primary responsibility (Ladson-Billings & King, 1990). Although we cannot describe assimilationist teachers as "technically poor," they do not challenge the way society categorizes or ranks various groups of people or the way that schooling has historically kept African Americans and other ethnic and social class groups in the lowest social categories, allegedly based on objective academic performance.

Assimilationist teachers are primarily concerned with maintaining the status quo rather than helping students learn to challenge it. Even though assimilationist teachers may overtly encourage African American students to do well in school, the more subtle, insidious message they transmit is one that has been transmitted for many generations—"Don't get out of your place."

The primary goal of culturally relevant teaching is to empower students to examine critically the society in which they live and to work for social change. In order to do this, students must possess a variety of literacies: language-based, mathematical, scientific, artistic, musical, historical, cultural, economic, social, and political. Culturally relevant teaching that is successful helps produce a relevant black personality (King, 1991).

CULTURALLY RELEVANT TEACHING IN ACTION

Since 1988 I have been working with a group of eight teachers in a small predominantly African American elementary school district in Northern California. The teachers were identified by parents and confirmed by principals as being especially effective with African American students. The criteria for effectiveness included student achievement; student attitude towards themselves, others, and school; parent-teacher interactions; and classroom management. Eight of nine teachers identified by both parents and principals agreed to participate in a study to examine the pedagogical excellence of teachers who are successful teachers of African American students.

During the first phase of the study, each teacher participated in an ethnographic interview (Spradley, 1979) to discuss her background, philosophy of teaching, and ideas about curriculum, classroom management, and parent and community involvement. After the interviews, the teachers were observed in the classroom and segments of their teaching were videotaped. The videotaped segments were viewed by the teachers collectively, who discussed their decision making and pedagogical reasoning (see Shulman, 1987, for a full description of this approach). After several collective meetings, the teachers were able to define dimensions of culturally relevant teaching that were important aspects of their teaching. During 1990–1991, I began to focus more intently on two of the teachers, Ann Lewis and Julia Devereaux,[1] and their teaching of language literacy.

ANN LEWIS

Ann Lewis is a 43-year-old Italian American teacher who has taught in this school district for 14 years. Prior to receiving her teaching credentials, she worked in the district for several years as an instructional aide. Ann has lived in the school community her entire life and attended the district's schools. A few of her older colleagues remember her as a student. She is politically active in the community and the school district, has served several terms as the teachers' association president, and currently holds an office in the association. Despite her Italian American heritage, Ann might be categorized as culturally African American. Her use of and facility with black language along with her close social contacts with African Americans are two examples of her identification with African American culture. She was formerly married to an African American man and has reared her children with a strong sense of their African American heritage. Her teaching experience has been in the intermediate grades (4–8). She is currently teaching grade 6.

Ann's classroom is busy—visually and aurally. Examples of student-initiated projects and papers are visible throughout the classroom. Additionally, there are displays on cognition—Bloom's taxonomy—and the parts of the brain. The 29 students in the class include 17 African Americans, 9 Mexican Americans, 2 Pacific Islanders, and 1 Vietnamese. The class has 16 boys, 9 of whom are African Americans, and 13 girls, 8 of whom are African Americans.

Ann is using a whole language, or literature-based, approach to teaching. During my visits, the students were reading a book entitled *Charlie Pippin* (Boyd, 1987). The book is the story of an 11–year-old African American girl whose relationship with her Vietnam War veteran father is strained. As the weeks go by, the students in Ann's class develop "webs" and "mind maps" to categorize and classify their thinking about various aspects of the book. They work in groups to write letters to the main character and to the author. Their interest in the Vietnam War (and their Vietnamese classmate's experiences in Vietnam) culminates in the development of a Vietnam War display that contains books, posters, pictures, maps, and student writing.

The nine African American boys in Ann's class are the intellectual leaders of the classroom. Ann promotes student discussion and sharing of ideas and opinions, and these boys dominate most discussions. In one discussion about whether there was an alternative to war, one boy, Jerry, argued that sometimes war can help solve problems. Although most of the girls disagreed with his position, Jerry's ability to articulate his position forcefully made his argument seem logical and persuasive. Ann tried to prompt some of the other students to challenge Jerry's position, but Jerry continued to dominate the discussion with clear examples and a somewhat simplistic logic.

During each of my visits, Jerry, Andre, Eric, Calvin, Larry, Sonny, Randall, David, and Sugar Ray were active participants in every discussion. The interesting thing about the boys' intellectual leadership is that each of these boys had been regarded as a "trouble-maker" in previous years.

> *Girl student:* Jerry was really *bad* last year!
> *Mrs. Lewis:* That was *last* year. *This* year he's a really great student!
> (fieldnotes, October 24, 1990)[2]

Another student, Larry, has experienced several personal traumas. An aunt who was particularly close to him was killed in a drug-related shooting. Although he is small for his age, at 13 years old, he is the oldest student in the class. He has been retained a year in school. Ann Lewis believes he is one of the brightest students in the class, and he does everything possible to confirm that belief. He is currently the sixth-grade class president, having run a skillful campaign with Ann's assistance. Ann uses his responsibility as an elected leader to help him monitor his behavior and mediate disagreements (e.g., "What do you, as sixth-grade president, think should be done about this?").

While working with *Charlie Pippin*, Ann requires the students to maintain a "metacognitive journal." In the journal the students divide the pages into two columns, one labeled "note-taking" and the other, "note-making." The note-taking side is for thoughts and questions about references on specific pages in the book. The note-making side is for reflections and ideas about those thoughts. For example, one student wrote on his note-taking side, "What are guerrilla movements?" After some class discussion about what the word might mean, Ann presented the students with the Spanish word for war, *guerra*. The students surmised that guerrilla movements are related to war and wrote some comments on the note-making side of their journals.

As Ann's class began to realize how real the threat of war was in the Persian Gulf, Ann encouraged them to think of ways in which they could express their fears and opinions. The students decided to imitate the talent of the book's character, Charlie, for origami to make their own paper cranes, matching Sadako's thousand cranes. The students reasoned that if Sadako could make 1,000 cranes alone, they could easily make 1,000 collectively. They also felt that making the cranes would be a message to everyone in the school community about how serious they were about stopping the war.

As the January 15th war deadline approached, the students worked frantically at completing the cranes, despite the fact that Ann provided them with no special time to make them. At every spare moment, students worked on folding paper into little birds. Even Jerry, who declared that sometimes war was inevitable, joined in the origami crane effort. Some of the cranes were made from magazine pages, others from loose-leaf binder paper. Ann displayed the cranes on pieces of twine strung across the room in front of the classroom windows, readily visible to passersby. By Monday, January 14, Ann's students had completed 1,039 paper cranes. They were certain that their "no war" effort would make a difference. Ann was able to soothe their disappointment by promising to send their cranes to the Sadako Memorial in Japan and assuring them that there were people throughout the world who shared their sentiments.

JULIA DEVEREAUX

Julia Devereaux, an African American woman, shares many of Ann Lewis's characteristics. Like Ann, she is 43 years old, has lived in the school community all of her life, and attended school in the district. She and Ann were classmates and share a number of common friends. Also active in school district politics, she has just succeeded Ann as the teachers' association president. Julia and Ann attended the same local state university. However, Julia entered school right after graduating from high school whereas Ann entered after marrying and becoming a mother. Both Julia and Ann were identified by a number of parents as excellent teachers. But unlike Ann, Julia believes that the way to ensure language literacy is through the use of a basal text.

Julia's fourth-grade classroom is located in a small, modular building commonly referred to as a "portable." The room seems small for Julia's 25 students, 21 of whom are African Americans (12 girls and 9 boys) and 4 of whom are Latinos. Julia is teaching in a school that has adopted a "back-to-basics" approach to teaching and learning. She voluntarily transferred to this school that offers its students the option of wearing school uniforms. Despite the bookshelves crammed with class sets of literature selections (e.g., *The Black Pearl, The Trouble with Tuck, Annie and the Old One*), Julia relies primarily on the reading textbook, *Burning Bright* (1988), and the accompanying skills book.

Julia begins her reading lessons by identifying the new vocabulary words and developing a purpose for reading the story. The class is not divided into reading groups (as a part of the school's philosophy), but Julia has seated the students in groups approximating their reading levels. Julia calls on students to read aloud in turn and asks periodic comprehension questions. When students are unable to decode a word, Julia helps them by using phonics.

In Julia's class the intellectual leadership comes from the 12 African American girls. They ask and answer most of the questions. Many of Julia's questions are centered around themes of moral and ethical behavior (e.g., "The girl in the story didn't really like herself. How many people here like themselves? How many people put out their best effort each day? How many people did their best during the time I was absent? So you *know* when you're misbehaving?"). At the end of the reading, Julia assigns pages from the student workbook.

A few months after I began visiting Julia's classroom, she introduced the students to a piece of literature entitled *The Trouble with Tuck* (Taylor, 1983). The book is a memoir about a golden retriever who is going deaf. Julia taught the book in much the same way she did the stories in the reader. She introduced the students to vocabulary words in the first chapter, set a purpose for reading, began to call on various students to read aloud, and asked questions to check students' comprehension.

Julia's teaching appears more discrete than Ann's, that is, she makes clear distinctions among activities such as reading, spelling, writing, and mathematics. She appears to place more emphasis on assessing students' skills and mastery of the individual elements taught each day. She does not have her students construct "webs" or "maps" or develop writing activities "out of their own experiences." Instead, Julia often sets up competitive structures in her classroom but builds them within a cooperative framework (e.g., team contests, individual quizzes followed by group checking).

DIFFERENT YET THE SAME?

Despite the different approaches to literacy teaching, African American students in both Ann's and Julia's classrooms are literate and performing on grade level. What commonalities exist that support the notion that they both practice culturally relevant teaching? The whole language or basal text approach used by these teachers is merely a veneer for the *real* teaching that is facilitating African American students' learning. In both of the classrooms, the teachers legitimate African American (and Latino) culture by making it a frame of reference for all texts. In both classrooms, the teachers do not shy away from issues of race and culture. Students are appreciated and celebrated both as individuals and as members of a specific culture.

Even though the students are in the intermediate grades, their teachers are in constant physical contact with them. The students are hugged, touched, and kissed as signs of approval and self-worth. The teachers wrap their arms around the students to both praise and admonish. Although the teachers speak and instruct in standard English, students' home language is incorporated into the conversations of the classroom without reprimand and correction. Thus, these classrooms are lively and buzz with student language.

Because both Ann and Julia are fluent in Black English, they freely banter with the students on the playground and in noninstructional conversations using black English. This linguistic ability allows the teachers into the students' world and provides the students with easy access to standard forms of English. Vocabulary words, word definitions, story plots, and themes can be translated easily so that students understand what something means while they appreciate that their own language has meaning and is not merely a corruption. This linguistic code-switching is a skill the teachers teach by both precept and example. Students experience the usefulness and appropriateness of the black linguistic style as they learn about a standard form of English.

Both Ann and Julia spend a good deal of time in the early part of the school year building an atmosphere of academic achievement, support, and trust among students, parents, and themselves. Ann calls it "team build-ing." "It's a feeling of camaraderie . . . teamness . . . a feeling of wanting everybody to succeed" (sp9–1). Julia refers to it as "extended family," and reflects on ways in which she maintains open lines of communication with the students' parents. "I'm accessible to them. They have my phone num-ber [at home] and I tell them it's just important for us to keep an open com-munication going" (sp6–6). That open communication became crucial when one of Julia's students was missing one Friday afternoon. Julia initiated a telephone tree and a search party that spent all of Friday night looking for the youngster. He turned up the following morning, having spent the night with a friend (not from the class). Julia recalled that she and several of the parents did not sleep that night.

Despite a recent study of teachers in New Orleans (Harris, 1990), which reported that 6 out of 10 teachers did not think their black male students would go to college, failure is not an option in either Ann's or Julia's class-rooms. Ann remarks, "I believe all children can learn . . . maybe not every subject matter to the same degree but all children can find a link that con-nects to another and so I don't give up on anyone" (sp9–1). Julia comments, "I'm constantly telling the children you can do whatever you set your mind to do. You know, you're capable of doing it. . . . These kids are very intel-ligent" (sp6–2, 3).

Both teachers work hard to create what might be termed a *literate en-vironment*.[3] In both classrooms it is difficult *not* to become literate. The class-rooms are filled with books and various forms of print matter, including trade books, comic books, pamphlets, journals, magazines, letters, and stu-dent-developed bulletin boards. In addition to these specific examples of similarities, Ann and Julia are alike along the broad categories of behav-iors referred to previously as culturally relevant teaching. These catego-ries include: (a) culturally relevant conceptions of self and others, (b) cul-turally relevant conceptions of classroom social relations, and (c) culturally relevant conceptions of knowledge.[4]

Conceptions of Self and Others

Both Ann Lewis and Julia Devereaux are proud to be teachers. They see their work as worthwhile and gratifying. As teachers of African Ameri-can students, they cultivate a strong identification and solidarity with their students and with African American culture. In Ann's case, her bio-logical whiteness does not impede what might be thought of as her so-cial, emotional, and perhaps intellectual blackness. Both teachers provide support for the students to "be themselves" and choose academic excellence rather than allow academic achievement to seem alienating and foreign.[5] Both of these teachers teach in the community in which they were raised and continue to live. Despite the challenges of living in an urban setting, they see this community as a good place to live and work.

Conceptions of Classroom Social Relations

Neither Ann nor Julia has difficulty managing a classroom. Their students respond positively to their requests and behave respectfully toward them. However, these classrooms are not rigid or authoritarian. The classroom relations are "humanely equitable" (King & Wilson, 1990), fostering positive student-to-student and student-to-teacher interactions. Ann and Julia assume responsibility for what transpires in the classroom without absolving students of personal and group responsibilities.

The teachers share power with the students because they understand that education is an empowering force, not merely a job prerequisite. Both teachers recognize the importance of creating a "community of learners," and both nurture cooperative, supportive classroom arrangements that resemble students' "home-living" experiences more than typical "school living" (Gay, 1975).

Conceptions of Knowledge

Both Ann and Julia make their own decisions about what content to teach their students. Often they decide to teach content that exceeds district and state mandates. They are neither motivated nor intimidated by standardized tests. They work to insure their students learn and expect that learning to be evident in a variety of ways, including formal tests. Because they are aware that state and local curriculum mandates may fail to include the experiences of African American students and, consequently, fail to engage the students in meaningful learning, they purposely design curriculum that makes their students (and their heritage) the focus of curriculum inquiry (see Asante, 1991).

In both classrooms, the content of the curriculum is viewed critically and examined by both teachers and students. Ann and Julia constantly ask their students to examine the validity, reliability, and logic of what they read. The students are asked to compare their own experiences with what they read and to make assessments about the value of their readings. For these teachers, being literate assumes being able to evaluate critically and make decisions about what you read.

EPILOGUE

The debate on the "best" way to teach reading continues to rage. Like clockwork we hear of new techniques and strategies followed by a reprise of alleged tried-and-true methods. Some techniques involve expensive and intensive one-on-one instruction. Others merely require enough copies of interesting books. However, rarely does this debate ask the question "Why become literate?" For many, this question may seem so obvious as to be meaningless. Of course one should be literate in a highly complex, technological society. However, we may be able to argue convincingly that this high degree of technology has changed what we mean by literacy in dramatic ways. The pervasive use of symbols and video technology allows the average person to take in and process a vast amount of information without actually reading it.

Thus, the question "Why become literate?"—or "Literacy for what?"—is both real and salient in communities for which the promise of an education has been elusive. The two teachers described in this article have asked and answered this question with their students. Rather than attempt to tie their students' literacy to vocational aspirations ("You need to learn to read so you can get a good job"), they assert that literacy is a tool of liberation, both personal and cultural. Thus, their pedagogy is embedded in the premise of this article—not simply *what* and *how* successful teachers of African American students achieve success but also *why* they do it. It has been less about what is *on* the lines and pages than what is *between* the lines and *beyond* the pages.

NOTES

Portions of this article are from an earlier paper, "A tale of two teachers: Exemplars of successful pedagogy for Black students," presented at the tenth Educational Equality Project Colloquium, "Celebrating diversity: Knowledge, teachers, and teaching," The College Board, May 5, 1989, New York.

1. The teachers' identities have been protected by the use of pseudonyms.

2. Two types of data citations are used in this article. Those with dates indicate fieldnotes taken during observation. Those with a code (e.g., sp-3) represent quotations taken from the ethnographic interviews.

3. A portion of the Stanford Teacher Assessment Project's (Stanford University) Elementary Literacy Assessment included a section entitled "Creating a Literate Environment," which assessed the teachers' abilities to design classrooms that encouraged and invited students to participate in literacy activities.

4. See Ladson-Billings citations in the reference section for a more detailed description of these categories.

5. This choosing of academic excellence contrasts with the work of Fordham and Ogbu (1986), which suggests that African American students who do well in school are thought to be "acting white."

REFERENCES

Arnove, F., & Graff, H. (1987). National literacy campaigns: Historical and comparative lessons. *Phi Delta Kappan, 69*, 202–205.

Asante, M. K. (1991). The Afrocentric idea in education. *Journal of Negro Education, 60*, 170–180.

Au, K., & Jordan, C. (1981). Teaching reading to Hawaiian children: Finding a culturally appropriate solution. In H. Trueba, G. Guthrie, & K. Au (Eds.), *Culture and the bilingual classroom: Studies in classroom ethnography* (pp. 139–152). Rowley, MA: Newbury House.

Boyd, C. D. (1987). *Charlie Pippin.* New York: Macmillan.

Burning bright. (1988). LaSalle, IL: Open Court Reading Series.

Carbo, M. (1987). Deprogramming reading failure: Giving unequal learners an equal chance. *Phi Delta Kappan, 69*, 197–202.

Cazden, C., & Leggett, E. (1981). Culturally responsive education: Recommendations for achieving Lau remedies II. In H. Trueba, G. Guthrie, & K. Au (Eds.), *Culture and the bilingual classroom: Studies in classroom ethnography* (pp. 69–86). Rowley, MA: Newbury House.

Cuban, L. (1990). Four stories about national goals for American education. *Phi Delta Kappan, 72*, 264–271.

Delpit, L. (1986). Skills and other dilemmas of a progressive Black educator. *Harvard Educational Review, 56*, 379–385.

Edelman, M. (1987). *Families in peril: An agenda for social change.* Cambridge, MA: Harvard University Press.

Edelsky, C. (1990). Whose agenda is this anyway? A response to McKenna, Robinson, and Miller. *Educational Researcher, 19*(8), 7–11.

Erickson, F., & Mohatt, G. (1982). Cultural organization and participation structures in two classrooms of Indian students. In G. Spindler (Ed.), *Doing the ethnography of schooling* (pp. 131–174). New York: Holt, Rinehart & Winston.

Fordharn, S., & Ogbu, J. (1986). Black students' school success: Coping with the burden of "acting White." *The Urban Review, 18*(3), 1–31.

Foster, M. (1991). Constancy, connectedness, and constraints in the lives of African-American teachers. *National Women's Studies Journal, 3*, 233–261.

Gay, G. (1975, October). Cultural differences important in the education of Black children. *Momentum,* 2–5.

Goodman, Y. (1989). Roots of the whole language movement. *Elementary School Journal, 90*, 113–127.

Harris, R. (1990, July 10). NAACP discusses threat to Black American males. *San Francisco Chronicle,* p. A–9.

Irvine, J. (1990). *Black students and school failure.* Westport, CT: Greenwood Press.

Jordan, C. (1985). Translating culture: From ethnographic information to educational program. *Anthropology and Education Quarterly, 16*, 105–123.

King, J. (1991). Unfinished business: Black student alienation and Black teachers' emancipatory pedagogy. In M. Foster (Ed.), *Readings on equal education: Qualitative investigations into schools and schooling* (Vol. 11, pp. 245–271). New York: AMS Press.

King, J., & Wilson, T. L. (1990). Being the soul–freeing substance: A legacy of hope in Afro humanity. *Journal of Education, 172*(2), 9–27.

Kunjufu, J. (1984). *Developing discipline and positive self images in Black children.* Chicago: Afro American Images.

Ladson-Billings, G. (1990a, Spring). Culturally relevant teaching: Effective instruction for Black students. *The College Board Review, 155*, 20–25.

Ladson-Billings, G. (1990b). Like lightning in a bottle: Attempting to capture the pedagogical excellence of successful teachers of Black students. *The International Journal of Qualitative Studies in Education, 3*, 335–344.

Ladson-Billings, G. (1991). Returning to the source: Implications for educating teachers of Black students. In M. Foster (Ed.), *Readings on equal education: Qualitative investigations into schools and schooling* (Vol. 11, pp. 227–244). New York: AMS Press.

Ladson-Billings, G. (1992). Culturally relevant teaching: The key to making multicultural education work. In C. Grant (Ed.), *Research and multicultural education* (pp. 106–121). Washington, DC: Falmer Press.

Ladson-Billings, G., & King, J. (1990). *Cultural identity of African-Americans: Implications for achievement.* Aurora, CO: Mid-Continent Regional Educational Laboratory (MCREL).

Larrick, N. (1987). Illiteracy starts too soon. *Phi Delta Kappan, 69*, 184–189.

Mikulecky, L. (1990). National adult literacy and lifelong learning goals. *Phi Delta Kappan, 72*, 304–309.

Mohatt, G., & Erickson, F. (1981). Cultural differences in teaching styles in an Odawa school: A sociolinguistic approach. In H. Trueba, G. Guthrie, & K. Au (Eds.), *Culture and the bilingual classroom: Studies in classroom ethnography* (pp. 105–119). Rowley, MA: Newbury House.

National Assessment of Educational Progress (NAEP). (1986). *Profiles of literacy: An assessment of young adults.* Princeton, NJ: Educational Testing Service.

Quality Education for Minorities Project. (1990). *Education that works: An action plan for the education of minorities.* New York: Carnegie Foundation.

Shulman, L. (1987). Knowledge and teaching: Foundations of the new reform. *Harvard Educational Review, 57*, 1–22.

Spradley, J. (1979). *The ethnographic interview.* New York: Holt, Rinehart & Winston.

Taylor, T. (1983). *The trouble with Tuck.* New York: Avon Books.

Vogt, L., Jordan, C., & Tharp, R. (1987). Explaining school failure, producing school success: Two cases. *Anthropology and Education Quarterly, 18*, 276–286.

Whitaker, C. (1988, August). A generation in peril. *Ebony*, 34–36.

9

Portfolios as Literacy Conversations Among Parents, Teachers, and Children

Collaboration, Negotiation, and Conflict

DARLENE BRESSLER AND
MARJORIE SIEGEL

In classrooms where teachers are exploring the possibilities of portfolio evaluation, new conversations can be heard as teachers and students talk together about what to include in portfolios and how to interpret the artifacts that are selected (Graves & Sunstein, 1992; Mills, 1989; Simmons, 1990; Tierney, Carter, & Desai, 1991; Wolf, 1989). On the face of it, these conversations may seem straightforward. But, in fact, each decision that is made about the content and meaning of a student's portfolio expresses a particular view of literacy and literacy learning. The significance of the literacy conversations produced by portfolio evaluation thus extends beyond the technical question of how to construct a portfolio to ideological questions about what counts as literacy and what it means to grow as a literacy learner. Given the importance of conversations about literacy that arise from portfolio evaluation, we must ask why parents—key stakeholders in the evaluation process—are so often excluded from portfolio literacy conversations and why their observations and perspectives fail to influence the classroom curriculum even when they do participate in discussions of their children's portfolios (Paratore, Homza, Kroi-Sinclair, Lewis-Barrow, Meizi, Stergis, & Haynes, 1995). The absence of parents' voices in portfolio conversations is even more ironic considering the fact that for many educators improving parent-teacher communication through portfolios is a goal second only to increasing student-teacher interaction (Calfee & Perfumo, 1993; cf. Au, Scheu, Kawakami, & Herman, 1990; Flood & Lapp, 1992; Hebert, 1992). Even when parents are invited to participate in the

What Counts as Literacy: Challenging the School Standard. Copyright © 2000 by Teachers College, Columbia University. All rights reserved. ISBN 0-8077-3972-3 (paper), ISBN 0-8077-3973-1 (cloth). Prior to photocopying items for classroom use, please contact the Copyright Clearance Center, Customer Service, 222 Rosewood Drive, Danvers, MA 01923, USA, telephone (508) 750-8400.

portfolio process, it is often assumed that they will accept and act on school-based definitions of literacy (Dillon, 1989). In these situations, teachers and administrators may view portfolio evaluation as an opportunity to educate parents about school-based definitions of literacy and literacy learning so that parents will be able to understand better the teacher's evaluation of their child's growth and to support the classroom literacy curriculum. Yet, privileging educators' values and views about literacy over those of parents undermines the claim that portfolios produce authentic assessments of students' literacy learning. That is, even if a student's portfolio shows what she or he can do when engaged in "meaning-ful" literacy experiences (e.g., writing an original story, reading self-selected books, discussing literature), the portrait of literacy learning that results may not include representations of the student's knowledge and use of community and peer group literacy practices. As a result, educators may unwittingly reinforce a single standard for literacy learning even as they challenge so-called traditional views of literacy (Willis, 1995).

Like others in this volume who believe that literacy instruction in schools reflects a "selective tradition" (Luke, 1991, p. 134), we think there is a need to move beyond school-centered interpretations of portfolio evaluation to those that incorporate parents' knowledge and values about literacy (e.g., Austin, 1994; Howard & LeMahieu, 1995; Paratore et al., 1995). Developing portfolio practices that cross the boundaries between schools and communities may offer a way to expand the terms upon which teaching and evaluating literacy in schools are based. The purpose of this chapter, therefore, is to explore the possibility of redefining portfolio evaluation practices in ways that value multiple voices and multiple literacies. To do so, we draw on findings of a year-long research project in which university researcher Darlene Bressler joined with second-grade teacher Carol Harris to use portfolios as a site for literacy conversations—conversations in which parents, as well as teachers and children, could express their values and understandings of literacy and literacy learning and consider the perspectives of others. Our exploration of the possibilities and challenges of a collaborative approach to portfolio evaluation will have three parts. We begin with a brief description of the practices Carol and Darlene[1] developed to involve parents in portfolio evaluation and in the literacy conversations portfolios produced. This is followed by two vignettes that show how parents, the teacher, and the children shared and negotiated their perspectives on literacy in an effort to construct multi-dimensional portraits of children as literacy learners and to develop a literacy curriculum that represented the values held by parents and children as well as the teacher. Finally, we draw on the work of Foucault (1977, 1979)

to look critically at the collaborative portfolio practices described throughout the chapter, especially the ways that power and conflict were embedded in these events.

DEVELOPING COLLABORATIVE PORTFOLIO PRACTICES

Inviting parents to participate in the ongoing classroom conversation about
what "counts" as literacy and growth in literacy meant developing portfolio practices that involved parents in all aspects of the evaluation
process, from making observations and contributing samples to noting
progress and identifying goals for literacy learning. This project became
the focus of Darlene and Carol's research during the 1992–1993 school year
(see Bressler, 1994, for a complete report).

The study grew out of Carol's previous experiences with portfolio
evaluation and Darlene's desire to better understand how portfolio evaluation might serve as sites for conversations among parents, teachers, and
children about literacy and literacy growth. The setting for this study was
Hillsview,[2] the largest (pop. 8,116) and most prosperous town in a rural
county that ranks among the ten poorest in New York State. All 21 children (12 boys, 9 girls) in Carol's classroom that year were European American, but represented a range of socioeconomic backgrounds.

Throughout the fall semester, Carol introduced students and parents
to collaborative portfolio practices, and these initial events marked the
beginning of conversations about teaching and evaluating literacy in her
classroom. Students were introduced to the concept of a portfolio in October when Carol invited the art teacher to present her artist's portfolio. To
help the children make the connection between an artist's portfolio and a
literacy learner's portfolio, Carol organized a follow-up presentation in
which she and Darlene shared the personal literacy portfolios they had
constructed. Parents were introduced to portfolios and to Carol's perspective on literacy during an evening meeting in early November. At this
meeting, the children and Carol demonstrated the daily routines of the
classroom, including a shared reading lesson and a "guided tour" of the
five learning center experiences (listening center, book center, science and
social studies center, math center, and art center), and parents also watched
a short video of a literature discussion group. In addition, Carol explained
her perspective on literacy evaluation by showing parents the kind of observations she made and the way she interpreted those observations. She
demonstrated how she kept running records and anecdotal records and
displayed two entries from a literature response log kept by a child the

previous year. For each example, Carol explained what she regarded as signs of growth, referring each time to the literacy learning continuum she had developed as a framework. When her presentation was completed, she and Darlene enlisted parents' involvement in defining portfolio evaluation by asking them to observe and think about the reading and writing their children engaged in outside of school over the next 10 weeks.

Starting in early January, the process of developing portfolios together began when Carol and Darlene sent home the first in a series of three parent response forms inviting parents to record their observations and perspectives on their child's literacy activities outside of school. Parents were asked to identify strengths the child demonstrated, suggest goals for the child's literacy learning, and recommend artifacts for inclusion in the portfolio.

While parents began to observe, document, and reflect on their children's literacy experiences, the children began to select artifacts to include in their portfolios. The portfolios were part of the daily instructional life of the classroom and reflected student choice and ownership. Among the artifacts students included in their portfolios were "published" editions of stories they had written, texts representing work they had completed at the five classroom learning centers, excerpts from literature response logs, and photographs of dramatic and artistic responses to literature. Also included were letters the children had written to parents explaining their own growth as well as a learning biography the teacher had prepared (which included a statement of goals for the next 8–10 weeks). Before the children took home their first portfolio collection in February, each participated in a conference with either Carol or Darlene in which they explained the processes and products of their literacy learning; these conferences were planned to prepare the children for a similar conference with their parents. The response sheet the children took home with their portfolios asked parents to discuss the portfolios with their children, record their observations about their child's literacy learning (pointing out the child's strengths as well as one area needing attention), and make suggestions for the next portfolio selections. Parents were asked to return this second response sheet to Carol and Darlene at the end of February.

The children continued developing their portfolios during March and April, and by the end of April they were ready to present their second portfolio collection to their parents. This time, however, the child-parent portfolio conferences were held during an evening conference time in the classroom—a time that replaced traditional teacher-parent conferences for over 75 percent of the parents. This evening conference provided another occasion for parents and children to talk with each other about the literacy learning documented in the child's expanding portfolio. As in February, parents were asked to reflect on the portfolio conference and record their reflections afterwards on a parent response form. The response form Darlene and Carol had prepared asked them to list any strengths they had noticed in their child's portfolio and discussed with him or her during the conference, identify learning goals they wanted their child to work on for the remainder of the school year, and react to the conference in general.

The process of selecting artifacts for portfolios was repeated in May and June, and culminated in another round of child-teacher portfolio conferences in June. During this time period, Carol and Darlene also paid a visit to the homes of selected children to discuss the child's growth with the child and his or her parents. Each child took home his or her final portfolio collection at the end of the school year.

NEGOTIATING UNDERSTANDINGS OF LITERACY AND LITERACY LEARNING

As parents began to observe their children's literacy at home and identify goals for their literacy learning and as children began to select artifacts for inclusion in their portfolios, it became evident that even within what appeared to be a homogeneous community, the stakeholders had different understandings of literacy. The literacy conversations that occurred as the children, parents, and the teacher began to construct portfolios together were pivotal to building collaborative relationships between home and school. It was in these settings that parents could express their views about literacy, learn how Carol thought about their children's literacy learning, and attempt to come to some agreement about what might be best for their children. At the same time, they could begin to see that Carol genuinely valued their perspectives and was open to rethinking her own ideas. These conversations also helped Carol develop an understanding of parents' perspectives on their children's literacy learning and the connections they envisioned between learning at home and at school. Finally, these literacy conversations provided parents and teacher with an opportunity to view literacy and the learning process through the eyes of the child.

In the vignettes that follow, we will look more closely at excerpts from literacy conversations with two families to show how portfolios became a site for negotiating understandings of literacy that would support each child's development as a reader, writer, and learner. The first vignette, drawn from a home visit that occurred near the end of the school year, shows how a parent's concern for growth in the use of conventional spelling inspired Carol to rethink her ideas about what should be included in the portfolios, and prompted the child to think more about the role of conventional spelling in her writing. The second vignette, which also took place during a home visit, illustrates how both Carol and the parent had to expand their views of literacy at school and at home to include the child's perspective and, in so doing, acknowledge the child's special strengths, which had often gone unrecognized in the classroom.

Vignette 1: Erin

Having experienced little or no difficulty in her development as a reader and writer, Erin, a child from a working-class family, enjoyed reading and writing independently at school and at home. Throughout the year, she made exceptional progress in her ability to evaluate her own development and to "read" her portfolio (Graves, 1992). When Carol and Darlene talked with Erin's mother about the portfolio, she indicated that she was pleased with her daughter's interest in reading and writing and the ways in which her writing had improved. She also believed that the portfolio had improved communication among the teacher, the parents, and the child. However, unlike other parents, Erin's mother expressed concern that the portfolio did not reflect the traditional "work" (i.e., worksheets) that her older children had brought home or that other second-grade children in the neighborhood brought home to their parents. Of particular concern was spelling.

> *Mother:* I'm real worried about the spelling because I don't see the spelling list. When she writes something, I think I need to correct it so that she is looking at the proper spelling of a word because I can see her writing the same misspelled word over and over again. I don't think that is helping her, you know, by seeing the misspelled word. And I also worry because [of] when she is in third grade next year. I have other friends who have children who are in second grade who have spelling lists. And this is what is expected of them and their spelling tests.
>
> *Carol:* In actuality we've spent the whole year with spelling through the writing. And in any of Erin's published work that she has done, she has done with me, and we talk about spelling strategies, and we put the correct spelling in her spelling dictionary, and then when she publishes something, it has to be correct. So we are moving toward [conventional spelling]. But it is so different from what you as a parent and what we as teachers have been used to with spelling. It does make you sit back and say, "Hey, what is happening?" And that's what we

need to hear from you, too. I think that is an area where we were weak in communicating with parents. We had another parent suggest the spelling dictionary idea—to put it in the portfolio with their published work plus their "sloppy copy" or rough draft.

Mother: Right. Then you would get the idea of those coming together.

Carol: Those three things, then you would have seen that whole picture. And we didn't get that. So we're learning too what works and what will give you a better picture.

In this vignette, we see how parental concerns about literacy and evaluation surfaced in conversations about the portfolios. Although this parent felt comfortable challenging Carol's conception of literacy (due, perhaps, to the clear expectations for schooled literacy she developed through volunteer work in the classrooms of her three children), it seems likely that without the portfolio she might not have had the opportunity nor taken the initiative to express her concerns about her child's spelling. Moreover, this vignette shows how negotiations over different views of literacy influenced the teacher's thinking. As the conversation with Erin's mother indicates, Carol's beliefs about the development of conventional spelling and the usefulness of invented spelling for young writers meant that she did not use weekly spelling lists and tests to teach spelling. However, hearing this parent's concerns enabled her to develop a better understanding of parent perspectives than she had when the school year began. As a result, she acknowledged her responsibility to communicate clearly with parents, affirm that spelling was an important part of literacy, and develop a means of evaluating spelling that documented progress toward conventional spellings over time. Parents' perspectives were also influenced by negotiations of literacy that occurred in the conversations about portfolios. In this case, Erin's mother not only asserted the need for more information about spelling, but acknowledged that the portfolio had helped her see her daughter's improved ability to "develop more of [her] ideas," "use her own thoughts and ideas," and "expand her vocabulary." Erin's mother thus seemed to recognize and value her daughter's developing ability to convey meaning through writing.

Like all of the other children whose homes Carol and Darlene visited, Erin participated in the conversation described above and listened as both of her parents, Carol, and Darlene discussed literacy and how it was evaluated in and out of school. Later, it became evident that this dialogue had influenced the choices Erin made for her final portfolio collection of the year. Unlike earlier collections, she included her spelling dictionary (consisting of words she was learning to spell through her writing) and "sloppy copies" of her published works. These rough drafts showed where Erin and Carol had identified invented spellings that needed to be corrected and had then recorded the conventional spellings. Further evidence that Erin had been influenced by the discussion of spelling could be seen in the letter she wrote to her parents in June explaining her portfolio. Unlike the letter she had written her parents in April, in which she had relied solely on invented spellings (even though she could have easily searched the environmental print in the classroom to find conventional spellings for all the words she used), this time she used only conventional spellings. Thus, it seems likely that Erin's attention to conventional spelling in her final letter was motivated by her mother's concerns. The final portfolio conference Carol had with Erin also reflected Erin's new awareness of spelling as an important part of writing. Although she did not focus on spelling to the exclusion of other aspects of reading and writing, she did trace her growth as a speller and commented on it five times. These comments indicated more attention to spelling than she had shown in her previous portfolio conference and more self-evaluation of spelling than other children had demonstrated. Taken together, these data suggest that the negotiations of literacy and evaluation that occurred during portfolio conferences not only influenced the teacher's and the parents' perspectives, but the child's as well, resulting in changes in her literacy practices and in the criteria she established to evaluate her own progress.

Vignette 2: Jason

A struggling reader and writer from a poor working-class background, Jason exhibited a high level of physical activity that made it difficult for him to concentrate and complete activities involving reading and writing. Only by dictating the story line to Carol was he able to publish his first book, one of the highlights of his second-grade experience. Although all the other children in the room, with the exception of one, published multiple stories, poems, and informational pieces over the course of the school year, Jason was unable to publish any other written text. In general, he coped with reading and writing by doing everything possible to avoid print. During independent reading time, for example, he always chose books containing little or no print (*Where's Waldo* [Handford, 1990] was one of his favorites), or he would study the maps in a world atlas.

His preference for reading pictures and maps undoubtedly reflected his exceptional ability to understand and visualize spatial relationships, solve two-dimensional puzzles, and construct three-dimensional models. This strength became strikingly evident during a science unit on flowering plants. The class had discovered an informational text about the world's largest flowers, and because of their fascination with the topic, many of the children explored a variety of nonfiction books about flowers and wrote brief reports. Jason chose not to read any print, but instead listened to class discussions, studied pictures, and without any prompting gathered several dozen pieces of construction paper and constructed a three-dimensional model—approximately 4 ft. × 5 ft. × 2 ft.—of the rafflesia plant, a gigantic and often foul-smelling tropical species. As he went about this process, Carol watched and waited until he announced his intentions and explained the final product. Once the project was completed, Carol not only encouraged the class to celebrate his accomplishment, but provided more opportunities for Jason to use his spatial abilities to demonstrate his learning. Although she continued to encourage him to read and write narrative and expository texts, Carol came to realize that from his perspective, literacy was a way to use and interpret images rather than print. What held the most value for him was to use pictures, diagrams, and a limited amount of printed text to make something or to visualize spatial relationships.

The conversation that occurred during Carol and Darlene's visit to Jason's home demonstrates how Carol negotiated this view of literacy with Jason's mother.

> *Carol:* [addressing Jason] Have you told Mom how much you are enjoying the map and atlases at school? [silent pause] Have you said anything about that to her? No? [to Jason's mother] He is really into looking at atlases and globes in our classroom.
>
> *Darlene:* Jason has displayed such a wonderful spatial ability. Today I noticed him working on a puzzle, and he has a very special gift in terms of seeing how things fit together.
>
> *Mother:* I know. One of [the] things is that he is building these Technic cars that have all the moving parts and the first diagram [was] of a steam roller and it had the directions to do that. Well he built that and the next day he took the whole thing apart and made a race car by himself. And it was really fascinating that he could actually get the gears in without following the instructions for it. . . . [He] has a set of encyclopedias that has these projects in it, like making batteries and doing all sorts of different types of projects. I am hoping to kind of get him into that next year. Then maybe he will be one of these kids who would rather give an oral speech with his projects instead of a written one.
>
> *Darlene:* Jason, do you prefer to read nonfiction or fiction?

Mother: When he goes to the library, he mostly goes into the
  dinosaur section, and then he's gotten a lot of carpentry books,
  you know for making things. The other day he got a car manual
  just to look through and see what it has to offer and everything.
  I'm the one who goes through and picks out the little fiction
  books that are his reading level and stuff, and I get those for
  him. But his big interest, and you know with maps, we've
  never really gotten into that section, so I'll make sure the next
  time we go down we'll go in and we'll find some books like
  that.

Carol: [addressing Jason] Do you remember when I read the book
  [about] buried treasures when the little girl was with her
  parents and they were archaeologists and they were out on the
  desert? You remind me and I'll give you that book tomorrow to
  look at because that is like what your mom is talking about. We
  did that [looked at the book] much earlier in the year when we
  were talking about India. That would be good for you to look at.

As Carol, Darlene, and Jason's mother articulated their perspectives
on Jason's learning in this literacy conversation, they attempted to understand Jason's view of literacy and his struggles to make sense of print. If
his mother and teacher had chosen to ignore Jason's perspective, with which
he had the most success, it is likely that he would have chosen not to read
at all and would have experienced a bigger sense of failure than he did.
Yet the success that he did experience at home and at school emerged because both his mother and Carol took into account his view of literacy
through ongoing conversations and negotiations that communicated their
acceptance and encouragement of his literate activity.

Reflections

The vignettes we have presented show that portfolios did become sites for
negotiating understandings of literacy. As each vignette demonstrates,
Carol did not just educate parents about her understandings of literacy,
but made genuine attempts to listen to and build upon their perspectives.
However, negotiating understandings across social groups often proves
more difficult to practice than to discuss on a theoretical level (Bigelow,
1992). Because Carol, as the teacher, represented the discourse that works
to produce "truth" (Foucault, 1977) and thus power and authority in relation to parents and their children's success in school, determining when
shared or negotiated understandings of literacy emerged proved to be
complex. It was dangerously easy for Darlene and Carol, who represented

positions of authority, to assume that understandings were shared when in fact they were imposed; yet, the vignettes show that each person who had a stake in the child's evaluation had an opportunity to explain his or her perspective on literacy learning. Nevertheless, the ultimate and most powerful participant in these conversations was always Carol, and in each case she had the option of taking the parent's suggestion into account or ignoring it. In the final analysis, she carried the responsibility for establishing the means of evaluating each child's literacy learning according to her professional judgment and for writing the child (Foucault, 1979) into the official literacy (i.e., permanent records) of the school. Her responsibility and authority thus invested her with the power to negotiate conflicting views of literacy and exercise her professional judgment in what she considered to be the best interests of the child.

CONFLICT IN LITERACY CONVERSATIONS

As noted earlier, the vignettes presented above show that literacy conversations created spaces where multiple voices and multiple perspectives could be expressed, heard, and negotiated. But if literacy conversations made visible the different knowledge and values about literacy each stakeholder brought to the table, they also made visible the complex ways in which social relationships among parents, their children, and the teacher involved both collaboration and areas of contest. Richard Ohmann (1985) articulates this point quite clearly:

> Literacy is an activity of social groups, and . . . like every other human activity or product, it embeds social relations within it [and] these relations always include *conflict* as well as cooperation. Like language itself, literacy is an exchange between classes, races, the sexes, and so on. (p. 685)

At the heart of the social conflict or areas of contest embedded in literacy learning and evaluation in schools is the question of "who is empowered to see, . . . to know and to be known as an authority" (Bissex, 1987, p. 17). In this section, we will explore the conflict embedded in literacy conversations, a conflict related to power and knowledge.

Foucault's (1977) explanation of power and knowledge (power-knowledge, *pouvoir savoir*) provides a means of analyzing the conflict that wove through the portfolio conversations. Foucault posits that power is diffused through all social relationships in concrete and detailed specificity (pp. 115–116). He thus rejects the notion that power is primarily repressive and juridical. He argues, rather, that power "traverses and produces things, it induces pleasure, forms knowledge, produces discourse. It needs to be considered as a productive network which runs through the whole social body" (p. 119). Knowledge or truth, on the other hand:

> isn't outside power or lacking in power. . . . Truth is a thing of this world: it is produced only by virtue of multiple forms of constraint. And it induces regular effects of power. Each society has its regime of truth, its "general politics" of truth: that is, the types of discourse which it accepts and makes function as true; the mechanisms and instances which enable one to distinguish true and false statements, the means by which each is sanctioned; the techniques and procedures accorded value in the acquisition of truth; the status of those who are charged with saying what counts as true. (p. 131)

Knowledge and power are thus inextricably tied in that what counts as knowledge is related to the ways in which power is diffused throughout society and within social relationships.

To clarify and understand the import of Foucault's concept, Lemert and Gillan (1982) suggest asking, "Where is the effect of power in this knowledge, or the displacement of knowledge in this power tactic?" (p. 136). A consideration of this question grounded in Foucault's concept of power and knowledge provides a basis for understanding conflict among parents, the teacher, and the children that became increasing visible as the year unfolded.

In reflecting on the collaboration that occurred in the conversations about portfolios, it is important to note three things. First, the particular knowledge each stakeholder contributed represents a particular kind of productive power (Foucault, 1977). Only the child, for example, could explain his or her perspective, and only the parents could describe their response to their child's learning. Disregarding for the moment that the teacher held the power to disenfranchise both of these perspectives, each of the participants possessed unique knowledge and consequently the power to produce particular understandings the other stakeholders could not develop. In the context of this study, the classroom teacher valued the knowledge and the democratic right of the other stakeholders to express their understandings and to contribute to decisions about the child's progress.

Second, as the vignettes presented earlier illustrate, Carol demonstrated that she valued the knowledge each stakeholder contributed to the portfolios by acting on her or his concerns. She acknowledged the need to include more documentation of Erin's growing awareness and use of conventional spellings in her portfolio and indicated her desire to support Jason's view of literacy in the classroom. Finally, collaborative relationships developed because the adult participants shared a common concern for the child and his or her progress. Because the child was the focus of the collaborative efforts around the construction and interpretation of portfolios, the adult stakeholders found common ground regardless of their social status or their perspectives on literacy.

Although the child-parent conferences revealed that social relationships among the stakeholders embodied a collaborative and democratic spirit, they also revealed the conflict and diffusion of power within the social context of the school and the classroom. As Foucault posits (1977), this power is specific, concrete, and inextricably tied to knowledge. An examination of Carol's role as a teacher brings to light how literacy evaluation embeds such conflict and power.

As a teacher, Carol stood in a position of authority and power in relation to both the children and their parents. By her very position, she represented the school and the gatekeeping power that the school wields in the lives of individual children. Carol's responsibility for evaluating individual children constituted a crucial part of her job and gave her the power to compare, rank, and sort them within the classroom if she so chose, and to make judgments about the normalcy of their progress. To borrow from Foucault's (1979) description of the examination, Carol's position as a teacher enabled her to cast "a normalizing gaze, a surveillance that makes it possible to qualify, to classify" (p. 184) her students. Not "triumphant," but "modest and suspicious" (p. 170), her power, nevertheless, was significant and this power was intuitively recognized to some extent by the children and more so by the parents. Simply put, Carol represented the authority and the power to pronounce children successes or failures in the literacy learning process. This power came not only from her position in the hierarchical structure of the school, but also from the knowledge she possessed about the child's literacy and learning in the context of the classroom—a process of knowing and constructing judgment that is not usually shared with parents or students.

In the parent-child portfolio conferences that took place in April, Jason and his mother recognized the specificity of Carol's power.

> *Mother:* The next paper is my reaction toward your portfolio and how I like it [she is referring to parent response form she will complete after the conference]. I think you are trying real hard. And I know you go up and down with your writing. Sometimes you can write real good so everybody can read it, and there are times when you just write everything all together. And that makes it hard for you to read it, doesn't it? Cause you had trouble on that one. It was all stuck together. I think you're doing real great on it. Your pictures are great on your story.

Maybe you'll be an artist, do you think? So a goal for what
you'd like to be at the end of the year?

Jason: I don't know.

Mother: Is there anything you want me to help you more with?

Jason: Not really.

Mother: OK. How about the computer. Is there anything more you
want to do on the computer? You just want to get to third
grade, huh? OK.

Jason's mother's observation, "You just want to get to third grade,
huh?" reveals that both recognized how the teacher can impede, in their
judgment, progress to the next grade. When Jason commented later that
his goal for the remainder of the school year was to "do my work harder,"
he undoubtedly understood that there were consequences for not working harder and that the power to decide what those consequences might
be rested with Carol. To both Jason and his mother, it was clear that Carol
functioned as a gatekeeper.

Both students and parents understood and valued the authority of
Carol's voice, the particular knowledge she held about the child, and the
power that knowledge gave her over the child's life and progress in school.
However, this power held disparate meanings for each family. For Jason
and his mother, Carol's power implied negative consequences, whereas
for Erin and her parents, the effects were more positive.

The power of Carol's position was also evident in the ways she conceptualized portfolio evaluation and invited parents to participate in
conversations about their child's learning. In the context of this classroom,
only Carol could invite parents and children to the educational roundtable
to dialogue about literacy and evaluation. Her philosophy of literacy, language, and learning compelled her to invite the other stakeholders to
construct knowledge with her about literacy and the child's progress, but
no one nor anything external to herself required her to do so. Parents' concern for their children undoubtedly motivated them to accept Carol's invitation to participate in the evaluation process, but it is possible and even
likely that some also feared the consequences for their children if they chose
not to participate. Even given assurances in writing that nonparticipation
carried no penalty, concern about the powerful position of the teacher may
have motivated some parents. Willingly or unwillingly, Carol wielded such
power, and, as Foucault (1977) explains, it was a productive power. In this
case, for better or for worse, it produced conversations, relationships, and
understandings.

Beyond Carol's powerful position, the structure and rules of the school
also wielded significant but less visible power in the child-parent confer-

ences about portfolios. This was most evident in the discussions of report cards that occurred during these conferences, especially since parent-child portfolio conferences replaced the traditional parent-teacher conference and came at a point during the school year when Carol was required to distribute report cards. Eliminating the traditional grading system had not been an option Carol could choose, but she tried to reduce the role that report cards played during the child-parent conferences by spending time with each child prior to the conference day, encouraging him or her to read and respond to the report card. It was significant that throughout the school year, the children had never received a grade except on their report cards; instead, Carol responded to all their work with written comments in an effort to help each child develop strategies for self-evaluation. But despite Carol's best efforts to downplay grades and the report card, the children and their parents valued the power of its message, and with good reason. In point of fact, the report card stood as the official and permanent evaluation of the child in the school records. Erin's conversation with her parents about her report card in the course of the portfolio conference shows how important grades were to her, just as they were to Jason. After she had explained her center work, read her literature study book, and talked about her published books, she focused on the report card:

> *Erin:* I got A's this time.
> *Mother:* Well, didn't you get A's last time? Sure you did.
> *Erin:* Yes, I did. I got three A's and like an improved mark. I improved a lot.
> *Mother:* You did. You went from a C to an A.
> *Erin:* I went really high, didn't I Mommy?
> *Mother:* You did real good. All A's.

Unlike the report card, the portfolio was unofficial and temporary compared to the official records of the school. It mattered only to the primary stakeholders (Carol, the children, and the parents), and regardless of how much they valued it, the portfolio did not become part of the child's permanent records. It is possible that the invisibility of the process used to assign grades contributed to the power parents and children ascribed to the report card. Grades represented a specialized kind of knowledge, and although parents appreciated the understanding of their child's progress that portfolio evaluation allowed, neither they nor the children had a part in constructing the official knowledge or truth about the child inscribed in the report card itself. In this way, the power of the report cards displaced the knowledge that parents, the children, and the teacher had used to construct and interpret the portfolios.

CONCLUSION

Throughout this chapter, we have tried to show that even in a seemingly homogeneous community, parents, children, and the teacher held different views about literacy and literacy learning. Yet, these differences would have remained hidden and largely unexamined had no vehicle existed that encouraged the participants to voice their perspectives on reading, writing, and learning. The collaborative portfolio practices Carol and Darlene developed provided the means and the opportunity for all those with a stake in the evaluation process to participate in conversations about what counts as literacy and as progress in literacy learning. As the vignettes presented earlier show, portfolios did become a site for negotiating views and values regarding literacy, and it seems clear that, without the portfolios, such conversations might not have occurred in an intentional and sustained way.

One outcome of portfolio literacy conversations was that negotiated understandings of literacy began to develop as each of the stakeholders influenced the others' perspectives on the nature of literacy learning. Viewing literacy through the eyes of the parents encouraged the teacher to alter her thinking and her practice to accommodate perspectives that did not necessarily align with hers, whereas considering the learning process through the eyes of the child enabled both parents and the teacher to think about reading and writing in new ways. And, because parents dialogued with the teacher about the processes and products of literacy, they too developed new frameworks for viewing their children's literacy learning. At the same time, our analysis of the vignettes has demonstrated that literacy conversations produced conflict as well as collaboration. One source of this conflict was differences in power and knowledge, which reflected the social structure of schools and the way parents, children, and the teacher were positioned within this institution. In calling attention to this conflict, we do not mean to suggest that it can somehow be eliminated through a teacher's practices alone, for such conflicts are reflective of a society in which language policies are often a way to maintain inequalities (witness the public response to the Oakland (CA) School Board's Ebonics policy and the elimination of bilingual education by California voters in 1998). Our purpose, instead, is to illustrate the complexities of opening the classroom door to include multiple voices and multiple literacies and point to the need for more research and theorizing on evaluation practices designed to challenge the use of a single standard for language and literacy achievement that sorts children into "successes" and "failures."

In conclusion, the collaborative portfolio practices described in this chapter are only a first step. Although conflict was embedded in collaborative portfolio practices, the literacy conversations produced by such practices did offer all parents an opportunity to respond to their child's literacy learning and express their perspectives. The fact that parents participated in this dialogue did not imply that all parents regarded their viewpoints or those of other parents as equally valid, nor did it imply that all parents had the same expertise as the teacher. It did mean, however, that the theory and practice of portfolio evaluation in this classroom acknowledged that each parent and child held equal stakes in the literacy learning process and represented an equally important perspective for the sake of enhancing the child's literacy learning. However, it will take more than one teacher working against the grain of the official system of school evaluation for collaborative portfolio evaluation to enlarge rather than limit the possibilities of children's lives. Without systemic change that challenges the dominant view of evaluation as noncollaborative and based solely on a single, schooled view of literacy, conversations that value multiple perspectives on literacy and learning will continue to be marginalized. One course of action might be to expand the focus of portfolio conversations so that portfolios not only become a site for negotiating literacy in and out of school but for making visible how evaluation works in schools and how literacy works in the world. In this way, the literacy conversations produced by portfolios could consider literacy and literacy evaluation in relation to ideology as well as individuals.

IF SCHOOLS / SOCIETY SHARED OUR PERSPECTIVE ON LITERACY, HOW MIGHT PEOPLE'S LIVES BE DIFFERENT?

The findings reported in this chapter lead us to be quite cautious in addressing this "what if" question, especially when we consider that U.S. society is more divided than ever with respect to race, class, and gender and that life in so many schools reflects those divisions. Still, we believe that collaborative portfolio practices are useful because they make visible the differences in the literacy perspectives of teachers, parents, and children as well as the differences in power and knowledge that serve as obstacles to genuine collaboration. Naming these differences and obstacles might enable all stakeholders to develop a conscious awareness of the cultural and political nature of literacy and literacy evaluation and thus achieve a clearer understanding of the ways in which traditional school assessment practices advantage some and disadvantage others, especially those who are not part of the so-called mainstream.

If teachers understood and valued the multiple literacies within the community and among the parents and children with whom they work, they might be able to develop a better understanding of children's responses to school definitions of literacy and to reconsider what has traditionally been labeled "success" and "failure" in literacy learning. School personnel might then be less inclined to fail children and blame them and their parents for their lack of success in school, focusing instead on the diversity of language and literacy that children bring to the classroom community and the possibilities such diversity affords for expanding the literacy of all children. Finally, the literacy conversations produced by collaborative portfolio practices could offer a very different "parent education" than is usually recommended, especially for those parents whose literacies and discourses have been marginalized by schools and society and who themselves may have experienced little success at school. In addition to serving as a site for negotiating perspectives on literacy, teachers could use portfolio conferences to make explicit the invisible ways in which schools work and in doing so offer parents the knowledge needed to make their voices count at schools. This kind of conversation might increase the likelihood that collaborative portfolio practices would enlarge the possibilities of children's lives, the choices that they make, and the opportunities they encounter. Although the literacy conversations described in this chapter did not result in the kind of collective action that may be needed to improve the life chances of children experiencing limited success at school, the potential for such action remains.

NOTES

1. We wish to acknowledge what we regard as a valid feminist critique of the textual practices educational researchers employ when writing about research carried out in classrooms. In particular, it has been suggested that the use of first names when referring to classroom teachers (who are overwhelmingly female) and last names when referring to "experts" (i.e., those cited in the text and references) perpetuates the hierarchical division between university-based researchers and school-based practitioners. Our use of first names is not intended to reinforce this division, but rather to signify the collaborative, conversational, and relational spirit that motivated this study.

2. To protect the identity of the children and their families who collaborated in this research, the names of the community and the children are pseudonyms.

REFERENCES

Au, K., Scheu, J., Kawakami, A., & Herman, P. (1990). Assessment and accountability in a whole literacy curriculum. *The Reading Teacher, 43*, 574–578.

Austin, T. (1994). *Changing the view: Student-led parent conferences.* Portsmouth, NH: Heinemann.

Bigelow, B. (1992). Inside the classroom: Social vision and critical pedagogy. In P. Shannon (Ed.), *Becoming political: Readings and writings in the politics of literacy education* (pp. 72–83). Portsmouth, NH: Heinemann.

Bissex, G. (1987). Why case studies? In G. Bissex & R. Bullock (Eds.), *Seeing for ourselves: Case-study research by teachers of writing.* Portsmouth, NH: Heinemann.

Bressler, D. (1994). *Opening conversations: Authentic evaluation as a site for negotiating understandings of literacy.* Unpublished doctoral dissertation, University of Rochester, Rochester, NY.

Calfee, R., & Perfumo, P. (1993). Student portfolios: Opportunities for a revolution in assessment. *Journal of Reading, 36*(7), 20–25.

Dillon, D. (1989). Editorial. *Language Arts, 66*(1), 7–9.

Flood, J., & Lapp, D. (1992). Reporting reading progress: A comparison portfolio for parents. *The Reading Teacher, 42*, 508–514.

Foucault, M. (1977). *Power/knowledge: Selected interviews and other writings (1972–1977).* (C. Gordon, L. Marshall, J. Mepham, & K. Soper, Trans.). New York: Pantheon Books.

Foucault, M. (1979). *Discipline and punish: The birth of the prison* (A. Sheridan, Trans.). New York: Vintage Books.

Graves, D. (1992). Help students learn to read their portfolios. In D. Graves & B. Sunstein (Eds.), *Portfolio portraits* (pp. 85–95). Portsmouth, NH: Heinemann.

Graves, D., & Sunstein, B. (Eds.). (1992). *Portfolio portraits.* Portsmouth, NH: Heinemann.

Handford, M. (1990). *Where's Waldo.* Cambridge, MA: Candlewick Press.

Hebert, E. (1992). Portfolios invite reflection from students and staff. *Educational Leadership, 49*(8), 58–61.

Howard, K., & LeMahieu, P. (1995). Parents as assessors of student writing: Enlarging the community of learners. *Teaching and Change, 2*(4), 392–414.

Lemert, C., & Gillan, G. (1982). *Michel Foucault: Social theory and transgression.* New York: Columbia University Press.

Luke, A. (1991). Literacies as social practices. *English Education, 23*(3), 131–147.

Mills, R. (1989, December). Portfolios capture rich array of student performance. *The School Administrator*, 8–11.

Ohmann, R. (1985). Literacy, technology, and monopoly capital. *College English, 47*, 675–689.

Paratore, J., Homza, A., Kroi-Sinclair, B., Lewis-Barrow, T., Meizi, G., Stergis, R., & Haynes, H. (1995). Shifting boundaries in home and school responsibilities: The construction of home-based literacy portfolios by immigrant parents and their children. *Research in the Teaching of English, 29*(4), 367–389.

Simmons, J. (1990). Portfolios as large scale assessment. *Language Arts, 67*(3), 262–268.

Tierney, R., Carter, M., & Desai, L. (1991). *Portfolio assessment in the reading-writing classroom.* Norwood, MA: Christopher Gordon.

Willis, A. (1995). Reading the world of school literacy: Contextualizing the expe-
    rience of a young African-American male. *Harvard Educational Review, 65*(1),
    30–49.
Wolf, D. (1989). Portfolio assessment: Sampling student work. *Educational Leader-
    ship, 46*(7), 35–39.

10

La Clase Mágica and *El Club Proteo*

Multiple Literacies in New Community Institutions

OLGA A. VÁSQUEZ AND
RICHARD DURÁN

As communities become increasingly diverse and information technologies enter into almost every aspect of everyday life, acting as competent and productive members of such communities becomes correspondingly complex. To be competent in such contexts means to be able to traverse skillfully a variety of culturally opposing learning domains ranging from the home to work, school, and recreation. Such competence affords the facility to interact with and interpret accurately the symbolic systems and social relationships of learning domains that reach beyond the home into the mainstream culture and the virtual world of telecommunication technology. In short, competent individuals have to be able to readily decipher and act upon the meanings and social dynamics of multiple cultural contexts.

This view of competence has powerful implications for members of communities not versed in middle-class norms or standard English. As a function of everyday life, individuals from ethnolinguistic communities routinely bridge the gap between the literacy practices of the home community and mainstream institutions (Heath, 1983; Vásquez, 1989; Vásquez, Pease-Alvarez, & Shannon, 1994). Frequently, however, their cultural knowledge is insufficient to transact their needs satisfactorily. Durán (1995), for example, argues that knowledge of basic literacy skills is not enough to interpret and by extension read and act upon the underlying social relationships and norms of interaction inherent in institutional cultures. Under such conditions, nonmainstreamed individuals typically

What Counts as Literacy: Challenging the School Standard. Copyright © 2000 by Teachers College, Columbia University. All rights reserved. ISBN 0-8077-3972-3 (paper), ISBN 0-8077-3973-1 (cloth). Prior to photocopying items for classroom use, please contact the Copyright Clearance Center, Customer Service, 222 Rosewood Drive, Danvers, MA 01923, USA, telephone (508) 750-8400.

communicate their needs for services or respond to bureaucratic demands for information and compliance incompletely or incorrectly. Although community members often make valiant efforts to pool the linguistic and social resources at their disposal, they rarely have the opportunity to acquire the cultural capital that could bolster their bargaining power (Vásquez, 1989). To complicate matters, most institutions are not prepared to bridge the gaps in knowledge and language found in interethnic communication; instead, each institution expects its client population to learn the nuances and implicit meanings that characterize written and oral communications.

This chapter focuses on a new type of community institution that not only is physically and intellectually situated at the intersection of the home and school but also supports the acquisition and transmission of the cultural knowledge found in these and other contexts. It is an institution that links the local university and a local community center. Specifically, the institution houses a computer club, combining an undergraduate university course and a computer-mediated after-school program for elementary-school-age children located within the local community center (Cole, 1991; Vásquez, 1993). This computer club galvanizes the needs and resources of its participant groups—children, parents, undergraduate student assistants, researchers, and an "electronic entity."

While the study of any one of these groups could provide interesting insights into the processes and outcomes of creating new community institutions, we have chosen to focus on the children's acquisition of mainstream literacy within the after-school computer clubs we have both independently directed for a number of years: *La Clase Mágica* and *El Club Proteo.* Our insights into literacy development within Spanish-speaking populations grow out of our careful analysis of our respective data, which is composed mainly of electronic texts written by undergraduate students, research staff, and the "electronic entity" described below.

La Clase Mágica and *El Club Proteo* are patterned after the Fifth Dimension Model developed at the University of California, San Diego (UCSD). The model links the university and a number of community institutions such as boys and girls clubs, churches, and schools through an after-school educational activity and an undergraduate course. Both clubs also form part of a research collective that examines learning and development in community-based contexts. Headed by collaborators at the Laboratory of Comparative Human Cognition (LCHC) at the University of California, San Diego, the Fifth Dimension initiative is composed of an increasing number of similar projects distributed both nationally and internationally. The after-school programs mix education and fantasy as a way to engineer learning environments that promote exploration and self-direction. Interpersonal communication between adults and children is guided by the theoretical notion that social relations are foundational to learning and development, prompting interactions that aim at enhancing learners' optimal performance (Vygotsky, 1978). Collaboration, self-reliance, self-expression, and intellectual development are goals embodied in the social and material content of the activities inherent to the daily life of the clubs. Children voluntarily attend these after-school programs because they enjoy participating in club activities with peers and young adults, and at times with parents and other family members.

Children are teamed with more knowledgeable individuals—usually undergraduate students—to play numerous computer games. (Much of this software is built around game environments; but some is in the form of tools for writing and artistic expression, or tied to use of the Internet and World Wide Web.) The activities give rise to opportunities for collaboration and decision making. For example, the children learn to operate computers and work with software requiring sophisticated forms of language use and unique problem-solving activities. They explore the world of the games through texts on the screen or through the accompanying bilingual instructional guidesheets. Although some of the games have little educational value (they are of the "shoot'em up" variety), the majority of them involve the children in some level of literacy practice, which is often mediated by the adults. Electronic communication, emblematic of the new information technologies, undergirds many of the literacy activities at the sites. Other activities build upon children's practical use of computer and telecommunication technology as part of their daily life. In effect, children practice manipulating multiple knowledge sources, each with its own interpretive and communicative traditions related to personal, school, and community literacies. In other words, they practice "multiple literacies" (Gallego & Hollingsworth, 1992; Hollingsworth & Gallego, 1996).

The life of the clubs is built around an imaginary culture stimulating creativity and spontaneity in both the children and adults. Its guiding force is a magical being—an "electronic entity" whose identity is held as a secret and known generically as the "Wizard"—who mysteriously oversees the activities at the club through various forms of communication. (Typically, a selected member of the staff does the "wizarding" from campus or outside the immediate context of the clubs.) At *La Clase Mágica*, *El Maga*, a multigendered bilingual entity, is known to be somewhat of a prankster that plays a powerful role in tapping children's background experience as a bridge to new knowledge and skills. For example, it/she/he—henceforth "it"—facilitates communication and cultivates children's use of both their home and school language by demonstrating the use of bilingualism as a resource for expressing sentiments and understandings. Acceptance of children's choice of language fosters the formation of a child's sense of self as an able learner and problem-solver (Vásquez, 1997). The electronic wizard at *El Club Proteo*, on the other hand, is named after Proteus, son of the Greek deity Poseidon, who possesses the power to shift identity and form at will. At *El Club Proteo*, the mythical *Proteo* guides children's activities and their exploration of their understanding of social identities in the world outside the computer club and its surrounding institutions.

COMMUNITY LITERACIES MEDIATED BY TECHNOLOGY

The intellectual environment of *La Clase Mágica* and *El Club Proteo* draws extensively on the literacies available to Spanish-speaking children and their families in two communities in Southern California. Both computer clubs provide access to technology and telecommunication services otherwise not available to Spanish-speaking children from lower socioeconomic backgrounds. Surveys of both sets of children indicate that few households have computers, and parents themselves express a need for tools to navigate competently the bureaucracies of institutions in their current communities. Access to computer and telecommunication activities at the clubs is one avenue by which children, and increasingly their parents, can have the opportunity to acquire the language forms required for transactions with mainstream institutions. Such access to technology and educational expertise provides marked contrast with the curriculum and interactional routines offered in typical classroom settings for bilingual children.

The activities at *La Clase Mágica* and *El Club Proteo* also help children experience the personal and global relevance of electronic media outside the club. They learn to rely on the Internet for key information to complete homework assignments, seek personal entertainment, and participate in cross-site related events such as visiting local businesses. They learn the objective and subjective use of information, giving them a real-life sense of how they themselves fit into the world as knowledgeable individuals. As part of these explorations, children have created publications and video recordings to distribute their new knowledge to other groups, including their families and children at other Fifth Dimension sites. On several occasions, children's writings in the form of newsletters have been displayed on the clubs' Internet Websites: <http://communication.ucsd.edu/lcm/index.html > (*La Clase Mágica*) and <http://www.ucsbngbgc.com/proteo1.html > (*El Club Proteo*).

DRAWING ON MULTIPLE RESOURCES

In contrast to the school classroom, activities at the computer clubs focus on topics and concerns that are of high motivational value because they pertain directly and immediately to children's areas and activities of interest. Rather than focus solely on English and knowledge of mainstream culture, the computer clubs draw extensively on the "funds of knowledge" relevant to children's sociocultural and linguistic heritage for their everyday activities and meaning making (Moll & Greenberg, 1990; Vásquez, 1993). The clubs are not organized around a context that is guided by a classroom agenda and managed authoritatively by a teacher who enacts a tightly regimented schedule and menu of teaching and learning activities. Instead, the activities of both *La Clase Mágica* and *El Club Proteo* shape a learning community based on collaborative relations of exchange in which children and adults learn from one another. Working together, they read and write their way through numerous computer games and telecommunication activities, sharing their respective knowledge and expertise. The undergraduates share their greater knowledge of the world and their more developed problem-solving skills. They share aspects of their life as university students, depicting for the children a possible life choice. Besides their knowledge and experience of bilingual communities, the children possess invaluable knowledge of the ways in which the clubs function culturally and technically. They help train each new set of undergraduate students, coach the younger and inexperienced participants, and mediate the difficulties posed by the technology.

PLAYING WITH POWER AT *LA CLASE MÁGICA*

An important characteristic of *La Clase Mágica* is the bilingual-bicultural character of the materials and intellectual resources made available to the child participants. All the activities draw spontaneously on the children's rich social and cultural knowledge embodied in their everyday life. Computer games are not just isolated games. They are embedded in an intricate web of meaning specifically designed to draw on the cultural and linguistic resources of the bilingual children. Accompanying materials— for example, instructional guides known as Task Cards—are designed to stimulate a bilingual-bicultural learning opportunity out of the most basic nonliterate games such as PacMan and Island Survivors, two games with little or no reading and writing. The electronic patron, *El Maga*, also becomes an additional important resource for enhancing the cultural relevance of learning and development. *El Maga* is produced by and for communication, and this is a language construction that enlivens the bilingual-bicultural character of the club through its use of multiple languages and cultural references. In every interaction, *El Maga* flits back and forth from Spanish to English and back again using both Mexicano and mainstream cultural referents as tropes or themes of discussion. In essence, *El Maga* models the effective use of code-switching and prior knowledge as viable intellectual tools.

El Maga exerts its nongendered power on social relations and individual accomplishment only in communication with participants. In a typical 10-week academic quarter, the electronic entity communicates with participants through numerous flyers, electronic and handwritten correspondence, and administrative forms. Real-time exchanges called *live chats* are another common form of *Maga*-child communication. During the 21 weeks (63 sessions) in which the site was opened during the 1995–1996 academic year, for example, *El Maga* received 103 letters from the children at our local site and 15 from outsiders—that is, from children at other sites and visitors to the Internet Website. In return, *El Maga* wrote 80 letters to child-participants, responded to all 15 messages from outsiders, and engaged in 36 electronic live chats lasting an average of one hour with the children from *La Clase Mágica*.

Live chats, or "on-line conversations," with *El Maga* often cover special interests or events. A widely recognized event is *El Maga*'s birthday, celebrated on November 2 every year. At the beginning of each new academic year, *El Maga* alerts all of the sites in the system to its upcoming celebration. In 1995, *El Maga* kicked off its birthday activities with a Scavenger Hunt competition that pitted children from all of the clubs against each other. The cross-site activity challenged the clubs to find each other's Websites and retrieve clues to solve a list of riddles. The coveted prize was a computer game of choice. A competitive frenzy across the sites spurred endless communication with *El Maga* seeking advice on new clues and the status of the competition. When *La Clase Mágica* won, this topic of discussion continued into the middle of the year between the children and the electronic pal.

Electronic correspondence with the Wizard at other sites has been found to enhance children's "development of writing skills" and the development of "voice" in written language (King & McNamee, 1994). Live chats, however, are relatively unexamined and potentially can provide unique insights into children's language and literacy development. Collected daily, notwithstanding technical glitches, these electronic dialogues serve as a less studied data source in the evaluation of program impact at *La Clase Mágica*. When examined closely, they provide interesting glimpses into the socialization to and through language.

Analysis of the most common topics of live chats indicates *El Maga*'s key role in encouraging children to follow the rules of behavior and thought basic to the culture of *La Clase Mágica*—that is, to stay within the rules, use both languages and cultures freely, and engage in constant deliberation and self-reflection. For example, *El Maga* designated November 2 as its birthday, a day celebrated as *El Día de Los Muertos* (Day of the Dead), a Mexican celebration in which families visit gravesites and construct altars with offerings of *antojitos* for those who have died. Analysis of live chats also point to *El Maga*'s role as a pal; one to whom children can turn to share their personal thoughts regarding such topics as love, marriage, school, and God. The electronic entity's ambiguous gender also spurs constant reaction from children. A curious youngster asked, "Hey El Maga are you a boy or a girl? Or are you bi?" These questions demonstrate linguistic play with the terms *bilingual* and *bisexual*.

The fictional death of *Maga* in a story written and published on the Internet by a child in another of the Fifth Dimension sites situated across the country confirmed its central role in communication and cultural production. When the story was posted on the project's listserve without a commentary on violence and violence-prevention, *El Maga* objected vehemently. In protest, it announced that until the children from the offending site sent it letters of remorse, it would cease to exist. When letters were not forthcoming, *El Maga* vanished from the wires, dying a quick and certain death. After several days without "chatting" with their electronic pal, the children at *La Clase Mágica* panicked and began a letter-writing campaign to revive it. It took over 60 letters and many exchanges with *El Maga*'s sidekick, *La Mosca* (the Fly), to convince Maga to come back to life.

El Maga's death exemplifies the role it plays as a motivating mechanism for encouraging children to engage in reading and writing activities. Through its literacy-mediated exchanges, it also functions as a powerful tool for cultural production. By reinforcing language choice as a norm in intercultural communication, *El Maga* helped transform the basis of the culture of collaborative learning noted by Nicolopoulou and Cole (1993) at the original Fifth Dimension site. As it prompts children to progress through the many activities of the club, *El Maga* draws on their multiple linguistic sources to create meaning, solve problems, and negotiate tasks (Vásquez, Pease-Alvarez, & Shannon, 1994). The electronic entity facilitates the ability of children to form relationships, and thus, according to McNamee's (1993) experience at her Chicago Fifth Dimension site, makes "possible new forms of skill and expertise in written communication and self expression" (p. 4). In using English or Spanish equally to communicate, *El Maga* also facilitates children's ability to express their ideas in a fluid manner without hesitation. As in other forms of computer-mediated communication, rather than being limited by language ability and other sentence-level concerns, children can concentrate on conducting and maintaining the written conversation (Colomb & Simutis, 1996). Translated from Spanish, the following segment of a longer conversation between *El Maga* and an expert child-participant, Nina, demonstrates the role the electronic entity plays in promoting language development and cultural production.

El Maga: Tell me in which part of the maze are you in?
Nina: I am in room 19.
El Maga: and tell me what is there to do there?
Nina: The game is called Limonade. I have to play with another person and I have to beat them. I like the game very much.
El Maga: Well, I think you are in the room named "Garibaldi," it is a plaza where mariachis sing very romantic and sad love songs to young couples. I want you to finish quickly so that you can go into the room called, "La Malinche." Do you know who she was? I'll give you a prize if you can answer the question and send it to me by next week if you want.
Nina: Well, I want to ask you one thing. Where are you going to put the photo? I am very happy.
El Maga: I am getting upset! I am not going to answer until you answer my question that I asked in the Last Message!!!!
Nina: I am sorry! I want to ask just one thing. Where are you going to put the photo?
El Maga: Why do you ask me the same thing? Now I am not going to answer until you answer my question!
Nina: No, I don't know who she is. Can you tell me? I am sad because you get upset.
El Maga: OK, don't get sad, I am not going to get upset any more but I do want to give you a prize if you ask your teacher who was La Malinche and you let me know. If you send me this information, I will send you a gift, OK?
Nina: Thank you, I will go do that. Good-bye.
El Maga: Adios.

In the omitted sections of the preceding live chat excerpt, Nina is distracted and repeatedly asks *El Maga* for a photo of itself. Exercising its role as task master, *El Maga* refuses to answer Nina's questions until she reflects upon her journey through the prearranged series of activities. *El Maga* directs the child to consider the corresponding knowledge elicited in the titles of games and rooms, prompting the child to explore meaning as it relates to Mexican history. Its goals are met when the child asks an adult in the vicinity for information on La Malinche, Hernán Cortez's interpreter. The question sparks a series of long conversations between the undergraduates and the parents detailing the history and lore of an indigenous woman who is blamed for the subjugation of the Indian tribes who inhabited the territory that is now Mexico. The discussion also led to evoking American history in the comparison that was made between La Malinche and Benedict Arnold, one of America's most infamous traitors.

In numerous interactions like the one cited above, *El Maga* organizes the social context in which cultural, intellectual, and technical resources are exchanged in the act of reading and writing. These interventions foster the development of multiple literacies extending across various cultural systems as well as types of study skills that include staying on task, data gathering, and the juxtaposition of historical facts. Children not only learn what is expected of them but also learn to appreciate the role of active participants in the pursuit of knowledge. Importantly, these activities provide an opportunity for children to acquire the love of learning outside of their required instructional activities.

ACTIVITY AND LITERACY AT *EL CLUB PROTEO*

El Club Proteo strives to broaden children's understandings of the "funds of knowledge" that are available in the various institutions in their community (Moll, 1992; Moll & Greenberg, 1990). Club children meeting in the Boys and Girls Club facility undertake field trips to local community institutions. Below, we describe the visits of *El Club Proteo* children to two community institutions—a car dealership and a Spanish-language radio station. Through the visits, the children learned about the various kinds of personnel and corresponding duties required to run a car dealership and a radio station.

The new car dealership, a highly visible and prominent institution in the neighborhood was located just a few hundred yards from the local boys and girls club where *El Club Proteo* is housed. Yet, culturally and economically, the dealership was inaccessible to young children or their families who come from low income backgrounds. Our purpose for the field trip was to provide a mechanism by which to extend the borders of the club, and, we hoped, to acquaint the children with literacy practices and corresponding literacy artifacts. College undergraduates aided the children during the field trip and helped them understand what they were seeing and how literacy was implicated in activities of the car dealership. The car salesman demonstrated how potential car buyers are informed about the costs and features of autos and how to read a sticker on a car window: By studying the sticker, the children learned where a car was manufactured, the various major components of a car, how much each component cost, and the overall cost of the car. The salesman also explained how computers guide the day to day operations of the dealership: Computers are used to maintain an inventory of new cars, parts in stock, and availability at other locations; to keep records of both buyers and sellers; and to help mechanics diagnose, repair, and catalog car problems.

Following their visit to the car dealership, the children wrote to *Proteo* (the site's electronic entity) about the field trip. In their correspondence with *Proteo*, the children were able to externalize what they had learned and to reflect upon the use of computer technology in real-world settings. Thus, the field trip and the follow-up writing activities set a pattern for how the computer club connected to real-world literacy in the external community and to the incorporation of the external community into the club as a community of literate action.

On another field trip, *El Club Proteo* participants visited a Spanish-language radio station located several miles from the computer club. The AM/FM radio station, known respectively as Radio Bronco and La Musical, was the major Spanish-language radio station in the region and thus was wildly popular in the Latino community. Our goals in undertaking the visit were to help the children appreciate how a media outlet is an active producer and communicator of popular culture practice and involves multiple forms of literacy. This station actively encouraged community participation in the programming and allotted time for dedications and the expression of opinions and announcements by neighborhood residents who called or visited the radio station. In addition, public service announcements often reported on cultural and educational events of significance to the Latino community at large.

The radio station visit began with an on-the-air interview of a select group of children and undergraduate staff members of *El Club Proteo* on the FM station. The announcer asked them to explain what *El Club Proteo* was about and how children in the community could join the club. Previously, club participants had answered similar questions in a presentation to parents but had never been asked to communicate this information in a medium broadcasting to the entire geographical region. The announcer conducting the interview was quite effective in overcoming the children's shyness in speaking up and modeled for them how to speak over the radio. The children were quite responsive; by the end of the live interview they eagerly requested permission to broadcast their hellos to family and friends.

Another portion of the radio station field trip involved children in the planning and live broadcast of a commercial on the AM radio station. The announcer planning the advertisement explained to the children that unlike television and live performance, radio requires special attention to the fact that an audience is able to attend only to sound. The announcer explained and demonstrated how pitch and intonation of speech, as well as the use of sound effects, helps listeners pay attention to what is said and what is important in a message. The announcer also showed the children how a commercial builds upon a script written in advance, oral practice of the delivery of the commercial, and finally study of a tape recording of the practice delivery. Children were given an opportunity to conduct a practice delivery and then were able to hear the announcer's actual delivery of the commercial on-the-air.

As at the car dealership, the children were shown how computers and other related technologies were used in a real-world setting. The visit to the radio station exposed the children to a rich literacy environment. As at the car dealership, the children saw how the competence of the radio station staff depended on knowing how to act and communicate in a manner requiring extensive collaborative problem solving among numerous persons. Many *El Club Proteo* children had listened previously to the radio station but, until the field trip, had not been aware of the variety and range of coordinated literacy skills required in the functioning of the radio station as a cultural activity setting within the community at large. Further, while it is fair to state that the children primarily viewed the radio station as a source for musical entertainment, the field trip made them more aware of the communication purposes and possibilities for a radio station.

Upon their return to the Boys and Girls Club home of *El Club Proteo*, the children were asked to write to *Proteo* about what they had experienced during their radio station field trip. In addition, they were asked to tell *Proteo* what they would broadcast if they had their own radio station. The children's initial communications to *Proteo*, to each other, and to club staff about the radio station are very interesting to consider. Below is an excerpt from a letter written by one child, Lupe.

> Hi Proteus it's Lupe. Sorry I haven't wrote to you in a long time. I have some ideas for the Radio Show like playing some cool music. And winning cool prizes if you answer some questions. Say what we do in the club. And we can say when and where it happens and maybe more people will come. But we don't have to do the same thing every day we can do different things if other kids have different ideas.

Two other children, Margaret and Nalloli, also wrote to Proteo:

The 2 thing was that some people just want Mexican and other
people want different kind of music. (I think that we should have 2
Radio shows one with mexican muci and a nother one with english
muci.) What do you think

Not unexpectedly, the children's initial concern was about what musical selections might be broadcast. Unexpectedly, this discussion produced
some controversy among the children centering on who would pick musical selections and what those musical selections would be. We were surprised by the children's intense feelings about this and reassured them that
everyone would get their turn. *Proteo* wrote back indicating that, before
too long, children would be given their own radio station based in the club
site. The plan for this possibility had begun developing among *El Club Proteo*
staff prior to the children's visit to the radio station and is currently in the
process of being implemented. The plan called for the installation of a
low-power FM radio transmitter at the club that did not require a Federal
Communications Commission license. The station would be capable of
being received only in the most immediately surrounding portions of the
community that, fortunately, includes the apartment dwellings housing
most of the *El Club Proteo* participants.

We see a number of radio station activities that might enhance *El Club
Proteo* and its theme of exploring the surrounding community and its institutions. But in carrying out these extensions, we see a need for developing
the radio station as a complex system of literate practices enhancing children's
understanding of their own roles and capacities in such a business enterprise.
While the use of computer technology and other electronic technology is
central to enacting this system, its bedrock rests on being able to collaborate
with other club participants in joint problem solving. Drawing on the radio
station field trip, we want children not only to plan the design of a radio
broadcast schedule but also to oversee the steps and materials ensuring high
quality broadcasts. There is a certain analogy to writing for publication here:
As with written publication, children need to learn how to reflect on the
purposes of communication, their intended audience, and how they might
effectively communicate to this audience. We envision, for example, that for
many communicative purposes children will need to design and revise written scripts that will be read over the air. Further, we envision that children
will need to stimulate an audience for their broadcasts and to incorporate
feedback from this audience in designing programming.

In light of the latter concern, the children will need to incorporate
programming beyond music to include general announcements of interests to other children and parents. Other programming possibilities include

poetry, drama fictional reading, and formal news broadcasts. Whereas *El Club Proteo* activities are not presently directly connected to school and classroom events, we see ways in which a radio station might facilitate such connections as in announcements of school activities and discussions of classroom learning activities. While the possibilities are numerous, the actual specification of programming needs to proceed with direct input from the children.

CONCLUSION

Together *La Clase Mágica* and *El Club Proteo* provide unique opportunities for children to learn multiple literacies to function well within and outside of their communities. Both clubs effectively merge the many literacies available to local bilingual children with new forms that grow out of the computer and telecommunication activities of the clubs. Rather than being held to the knowledge forms of one particular context or another, children's meaning making transcends space, culture, and language and incorporates the knowledge and skills of the multiple cultural domains found in the surrounding communities and increasingly in the world of the Internet. Thus, the activities draw upon the funds of knowledge found in community and university settings familiar to children. With incredible ease, they find themselves at home presenting to university classes, conference audiences, and various community meetings that often involve representatives from the funding agency, the school, and other state and international programs. A Latino undergraduate staff member said it best, speaking to 60 students in one of Vásquez's undergraduate classes at UCSD, when he noted the confidence that long-term participants, known as Wizard Assistants, demonstrate:

> Reflecting upon my own experiences as a Latino in the educational system, their poise was the most remarkable thing to me. These kids walked onto this University campus, and stood in front of this class, and seemed comfortable and in control. The strange thing to me was their level of confidence, for this was not an environment in which these kids had grown up. This has been, and for most part still is, a white (Anglo) institution. The university has historically been inhospitable to persons of color. I myself have to constantly resituate myself to maintain some kind of comfortable position within the university. However, they seemed oblivious to this fact. [UCSD staff member, November 25, 1991]

Such competence is also not lost on teachers and researchers who recruit these children to help in the computer room at school or consult for pay at other clubs and community activities.

The use of computers at the clubs provides new ways to look at how technology can serve a social as well as a pedagogical agenda. The use of computers and telecommunication technology facilitates new connections to the world through the function of internal planes of action—that is, the "ability to perform manipulations with an internal representation of external objects before starting actions with these objects in reality" (Kaptelinin, 1996, p. 51). Each participant at the computer club is presented with new ways to act in the world before actually taking action. Free from the immediate situation, according to Kaptelinin, the child avoids costly mistakes. The trips to the dealership and the radio station and the many interactions with *El Maga* provide children with a mental frame for the ways in which many worlds work. They have many opportunities to evaluate and manipulate their conceptions before they go out on their own and interact with institutional agents such as teachers, car salesmen, or disc jockeys.

La Clase Mágica and *El Club Proteo* represent new community institutions that prepare participants for the complexity of a technology-based society. Participants are not restricted to one knowledge base, nor one language, but are able to move in and out of the multiple learning domains that make up their daily life. They are at home in any number of geographical communities as well as those found on the Internet. These competencies have powerful implications for reforming education. Cummins and Sayers (1995) reflect the lessons we have learned at our respective research sites. They state:

> We [must] reframe education around critical inquiry and the collaborative generation of knowledge in such a way that the experience and cultural contributions of all students are valued. In this scenario, rather than passively internalizing the cultural literacy of socially powerful groups, students actively generate their own intercultural literacy through dialogue and collaborative research with colleagues in their own classroom and in classrooms across the globe (p. 13).

While Cummins and Sayers focus on schools, their message is just as applicable to other learning settings, including after-school computer clubs and other community settings where technology supports new forms of cultural practice and new learning. As we proceed to develop our computer clubs toward greater use of the World Wide Web and e-mail, we are keeping these comments in mind as central to the development of the literacies of the children we serve. Hopefully, our work has illustrated that the beginnings of new forms of literacy and self-identity originate fundamentally in social collaboration to make new sense out of the immediate communities we inhabit. The existence of a global community at our immediate access will remediate our understanding of how literacies can be used to construct cultural reality, human social identity, and human collaboration (Nardi, 1997).

IF SCHOOLS / SOCIETY SHARED OUR PERSPECTIVE ON LITERACY, HOW MIGHT PEOPLE'S LIVES BE DIFFERENT?

Our descriptions of the various activities and corresponding competencies that constitute the life of *La Clase Mágica* and *El Club Proteo* are informed by a view of learning and development that is not widely shared by practitioners and lay people. According to this view, learning and development are context specific and socially based. As individuals traverse the numerous cultural systems that make up their daily life, they learn the behavioral and epistemological norms and expectations of the respective contexts through meaningful social relations with key representatives. While individuals do have an active role in their own development, the guideposts they use have been formerly negotiated with those around them.

   If schools and society were to embrace our perspective on the ways in which the multiple literacies of the clubs are the medium and object of learning and development, then instructional methodologies and notions of cultural capital would radically change. First of all, teachers and other practitioners would expand their views about what knowledge is valued, where and how it can be acquired, and who possesses it. Instead of the teachers, the school, and the intellectual elite of Western canon being seen as the sole receptacles and disseminators of knowledge, other institutional agents, contexts, and forms of knowledge would be considered drawing on a broader range of social and cultural experiences. The "funds of knowledge" of the radio disc jockey, the car salesman, and even the electronic entity would be viable material for a fully integrated instructional program.

   Second, we imagine that if the conditions we propose were more widespread, "difference" would be less susceptible to distrust and apprehension. Knowledge of the "other" would translate to understanding, if not accepting, the "other." Boundaries and barriers would be less impenetrable, and psychological distances based on language, ethnicity, and class would be lessened. These are grandiose projections of our work, no doubt; however, our experiences in designing "ideal" learning environments, compel us to imagine the best of possible worlds.

REFERENCES

Cole, M. (1991). *Capitalizing on diversity: A proposal for a distributive literacy consortium.* Research Proposal (University of California, San Diego, 91–5215) submitted to the Andrew Mellon Foundation.

Colomb, G. G., & Simutis, J. A. (1996). Visible conversation and academic inquiry: CMC in a culturally diverse classroom. In S. C. Herring (Ed.), *Computer-mediated communication: Linguistic, social, and cross-cultural perspectives* (pp. 203–222). Amsterdam/Philadelphia: John Benjamins.

Cummins, J., & Sayers, D. (1995). *Brave new schools: Challenging cultural illiteracy.* New York: St. Martin's Press.

Durán, R. P. (1995). *Cultural accommodation and family literacy among English immigrant language learners.* Paper presented at the Family Literacy Research Symposium, U.S. Department of Education.

Gallego, M., & Hollingsworth, S. (1992). Multiple literacies: Teachers' evolving perceptions. *Language Arts, 69,* 46–53.

Heath, S. B. (1983). *Ways with words: Language, life and work in communities and classrooms.* Cambridge, U.K.: Cambridge University Press.

Hollingsworth, S., & Gallego, M. (1996). Toward a collaborative praxis of multiple literacies. *Curriculum Inquiry, 26*(3), 265–292.

Kaptelinin, V. (1996). Activity theory: Implications for human-computer interaction. In B. Nardi (Ed.), *Context and consciousness: Activity theory and human-computer interaction* (pp. 103–116). Cambridge, MA: MIT Press.

King, C., & McNamee, G. (1994, April). *The development of children's voice in written language in their home community and in far away places.* Paper presented at the annual meeting of the American Educational Research Association, New Orleans, LA.

McNamee, G. D. (April, 1993). *Written language development of school-aged children in an African American community.* Paper presented at the annual meeting of the American Educational Research Association, Atlanta, GA.

Moll, L. (1992). Bilingual studies and community analysis: Some recent trends. *Educational Researcher, 21*(2), 20–24.

Moll, L., & Greenberg, J. (1990). Creating zones of possibilities: Combining social contexts for instruction. In L. C. Moll (Ed.), *Vygotsky and Education* (pp. 319–348). Cambridge, U.K.: Cambridge University Press.

Nardi, B. A. (1997). Activity theory and human-computer interaction. In B. A. Nardi (Ed.), *Context and consciousness: Activity theory and human-computer interaction.* Cambridge, MA: MIT Press.

Nicolopoulou, A., & Cole, M. (1993). Generation and transmission of shared knowledge in the culture of collaborative learning: The Fifth Dimension, its playworld, and its institutional contexts. In E. A. Forman, N. Minick, & C. A. Stone (Eds.), *Contexts for learning: Sociocultural dynamics in children's development.* New York: Oxford University Press.

Vásquez, O. A. (1989). *Connecting oral language strategies to literacy: An ethnographic study among four Mexican immigrant families.* Unpublished doctoral dissertation, Stanford University, Stanford, CA.

Vásquez, O. A. (1993). A look at language as resource: Lessons from La Clase Mágica. *Bilingual education: Politics, research, and practice, 17*(2), 199–224. Chicago: National Society for the Study of Education.

Vásquez, O.A. (July, 1997). Negociando identidad en un media bilingüe. *Morphé: Ciencias Del Lenguaje, Revista del Centro de Investigación y Docencia en Ciencias del Lenguaje,* (15/16), 231–247. (Published by Instituto de Ciencias Sociales y Humanidades, Universidad Autónoma de Puebla, Mexico).

Vásquez, O. A., Pease-Alvarez, L., & Shannon, S. M. (1994). *Pushing boundaries: Language and culture in a Mexicano community.* Cambridge, U.K.: Cambridge University Press.

Vygotsky, L. S. (1978). *Mind in Society: The development of higher psychological processes.* In M. Cole, V. John-Steiner, S. Scribner, & E. Souberman (Eds. & Trans.). Cambridge, MA: Harvard University Press.

11

Examining the Research Narrative in Early Literacy

The Case of Parent-Child Book Reading Activity

CAROLYN P. PANOFSKY

In the United States today, the idea of parents' reading to children seems to be taken as axiomatic of "good parenting." In the late 1980s, for example, First Lady Barbara Bush took to the television airwaves to urge parents to read to children. Public service announcement campaigns, of course, are an interesting phenomenon: they seem to speak to and for *all* of us while at the same time exhorting *some* of us to change our behavior. While some public service campaigns are more controversial than others, the reading campaign must have seemed utterly uncontroversial, so much so that Mrs. Bush, never one to engage controversy, was ready to lend her grandmaternal image to the cause. And yet in speaking to and for all of us, she *was* urging some of us to change—otherwise why the campaign in the first place?

Early in 1997, First Lady Hilary Rodham Clinton also took up the cause, writing in a popular news magazine about the virtues of parents' reading to children and offering the suggestion (astonishing to some) of "reading as an easy way to help a baby's brain grow." In contrast to controversial issues such as health care, the topic of parents' reading to children appears to be on unassailable high ground, like motherhood and the flag.

Inscribed in Mrs. Bush's campaign of public service announcements and in Mrs. Clinton's personal essay is a kind of "narrative of guidance" about parents' reading to children, a story about the activity which is generally accepted, not seen as problematic. Yet I want to problematize the narrative, not because it promotes a "wrong" idea or view, but because it supports a set of misunderstandings and a misguided agenda. Although

What Counts as Literacy: Challenging the School Standard. Copyright © 2000 by Teachers College, Columbia University. All rights reserved. ISBN 0-8077-3972-3 (paper), ISBN 0-8077-3973-1 (cloth). Prior to photocopying items for classroom use, please contact the Copyright Clearance Center, Customer Service, 222 Rosewood Drive, Danvers, MA 01923, USA, telephone (508) 750-8400.

the idea that parents should read to their children may seem unassailable in its common sense, I suggest that it is grounded in an ethnocentric perspective on education, and family and culture. In addition, by diverting attention from analysis and critique of schooling, it promotes misguided thinking about how to address issues of literacy instruction.

Although never directly stated, the guidance narrative on parents' reading consists of a set of assumptions. A primary assumption connects parent's reading to children with children's learning to read. An attendant assumption is that children will not succeed in literacy if their parents do not read to them. A further assumption seems to be that parents who do not read to their children are neglectful and, by not doing all that parents should do, are by implication "bad" parents. So there is an implied "right parenting." From these assumptions, questions about literacy can subtly shift to matters of morality. While it is difficult to track such a narrative through the culture, it has an impact. When a child is having difficulty learning to read in school, other assumptions are made: "His mother doesn't read to him."[1]

Various elements, when added together, create a collectively composed narrative about literacy and literacy learning in our society. Taken as a whole, this narrative reveals that reading is not only a cognitive or a social-cognitive process, but is embedded in larger political, cultural, and historical frames which cannot be separated from the processes of an individual's development.

BACKGROUND

In recent decades, research in the broad field of literacy has made tremendous strides in both expanding and transforming earlier views. This has been true particularly in understandings of the development of literacy during the preschool years. An expanded view of literacy has the reconceptualization of literacy development during the preschool years now referred to as "emergent literacy" (e.g., Sulzby & Teale, 1991). Revised perspectives in literacy research have constructed a more socially oriented perspective, informed by theories of language and communication developed in the ethnography of communication and language socialization (e.g., Cazden, John, & Hymes, 1972; Heath, 1982a, 1982b, 1983; Ochs, 1987) as well as in developmental psycholinguistics (e.g., Snow & Ferguson, 1977; Bruner, 1983).

At the same time, others, working in the historical and political analysis of literacy in society, have uncovered myths about literacy that have led to other fundamental revisions in understanding. For example, Harvey Graff (1981) has examined what he calls "the literacy myth" to illuminate "the contradictions in the perceived connections between education, employment levels, and economic development, to argue that literacy was not always central to jobs, earnings and industrialization in the nineteenth century in the manner typically assumed" (p. 233). In particular, Graff shows that the lines of causality may work differently from what is often assumed, with increased levels of literacy following, rather than preceding, increased levels of employment. In addition, the work of others has shown that literacy in particular and education in general seem to "offer less in rewards than [they engender] in expectations, making underemployment a serious concern" (p. 242) today. Graff's work problematizes certain assumptions and reveals some commonsense understandings to be myths. Such myths circulate as privileged assumptions in collective societal narratives about literacy, as stories constructed to make sense of research, and as routine ways of talking and thinking about literacy and education in the United States. Such revisionist activity of Graff suggests the need to reconceptualize ways of understanding relationships between literacy and life.

Another important contribution in this area is a discussion by Sylvia Scribner (1984) in which she points out the privileged status given by those in positions of power in society to their *own* forms of literacy, an insight which bears much reflection from literacy researchers. Scribner discusses literacy in terms of three metaphors, one of which is particularly relevant here. This metaphor she calls variously, "literacy as salvation" and "literacy as a state of grace." However, neither metaphor quite captures the meaning she intends; she writes: "Both labels are unsatisfactory because they give a specific religious interpretation to the broader phenomenon I want to depict—that is, the tendency in many societies to endow the literate person with special virtues" (p. 13).

Scribner (1984) goes on to show that "the attribution of special powers to those who are literate" has roots in secular as well as sacred traditions and in both Western and non-Western traditions. She produces examples from the worlds of post-Luther Protestantism, the older religious traditions of Judaism and Islam, the writings of Plato and Aristotle, and finally the perspective of Western humanism, where

> literateness has come to be considered synonymous with being "cultured," using the term in the old-fashioned sense to refer to a person who is knowledgeable about the content and techniques of the sciences, arts, and humanities as they have evolved historically. The term sounds elitist and archaic, but the notion that participation in a literate—that is, bookish—tradition enlarges and develops a person's essential self is pervasive and still undergirds the concept of liberal education. (p. 13)

It seems plausible that the powers attributed to literacy, which Scribner finds inscribed in various traditions, help to account for what Graff identified as "the literacy myth." So too, "literacy as salvation" seems inscribed in collective assumptions about parents' reading to children. While it may be impossible to separate such deeply embedded beliefs from our scholarly and scientific activity, it is nevertheless imperative that we attempt to identify and to acknowledge the varied and often out-of-awareness ideological dimensions in our research and to explore the implications of this imperative. This discussion is such an exploration.

Echoes of Mythology: Problematizing Research on Parents' Reading to Children

Research on parents' reading to children has been a rich source for producing new understandings about children's literacy development during the preschool years and has been important in amassing a knowledge base on what has become known as "emergent literacy" (Sulzby & Teale, 1991). Much of the research in this area has claimed to examine literacy from a "cultural perspective": Sulzby and Teale (1991) state that

> studying literacy development is basically an investigation of the acquisition of culture. The task for researchers is not merely to study in isolation the cognitive operations of children, but rather to understand cognition in terms of the social systems for utilizing literacy. In other words, motives, goals, and conditions are intrinsic parts of the processes of reading and writing (and of becoming readers and writers); and they cannot be abstracted away without losing characteristics essential to the attempts to analyze literacy and literacy development. (pp. 744–745)

In this passage, the authors stress the "wholism" that is a key element in understanding literacy as cultural activity, which, as they say, includes motives and goals of actors in meaningful contexts. Such wholism is integral to describing and understanding the development of the child in cultural context. However, the account of early or emergent literacy has sometimes been constructed in a way that contradicts a cultural perspective—with a relativistic view of differences. Instead, the cultural practices of a particular sociocultural group have been treated as "natural" and as "normal"—that is, practices of the dominant cultural group, the middle-class mainstream, have been referred to as "natural." This naturalizing of the dominant group can be seen in summative statements such as the following:

Thus, research shows that the home plays a key role in emergent literacy. For literacy education, perhaps the most striking implication is the extreme importance of getting literacy embedded in children's social lives. It is this fundamental orientation that provides the foundation for subsequent academic growth in literacy. In fact, Teale (1988) has argued that essentially *the first step* in children's literacy is learning that literacy serves to mediate a variety of cultural activities in their everyday lives. However, insufficient research has been done with children in homes and cultures in which children are not heavily involved in literacy. (Sulzby & Teale, 1991, p. 745, emphasis added)

The repeated reference to "children" and "children's" literacy and social lives in this passage seems to be referring to *all* children, but actually shifts subtly in ways which confer value on some and stigmatize others. One minute the reader is told about "the" first step, but then it is suggested that some children do not take that "first step." There is a gap in logic here. The shift from an implied *all* with their essential first step to some implied *others* who are "not heavily involved" seems to fill the gap with old beliefs rather than to actually establish or describe a knowledge base. The child-rearing practice of bedtime storybook reading is in this way privileged by researchers. A particular cultural practice comes to be taken as both natural and normal in the research literature, especially because this practice appears to prepare children for success in schooling, particularly in learning to read. In this way, other cultural forms of literacy come to be referred to as "nonmainstream," "marginal," "atypical," deemed "inappropriate," "deficient," "lacking," or "wrong," and children whose experiences are so characterized become "other"—"children [who] are not heavily involved in literacy." It seems that differences in practices and families are being viewed as deficits in the implicit narrative of this account.

CORRELATION OR CAUSATION? REEXAMINING *BECOMING A NATION OF READERS*

An example of the claim that reading to children is preparation for school success is found in *Becoming a Nation of Readers* (Anderson, Hiebert, Scott, & Wilkinson, 1985). In this national report, widely viewed as having had a major impact on public and academic discussions of literacy, the authors of the report make this unequivocal claim: "The single most important activity for building the knowledge required for eventual success in reading is reading aloud to children. This is especially so during the preschool years" (p. 23). The preschool context the report refers to here is the home, with parents reading to children (that is, the reference is not to schools for the preschool-aged group). It is worth noting that the National Commission on Reading locates reading *outside of schools* as the most important activity in the literacy learning process!

Apart from marveling at this implicit dismissal of the role of formal instructional institutions, another reason to examine this statement made in *Becoming a Nation of Readers* is that it sheds light on the mythology to be uncovered in the narrative being explored here. The statement appears to be making a causal claim, that is, *if* parents read to children, *then* children will succeed in reading instruction. Some may even infer the negative, namely, if parents do not read to children, then children will not succeed. In this way, the narrative comes to be invoked to explain school failure: "X hasn't learned to read because his mother (parents) doesn't (don't) read to him." Are these inferences what the report intends? If so, are such if-then claims legitimate? Researchers need to consider whether justification exists for such causal claims, and why or why not.

Principles of research design and scientific reasoning suggest that causal claims are not justified in this case: to justify causal inference, evidence would need to come from experimental studies, with randomized selection or assignment to treatments. But none has ever been conducted, for obvious reasons: to test the hypothesis that reading to children causes success in learning to read, researchers would need to randomly assign children either to a parental reading condition or to a nonreading control condition—which parents (who would otherwise practice bedtime reading with their children) would not consent to—nor would it seem an ethical course to ask them to do so.

Moreover, the negative or converse that children who have not been read to will not learn to read also seems unsubstantiated: many children who successfully learn to read were not read to by their parents. Over the years, as alluded to earlier, I have been approached by a number of teachers and college professors who have confessed to not having been read to. Indeed, it is partly due to their stories and their reports of the silencing taboo they have experienced on the issue that I have become convinced of the need to discuss the ideology and mythology surrounding the issue of parents' reading to children. To be as clear as possible, let me say that I am certainly not against parents reading to children. I am, however, opposed to the misinterpretation and misappropriation of research in ways that naturalize and normalize the cultural practices of some while stigmatizing and marginalizing the cultural practices of less-powerful others.

So, while the statement from *Becoming a Nation of Readers* has an "if-then" sound, and may be widely taken as such, in actuality only correlational and descriptive studies are cited by the authors as evidence—and as any beginning statistics student learns, "correlation is not causation." This is a second example of an explanatory gap being left for the ideology and mythology of the narrative to fill in.

If the statement about the importance of reading to children is not legitimate as an if-then relation, how does one make sense of it as correlational data? Looked at in a correlational way, the presence of these predictive factors does not assure success nor does the absence of these factors preclude success. To explore the interrelatedness, or specifically the activity of parents' reading books to children, requires enlarging the perspective to look at cause and effect in a sociohistorical way.

The data require a theory or framework that attempts to describe the cultural and political meanings and the origin as well as the interrelations of these so-called predictive or antecedent correlated variables. Such a framework would address not only the fact that parents read to children, but also the differences in "cultural capital" (Bourdieu, 1977) that parents bring to the activity, the school as a "cultural institution" and its match or mismatch with the cultural practices and cultural capital of the home, the differential relations between diverse home cultures and the culture of the school as an institution of the dominant society, and the role of power in privileging some cultural subgroups and their practices over others. One reason that such a theory or framework is needed is that a number of studies have shown quite clearly that not all parents read to children in the same way.

For example, Shirley Brice Heath (1983) found patterned differences between parents she identified as being of middle-class and working-class status in the ways they organized and conducted bedtime story reading with their preschoolers. Gordon Wells (1985) also found social class differences to be significant in ways parents read to their children, ways which correlated with success in school literacy. That is, some ways of reading to children are more successful than others. In Heath's research, both the parents of Roadville and the parents of Maintown read to their preschoolers—but only the Maintown children were successful in school. Similarly, all of the parents in Wells's research engaged their children in looking at books, but differences were found in the talk which accompanied the activity.

In intervention studies, researchers have sometimes found parents' ways of approaching book reading activity different from the researchers' expectations and rather resistant to researchers' attempts at modification. For example, Gallimore and Goldenberg (1993) conducted a study with parents they described as "low income, Spanish-speaking." The parents, who were encouraged to read with their children, engaged in the activity in a particular way that the researchers found to differ from their own conception and that they thought would not succeed in promoting success in school literacy learning.

There are, then, multiple ways of reading to children, not only one way. Differences in practices related to parents' socioeconomic class require us to problematize both the role of the school and the issue of parents' reading to children in ways that have often been ignored in other discussions. What is the origin of differences in how parents read to children? Why are schools able to "capitalize" only on some forms of reading to children and not others? There has been mostly silence on these issues, silence which reflects larger ideological biases in discussions of and narratives about literacy.

Several scholars have written about ideological dimensions of literacy that are helpful in this discussion. Linda Brodkey (1986), for example, has argued that literacy is a "social trope" and that the various and often conflicting definitions arrived at are "cultural Rorschachs." Her work suggests that differing cultural perspectives see different literacies. Echoing Brodkey's insight, Knoblauch (1990) declares, "Literacy is one of those mischievous concepts, like virtuousness and craftsmanship, that appear to denote capacities but that actually convey value judgments" (p. 74). Elaborating on this idea, Knoblauch continues his argument:

> Invariably, definitions of literacy are also rationalizations of its importance. Furthermore, they are invariably offered by the literate, constituting, therefore, implicit rationalizations of the importance of literate people, who are powerful (the reasoning goes) because they are literate and, as such, deserving of power.
> The concept of literacy is embedded, then, in the ideological dispositions of those who use the concept, those who profit from it, and those who have the standing and motivation to enforce it as a social requirement. . . .
>
> [I]f literacy today is perceived as a compelling value, the reason lies . . . in its continuing association with forms of social reality that depend on its primacy. (pp. 74–75)

These are strong words, but Knoblauch is reminding the reader that multiple ways of life are to be valued, not only the current dominant form. Further, Knoblauch points to "ideological dispositions" in theories and research that may be involved in the tendency noted here to suggest causation when only correlation is warranted by data. How do ideology and mythology play out in the area of emergent literacy research?

DIFFERENCES OR DEFICITS? THE VIEW
FROM EMERGENT LITERACY RESEARCH

If the exemplar of an official account, *Becoming a Nation of Readers*, failed to provide an adequate analysis of reading to children, what of the accounts provided by academic scholarship that have come out since that report? How, for example, have prominently placed review articles represented the findings on social class differences in bedtime storybook reading? What about the role of school instruction in building on children's prior experiences? A number of review articles have appeared; prominent among these are those by Mason and Allen (1986), Sulzby and Teale (1991), and a somewhat shorter review by Bus, Van Ijzendoorn, and Pellegrini (1995). Of the three, Sulzby and Teale's article seems most relevant to examine here, because of its prominence and comprehensiveness and because of the leading role that Sulzby and Teale have had in constructing the emergent literacy conception as an area of research.

In the section of their review titled "Variability in Storybook Reading," Sulzby and Teale discuss studies that identified social class differences in parents' activity. They focus initially on two studies that are similar in taking a comparative approach to middle-class and working-class (or "lower"-class) differences, but quite dissimilar in their methodological assumptions. One is a psycholinguistic study conducted by Ninio (1980); the other is an ethnographic study conducted by Heath (1983), mentioned earlier. In the psycholinguistic study, Ninio compared middle- and lower-SES mothers' verbal interaction with their preschooler during a school-like laboratory task conducted in an experimental setting. In the task, Ninio found the lower-SES mothers to be "less skilled."

In the other study, ethnographic field research conducted in homes, Heath took a long-term perspective to try to understand the socially and culturally situated literacy experiences of preschoolers growing up in several different communities. Heath reports many differences between the three communities she studied, but she explicitly cautions against evaluative comparisons. Although her comparisons may at times appear to find the middle-class "Maintowners" to be "better" equipped *for the culture of schooling* and the others "less equipped" by comparison, she also sees the white children of low-income families from Roadville and the black children of low-income families from Tracton as developing narratives and ways of knowing that the mainstream middle-class children do *not* have and that they would be enriched by. In such a view, no group has a monopoly on "best" linguistic or social practices, but each group has something to offer, something that others could be seen to "lack." Heath concludes her discussion by explicitly cautioning against universal, unilinear, and normative perspectives on development.

Thus, Heath seems to be suggesting a stance that resists viewing differences as deficits, while recognizing that, in the context of schooling, differences are often "mis-taken" as deficits and in turn are taken to "construct" disadvantage for learners. In this way, she appears to support a multiple literacies perspective and to resist a universal and unilinear view of development that sees dominant culture life-ways as the norm. Ninio's account, by contrast, appears to accept as unproblematic a single path of development and a single norm for development, with that norm set by the middle class.

Critics for some time have pointed to a normative bias that is methodologically embedded in much of the research in the fields of developmental psychology and psycholinguistics (e.g., Broughton, 1987; Burman, 1994; Parker & Shotter, 1990). In a striking opening to their recent volume, Greenfield and Cocking (1994) have asserted, "The field of developmental psychology is an ethnocentric one dominated by a Euro-American perspective" (p. ix). By contrast, research building on anthropological perspectives more often has attempted to work from a stance of cultural relativism in such matters, and this perspective is an implicit element of ethnographic method. In their discussion, Sulzby and Teale make no reference to the methodological, epistemological, or paradigmatic differences between the ethnographic anthropological research of Heath and the experimental psycholinguistic research of Ninio, and they seem to take the social class comparisons in the two articles as similar in their findings. As a result, Sulzby and Teale appear to miss the anthropological message of Heath's article and the multiple literacies perspective it supports. Rather, their discussion ignores the strengths in the language of children from Tracton and Roadville highlighted by Heath, and instead they note only deficiencies in what the parents and children do. Some readers may see it as unfair to cast Sulzby and Teale as constructing differences as deficits or deficiencies, but their treatment has a pattern: they repeatedly provide comparisons that highlight what middle-class parents do and what working-class parents "tended not" to do; yet they never address these problematic comparisons directly. The absence of any explicit commentary on such an issue, in a review article of such prominence, is a troubling silence.

My suggestion, then, is that the field of early literacy research needs to be significantly reenvisioned from a perspective that is able to see the kinds of ethnocentrism to which Greenfield and Cocking (1994) refer. To be able to do so may require taking the kind of social, historical, and political perspectives suggested by growing numbers of literacy theorists (discussed below). With such perspectives in mind, and recalling also the ideological sensitization provided by Knoblauch (1990) and Brodkey (1986), this discussion turns next to an account of the possible *origin* of the social class differences in parents' reading to children.

Toward a Sociohistorical Account
of Parents' Reading to Children

Sociohistorical theory, drawing on the foundation of L. S. Vygotsky's writings, proposes that mental processes emerge sociogenetically: that is, thinking develops in and through the processes of social interaction. In the logic of this theory, one looks to the context or contexts of social interaction in which parents earlier in life developed the understandings that are reflected in their differing ways of reading with their children. That is, to try to discover an explanation of why research appears to have found patterned differences between middle-class and working-class parents' ways of engaging in book reading activity with their children, one may consider possible sociogenetic differences in the parents' own literacy learning experiences. While the more typical line of reasoning would be to look to home, family, and parent-child interaction for possible differences, another body of research draws one to consider parents' own experiences in school and specifically in reading instruction.[2] This line of reasoning leads to a consideration of differences in school experiences based on curriculum differentiation, especially grouping and tracking. In respect to parents' styles of reading to and with their preschoolers, the differences between parents identified in research as middle class and working class, as found by Heath (1982a, 1982b), Wells (1985), and Gallimore and Goldenberg (1993) referred to above, bear a striking resemblance to the high group/low group differences reported in numerous studies on differential curricula in reading groups: instruction in high groups has been found to focus on meaning and interpretation—on high-level skills; instruction in low groups has been found to focus on decoding and word attack skills—on low-level skills. In related research, Collins (1986) reports similar differences between high and low groups in allocation of time for instruction in these skills (see Table 11.1).

The high group is receiving what educators usually value as "quality" instruction. Collins (1986) speculates on these differences as producing different "conceptions of the task of reading [that] are being formed by the differing emphases on decoding versus meaning" (p. 124). This possibility of a link between distribution of activities during instruction and conceptions of reading leads Collins to examine studies of children's conceptions of reading, in particular, comparisons of the conceptions of read-

TABLE 11.1. Percentage of Instructional Time

	High Group	Low Group
Dictation, penmanship	0	16
Sound/word identification	17	31
Sentence completion	13	16
Passage reading	49	31
Comprehension questions	21	6

Source: Collins, J. (1986), p. 124. © 1986 Cambridge University Press. Adapted with permission.

ing held by "good" and "poor" readers. Citing several interview studies that examine children's conceptions of reading, he summarizes:

> [F]or poor readers, the final purpose and hallmark of proficiency is fluent and rapid reading aloud, with little concern evinced for possible meaning; for good readers, however, the goal of reading is extraction of meaningful content—and usually they view reading instrumentally, as a means of attaining further information. (pp. 124–125)

Collins's point is that if one views "cognition and ability as the outcome, at least in part, of social interaction," then differing "conceptions of the task of reading are being formed [at least in part] by the differing emphases" (p.125) on decoding versus meaning.

In a related discussion of literacy instruction, Allan Luke (1991) uses the concept of "selective traditions" in instruction. In clarifying his concept, Luke directs our attention to the ends or consequences of instructional variations:

> The literature we select, the methods and strategies we use to teach and assess, and the knowledges and competencies we disburse selectively to different groups of students, are selections from the plurality of cultures extant in modern Western nation states. Perhaps more importantly, these selections are not random, but selections which serve particular economic interests and political ends. (p. 133)

Luke refers to research such as Collins's (1986) as highlighting a form of selective tradition in which certain competencies are selected for distribution to some children, while other competencies are selected for others. Although, he comments, one can see an obvious explanation for how these instructional differences arise, "the effect is undeniable" in the sense of distributing different competencies—which constitute different "literacies"—to different groups. Ultimately, what Luke calls the selective tradition includes not only selection of texts and authors but also

> the selection and valorization of particular literacies, attitudes toward texts, degrees and kinds of social competence. . . . From this perspective, no approach to literacy is neutral. All are utterly implicated in distributing to and perhaps depriving children and adults of power, knowledge, and competence to particular economic and political ends. (pp. 134–135)

The differences in perspective held by so-called good and poor readers here have an intriguing resemblance to the differences in what parents emphasize when reading with their children that have been found between the parents of different social classes in the various studies by Heath (1982a, 1982b), Wells (1985), and Gallimore and Goldenberg (1993). Indeed, research has also suggested that children's group placements may be more closely related to family background and economic status than to achievement or aptitude. In Rist's (1970) classic study, children's group placement at school entry related to aspects of dress and physical appearance, apart from any measured "ability," with better-dressed children more likely to be placed in higher groups and challenged with higher expectations; moreover, group placement was quite likely to remain unchanged either in the short term or the long term. Subsequent studies have sometimes been mixed in their findings, and placement is certainly not always as found in Rist's study. Nevertheless, overall the outlook is not encouraging, with differential expectations connected to differential achievement in terms of grouping and tracking reflecting not only social class, but also race and gender hierarchies (Oakes, 1985; Wilcox, 1982).

Such findings are recalled here to provide a broader sociocultural and political frame to connect with Luke's (1991) point quoted above about the selectivity of curriculum differentiation as serving different ends. Larger social and economic patterns play out in education—even despite efforts to the contrary—and reveal cycles of advantage and disadvantage in the experience of schooling itself. Attempts to "compensate" or "remediate," guided by the best of intentions, may actually contribute to the *reproduction* of disadvantage in society. French social theorist Pierre Bourdieu offers the concept of "cultural capital" to help account for how the process of reproduction works (Bourdieu, 1986; Bourdieu & Passeron, 1977). The cultural capital of a group is comprised of its cultural patterns, summarized by Bennett de Marrais & LeCompte (1995) as follows:

> Cultural capital includes . . . language and social roles, but also the general cultural background, knowledge, and skills passed from one generation to the next. Cultural capital differs according to social class: Some has a higher "exchange rate" than others. High culture—that concerned with the arts, literature, and languages as well as communication skills, cooperative work patterns, creative endeavor, and what might be called "middle-class manners and behavior"—characterizes the middle and upper classes and is the most highly valued. This type of cultural capital forms the basis of the overt and the hidden curriculum in schools. . . . [W]orking-class children find that their stock is undervalued. . . . [C]hildren from lower social backgrounds who are not familiar with the codes [for speech and action] will have more difficulty understanding the schooling process. . . . [and because of their ways of speaking] will be perceived as less intellectually competent than their [middle class] peers. (pp. 15–16)

In the case of parents' reading to children, the "more highly valued" cultural capital consists of certain ways of interacting between children and adults and certain ways of talking about texts which are particularly highly valued in school contexts and thus confer advantage on those who are in possession of these forms of capital. Above, it was suggested that schools may be involved in producing through selective traditions the social class differences in cultural capital that are later reflected in the differential ways parents read with children. Clearly, the school is only one site in which individuals are socialized throughout the life cycle, with both family and work contexts and roles having significant influence as well. There is probably no ultimate solution to the "chicken and egg" question of the origin of differences in group practices. Rather, the patterns are multiply influenced in varied public and private sites. But research suggests the need for a *cyclic* sociohistorical perspective and correspondingly the need to reevaluate the role of the school in the cycle: while there are many caring teachers who contribute to children's growth, the overall outcomes are bleak, with mostly unchanging patterns of achievement reflected in test scores and high school graduation rates among students from low-income populations; rather than functioning, then, to interrupt the cycle in which disadvantage is reproduced, schooling frequently fails, reflecting the view of Bourdieu and others, and instead merely promotes reproduction of the status quo through the production of different curricular experiences. Such an analysis helps to explain the differences found by Heath (1982a, 1982b), Wells (1985), and Gallimore and Goldenberg (1993), mentioned earlier, but it also attempts to cast those differences in a larger sociohistorical context.

This sociohistorical analysis also suggests a number of implications. Parents—all parents—teach their children (in a relatively culturally "unconscious" way) what they believe needs to be known about literacy. Parents teach their children what they know and what they learned—their parent-child *activity* is likely to reflect the literacy values they learned and the activities in which they engaged, at home, but particularly in school—since school is the world parents attempt to prepare their children to enter. If parents' instructional experiences were focused on decoding, so that they learned to think of reading *as* decoding, and if most or primary value was placed *on* decoding, it is not surprising that they too focus on that dimension of reading.

In view of this analysis, programs that urge parents to read to their children need to be reconsidered. Rather than trying to enlist parents in the school's work, there may be alternate ways of constructing relations between schools and families. Moll (1996; Moll & Greenberg, 1990), for example, has conducted research with teachers in low-income community schools to help the teachers identify the "funds of knowledge" in children's homes and community, which can then be used to connect classroom instruction with children's out-of-school experiences and base of knowledge. Such an approach highlights two important points: first, it resists the notion of a single model or standard of development in the area of literacy or any other area of development; second, it resists the notion of a single "best" model of parenting, or of family life; third, it resists focusing on what children and families *lack* and instead focuses on what they *have*, and in this way seeks to connect the worlds of home and school in a new way and to reconstruct the home-school relation on a new basis.

Beyond this, an additional element is highlighted by this analysis. Luke (1991) points out that deeper questions need to be raised, questions which ask not only "how" to teach but "what is the goal?" One goal may be to diversify the curriculum, along the lines of Moll's research, by connecting schooling with the culture of the home and community. Diversifying the curriculum does *not* mean re-creating tracking, but does mean finding ways to give a highly valued curriculum to all—while at the same time both problematizing and transforming what "counts" as highly valued curriculum. Heath (1982a) has referred to the idea of "two-way intervention" in which the "ways with words" of the home and community are integrated into the curriculum. Such an approach aims to interrupt the cycle of failure: it seeks to break into the historical-sociogenetic process and teach all children in school in ways which provide them with knowledge or cultural capital that some children get at home and then find "reinforced" and "extended" in school, while at the same time transforming that cultural capital by valuing the knowledge and life ways of *all* groups and *connecting* knowledge from home and community with school learning.

At this point in the discussion, it seems necessary to ask "What does the cultural capital of dominant model parent-child book reading consist of?" In elaborating his conception of cultural capital, social theorist Pierre Bourdieu (1986, 1991) suggests that from the point of view of the *subject,* that is, the individual in possession of it, cultural capital consists of ways of behaving and uses of language which amount to

> *dispositions* which incline agents to act and react in certain ways. . . . Dispositions are acquired through a gradual process of *inculcation* in which early childhood experiences are particularly important. Through a myriad of mundane processes of training and learning, such as those involved in the inculcation of table manners, . . . the individual acquires a set of dispositions which literally mold the body and *become second nature.* (1991, p. 12, *emphasis in original*)

It seems particularly significant that Bourdieu refers to acquired dispositions as *"second nature"* because writers for both academic and popular audiences have so frequently characterized as "natural" both parents' reading to children and children's literacy learning. Such characterizations reveal that the learning and teaching embedded in this activity—what Bourdieu refers to as the "gradual process of inculcation"—is *invisible* to most observers. The claim by some researchers (Goodman & Goodman, 1979; Teale, 1982) that reading to children and learning to read are "natural" is simply evidence from Bourdieu's perspective of the cultural embeddedness of the observer, who mistakenly takes the cultural for the natural. The suggestion is that much of what takes place during the cultural activity of parent-child book reading is not readily apparent to one for whom the activity is a "native" cultural practice. As a consequence, when researchers have asked parents to "read to children," as Gallimore and Goldenberg (1993) did in their "training" study with Latino working-class families, the researchers were surprised when what parents did differed from what the researchers had expected. On the other hand, few researchers have seen "absences" in the verbal repertoires of children from mainstream backgrounds, although Heath (1982b) notes verbal skills specific to each of three communities she studied and absent from the other two, commenting that strengths of all three could be valued and taught in schooling. She writes,

> mainstream children can benefit from early exposure to Trackton's creative, analogical styles of telling stories and giving explanations, and they can add

the Roadville true story with strict chronicity and explicit moral to their
repertoire of narrative types. (p. 72)

All of these forms of talk can be taken into the curriculum as relevant
language development for all children.

Toward Reconceptualizing Early Literacy

What difference does it make how parent-child book reading activity is
viewed? Critical and uncritical views have differing consequences, which
are both analytic and programmatic.

Analytic Consequences

Earlier it was argued that statements in the report *Becoming a Nation of
Readers* imply a cause-effect analysis which mistakes correlation for cause.
When this cause-effect view is taken (often only implicitly), it may seem
easy to blame parents (or, more typically, the child's mother) when a child
has difficulty learning to read. It is not uncommon to hear, said of a child
who struggles with learning to read, "Well, you know, his mother probably doesn't read to him." Such a statement acts in three interrelated ways:
(1) it displaces responsibility onto the home and simultaneously minimizes
the school's role; (2) it naturalizes the practices of the school, rather than
considering possibilities for change; and (3) it recycles the logic of "blaming the victim," a way of interpreting difference that once again normal-
izes the mainstream and marginalizes and stigmatizes difference. This
analysis could also probe more deeply to find "methodological individu-
alism" in these ways of thinking: that is, a reading "problem" is identified
and located in an individual learner rather than in a learning context,
specifically, the school: in this way, it can be assumed that the child has a
reading-*learning* problem—rather than that the school has a reading-
teaching problem.

Programmatic Consequences

A particular kind of programmatic approach tends to be seen as following
from or at least accompanying the faulty reasoning under critique. The
frequently made programmatic assumption is that programs can and
should be developed to train parents to read to their children as a way to
solve, or perhaps prevent, reading problems of beginning readers. On the
one hand, such an approach might seem misguided on purely practical
grounds: how could all the parents who do not read to their children (or

who do not read "the right way") be trained? Beyond this, however, one may question such an approach because it diverts attention away from the school on the assumption that the "problem" originates in the home and because it assumes "right" and "wrong" forms of parenting, based on a dominant group model. If the sociohistorical analysis given earlier is considered, then social and historical scope would be enlarged to the earlier school experiences of parents. If it is in such experiences that parents learned to conceptualize the activity of learning to read as focused on the mechanics of reading, then programs which encourage parents to read to children may have predictably disappointing results, as in the study earlier referred to by Gallimore and Goldenberg (1993). That is, the sociohistorical analysis suggests that such results are predictable from the experiences that the target parents may have had in their own schooling. Parent-training programs have failed to take the larger sociohistorical perspective or to take account of the research on tracking and social class which suggests this analysis and what Luke (1991) has labeled the "selective tradition." Instead, the readily available pattern of thinking, long since dubbed "blaming the victim" by William Ryan (1971), leads to parents being blamed for not reading to their children, or not reading the "right way," instead of seeing that parents may have been recipients themselves of instruction which "selected" for them the less highly valued forms of literacy that focused on mechanics in the first place.

Thus, there is a potential self-fulfilling prophecy at work in parent training programs. By focusing attention on homes and ways of parenting, programs of parent training imply indirectly that "all's right with the school," that it is homes that need to be fixed. Moreover, parent training mistakenly tends to be seen as trying to attack "the root of the problem." Then, if parent training does not result in children's success, the logic of victim blaming suggests that all possible avenues of remediation and compensation have been exhausted: "we've tried everything," the logic goes, "even training the parents." But if the "roots" of parents' conception of learning to read are their own classroom experiences, then it makes sense that change needs to come in classrooms, not in homes.

After more than a decade of considerable research on parents' reading to children, it seems surprising that the insights gained from that research have been so little discussed as applicable to classrooms. A recent review by Bus, Van Ijzendoorn, and Pellegrini (1995), for example, concludes with the summary statement that research on parent-child book reading "support[s] intergenerational programs focusing on parent-preschooler reading" (p. 18). But the insights gained from research on parent-child book reading activity can be used to inform activity in kindergarten and first-grade classrooms, instead of focusing on parents who do not read to children or who read to children differently from what seems to be the dominant pattern. At the same time, the "two-way" process of change that Heath (1982a) referred to and the "funds of knowledge" explored by Moll (1996) are needed: multiple ways of life need to enter into our conceptions of schooling to find ways of connecting with the out-of-school experiences of learners from diverse backgrounds to the experience of schooling.

DISCOURSES AND LITERACY: THE POSSIBILITIES FOR LEARNING LITERATE DISCOURSE IN SCHOOL

What kinds of considerations are necessary in developing an approach for integrating the varied home literacy practices of parent-child book reading into school contexts? Although there are only a few illustrations of successful implementations of such strategies, an important conceptual resource for thinking about this topic is the idea that schools need to be more like homes in the sense of providing care and support, as sites for nurturance (Martin, 1992, 1994; Noddings, 1984). Teacher-researcher Carollyne Sinclaire (1994) shows the type of classroom that is possible when she says her "calling is one of preparing the child in my classroom for being at home in the world" (p. 29)—one not solely a place of instruction.

Anne Barry nurtures and welcomes children's personal lives in a way that builds a homelike community and invites each child to take up an identity as a reader. In contrast to the common classroom practice, yet similar to some family examples of storybook reading, Barry's students are free to break into the reading at any time with comments or questions, they are free to get up to retrieve other materials (books or other objects) that they find relevant to the talk about text in which all participate, and they are free to introduce experiences from outside the (classroom) reading activity into the read-aloud discourse, allowing them to connect text to their experiences of self and world at home and elsewhere (Oyler & Barry, 1996). While Anne Barry's ways of transforming her classroom may not have been explicitly guided by the attempt to model book reading activity on the pattern of parents and children, it appears to do so. Gee (1990) has offered the pessimistic prediction that schools are not likely to succeed in providing access to dominant literacy and discourse to learners from nonmainstream backgrounds. While Gee's analysis is compelling, it is possible for children from nondominant discourse backgrounds to acquire the discourse of school literacy when classroom literacy practices are modified. Research is needed to identify ways of interconnecting the forms of literacy traditionally valorized in school contexts with the literacy forms which children experience elsewhere. I suggest that the rewriting of the research narrative on early literacy can help to move us toward such possibilities.

IF SCHOOLS/SOCIETY SHARED OUR PERSPECTIVE ON LITERACY, HOW MIGHT PEOPLE'S LIVES BE DIFFERENT?

What I have been arguing is that the old narrative on reading to children has to be abandoned, and a new conception put in its place, as in the example of one classroom. If this were accepted, the assimilationist ideological cycle which judges ways of living and patterns of child rearing according to an assumed norm or single standard would be interrupted and abandoned, and it would be replaced with an alternative approach to pedagogy. This alternative approach would take teaching as an ongoing inquiry in which the goal of getting to know one's students would be understood by teachers as a *sine qua non* for children's successful learning in school. Integral to this perspective would be the valuing of the funds of knowledge in all communities and groups and a problematizing of the hierarchies of knowledge in which the abstract and academic is valued over the applied and practical uses of knowledge. An increasing range of scholars argue that these hierarchies are not natural, but cultural and political, and reflect the economic and political structures of society.

Thus, it is the larger structures of society that are finally responsible for the problems we face in education. Although it is possible to imagine that significant school change could have positive influences on society, no amount of school change in and of itself will produce fundamental change in society. But without significant changes in the economic and societal structures, improved schooling may bring greater inequities, as better educated groups of young adults are left to compete for the same fraction of high-skill jobs, expanding the ranks of the "well-qualified" and driving down wages.

I am not suggesting a one-dimensional, career-oriented purpose for schooling. However, I am suggesting that the problems posed by a single standard in schools must always be seen as part of much larger, systemic patterns in the society of which the schools are a part. Success in changing the practices and standards in schools will inevitably be linked to changes in other domains of society. Thus, many who work for change within schools also see a need for teachers and their allies to work for social change outside of schools as well.

ACKNOWLEDGMENT

I would like to thank Margaret Gallego, Eleanor Handerhan, and Marjorie Siegel for discussion and helpful comments on an earlier version of this paper, presented at AERA.

NOTES

1. The non-reading child is rarely "her." The non-reading parent is never "father" (though is sometimes plural). The gendered nature of the narrative is important, but will not be addressed here.

2. Much research has focused on variability in patterns of parent-child interaction across different groups. However, I am interested in this discussion to shift the emphasis away from a tendency to "blame" the family and instead to consider the possibility that schooling is implicated in the production and reproduction of inequalities. Heath's research (1982a, 1982b, 1983) is relevant here; see also the work of Tudge, Putnam, and Sidden (1993) for an attempt to develop a theoretical account of social class differences in parent-child discourse.

REFERENCES

Anderson, R., Hiebert, E., Scott, J., & Wilkinson, I. (1985). *Becoming a nation of readers*. Washington, DC: National Institute of Education.

Bennett de Marrais, K., & LeCompte, M. (1995). *The way schools work*. New York: Longman.

Bourdieu, P. (1977). *Outline of a theory of practice*. Cambridge; U.K.: Cambridge University Press.

Bourdieu, P. (1986). The forms of capital. In J. G. (Ed.), *Handbook of theory and research for the sociology of education* (pp. 241–258). New York: Greenwood Press.

Bourdieu, P. (1991). *Language and symbolic power*. Cambridge, MA: Harvard University Press.

Bourdieu, P., & Passeron, J. C. (1977). *Reproduction in education, society and culture*. London: Sage.

Brodkey, L. (1986). Tropics of literacy. *Journal of Education, 168*, 47–54.

Broughton, J. (Ed.). (1987). *Critical theories of psychological development*. New York: Plenum Press.

Bruner, J. S. (1983). *Child's talk*. New York: Norton.

Burman, E. (1994). *Deconstructing developmental psychology*. London: Routledge.

Bus, A., Van Ijzendoorn, M., & Pellegrini, A. (1995). Joint book reading makes for success in learning to read: A meta-analysis on intergenerational transmission of literacy. *Review of Educational Research, 65*(1), 1–21.

Cazden, C., John, V. P., & Hymes, D. (Eds.). (1972). *Functions of language in the classroom*. New York: Teachers College Press.

Clinton, H. R. (1997, February 3). Comfort and Joy. *Time*, 63.

Collins, J. (1986). Differential instruction in reading groups. In J. Cook-Gumperz (Ed.), *The social construction of literacy* (pp. 117–137). Cambridge, U.K.: Cambridge University Press.

Gallimore, R., & Goldenberg, C. (1993). Activity settings of early literacy: Home and school factors in children's emergent literacy. In E. Forman, N. Minick, & C. A. Stone (Eds.), *Contexts for learning: Sociocultural dynamics in children's development* (pp. 315–355). New York: Oxford University Press.

Gee, J. (1990). *Social linguistics and literacies: Ideology in discourses*. London: Falmer Press.

Goodman, K., & Goodman, Y. (1979). Learning to read is natural. In L. Resnick & P. Weaver (Eds.), *Theory and practice of early reading* (Vol. 1, pp. 137–154). Hillsdale, NJ: Erlbaum.

Graff, H. (1981). Literacy, jobs, and industrialization: the nineteenth century. In H. Graff (Ed.), *Literacy and social development in the West: A reader* (pp. 232–260). Cambridge, U.K.: Cambridge University Press.

Greenfield, P., & Cocking, R. (Eds.). (1994). In *Cross-cultural roots of minority child development* (pp. ix–xix). Hillsdale, NJ: Erlbaum.

Heath, S. B. (1982a). Questioning at home and at school. In G. Spindler (Ed.), *Doing the ethnography of schooling* (pp. 102–131). New York: Holt, Rinehart & Winston.

Heath, S. B. (1982b). What no bedtime story means: Narrative skills at home and school. *Language in Society, 11*, 49–76.

Heath, S. B. (1983). *Ways with words*. Cambridge, U.K.: Cambridge University Press.

Knoblauch, C. H. (1990). Literacy and the politics of education. In A. Lunsford, H. Moglen, & J. Slevin (Eds.), *The right to literacy* (pp. 74–80). New York: Modern Language Association.

Luke, A. (1991, October). Literacies as social practices. *English Education, 131*–147.

Martin, J. R. (1992). *The school home: Rethinking schools for changing families*. Cambridge, MA: Harvard University Press.

Martin, J. R. (1994). *Changing the educational landscape*. New York: Routledge.

Mason, J., & Allen, J. (1986). A review of emergent literacy with implications for research and practice in reading. In E. Rothkopf (Ed.), *Review of Research in Education, 13*, 3–47.

Moll, L. (1996, February). *Inspired by Vygotsky: Ethnographic experiments in education*. Invited paper presented at Vygotsky Centennial Conference of the Research Assembly of the National Council of Teachers of English, Chicago.

Moll, L., & J. Greenberg. (1990). Creating zones of possibilities: Combining social contexts for instruction. In L. Moll (Ed.), *Vygotsky and education* (pp. 319–348). New York: Cambridge University Press.

Ninio, A. (1980). Picture-book reading in mother-infant dyads belonging to two subgroups in Israel. *Child Development, 51*, 587–590.

Noddings, N. (1984). *Caring: A feminine approach to ethics and moral education*. Berkeley: University of California Press.

Oakes, J. (1985). *Keeping track: How schools structure inequality*. New Haven, CT: Yale University Press.

Ochs, E. (1987). Input: A socio-cultural perspective. In M. Hickmann (Ed.), *Social and functional approaches to language and thought* (pp. 305–319). Orlando, FL: Academic Press.

Oyler, C., & Barry, A. (1996). Intertextual connections in read-alouds of information books. *Language Arts, 73*, 324–329.

Parker, I., & Shotter, J. (Eds.). (1990). *Deconstructing social psychology.* London: Routledge.

Rist, R. (1970). Student social class and teacher expectations: The self-fulfilling prophecy in ghetto education. *Harvard Educational Review, 40*, 411–451.

Ryan, W. (1971). *Blaming the victim.* New York: Vintage.

Scribner, S. (1984, November). Literacy in three metaphors. *American Journal of Education*, 6–21.

Sinclaire, C. (1994). *Looking for home: A phenomenological study of home in the classroom.* Albany: State University of New York Press.

Snow, C., & Ferguson, C. (Eds.). (1977). *Talking to children.* Cambridge, U.K.: Cambridge University Press.

Sulzby, E., & Teale, W. (1991). Emergent literacy. In R. Barr, M. Kamil, P. Mosenthal, & P. D. Pearson (Eds.), *Handbook of reading research* (Vol. 2, pp. 727–757). New York: Longman.

Teale, W. (1982). Toward a theory of how children learn to read and write naturally. *Language Arts, 59*, 555–570.

Teale, W. (1988). Developmentally appropriate assessment of reading and writing in the early childhood classroom. *Elementary School Journal, 89*, 173–183.

Tudge, J., Putnam, S., & Sidden, J. (1993). Preschoolers' activities in socio-cultural context. *Quarterly Newsletter of the Laboratory of Comparative Human Cognition, 15*(2), 71–84.

Wells, G. (1985). Preschool literacy-related activities and success in school. In D. Olson, N. Torrance, & A. Hildyard (Eds.), *Literacy, language and learning* (pp. 229–255). Cambridge, U.K.: Cambridge University Press.

Wilcox, K. (1982). Differential socialization in the classroom: Implications for equal opportunity. In G. Spindler (Ed.), *Doing the ethnography of schooling: Educational anthropology in action* (pp. 268–309). Prospect Heights, IL: Waveland Press.

12

Literacy and American Indian Students

Meaning Making Through Multiple Sign Systems

ELIZABETH NOLL

Brad is hunched over a sheet of paper, drawing a valley dotted with pine trees and teepees and bordered by snowcapped mountains. He works slowly and deliberately, stopping occasionally to study his picture. Around him other students are completing a worksheet on sentence structure while the teacher moves about the room, quietly answering questions. As she nears his desk, Brad flips over his drawing to reveal the worksheet and begins working on it. His teacher pauses, glances at his worksheet, then moves on. After a moment, Brad returns to his picture (Figure 12.1).

Brad, a twelve-year-old Lakota boy,[1] enjoys drawing and spends a considerable amount of time in school creating pictures of realities far removed from the classroom. He explains, "When I'm in class and I don't feel right, I just start drawing like some stuff on the back sheet of my paper. And then I'll get it out of my mind and then I'll feel better. . . . I draw my culture. Usually I draw teepees, sweat lodges."

Brad struggles in school, both academically and socially, and drawing offers him temporary refuge. Moreover, through artistic expression Brad is able to express ideas that he often finds difficult to express through writing. "Writing is hard," he says. "I understand things better in pictures than, like, in words . . . and I can say it better that way—in my drawings and sometimes [in] cartoons I copy from TV."

Brad is one of 34 American Indian students, mostly Lakota and Dakota (Sioux), at his predominately white middle school. Growing up in a rural, nonreservation community in the upper mid-West, he and most of his Indian peers speak English as their first language though most also

What Counts as Literacy: Challenging the School Standard. Copyright © 2000 by Teachers College, Columbia University. All rights reserved. ISBN 0-8077-3972-3 (paper), ISBN 0-8077-3973-1 (cloth). Prior to photocopying items for classroom use, please contact the Copyright Clearance Center, Customer Service, 222 Rosewood Drive, Danvers, MA 01923, USA, telephone (508) 750-8400.

FIGURE 12.1. Brad's Drawing

maintain strong ties to Native culture and traditions. I came to know Brad during a 9-month study I conducted in his school and community. The focus of my study was on the role of literacy in the lives of American Indian young adolescents. I wanted to understand the ways in which they use literacy in and out of school as well as the meaning they make of their literacy experiences.

CONCEPTIONS OF LITERACY

As a former language arts and reading teacher at the middle school where much of this investigation took place, I had been guided by the work of Graves (1988), Goodman (1982), Freire & Macedo (1987), Smith (1983) and others who write about language and literacy learning from social and political perspectives. My conception of literacy was influenced by their research and by my own teaching practice. Thus, as I began this study, my view of literacy was language-based, and my aim was to explore how these particular American Indian adolescents use literacy—specifically reading and writing—to construct meaning in their lives.

Early in the study, however, my view of literacy was challenged by my findings and I was pushed to reconsider and eventually to broaden my conception of literacy. According to plan, I observed the American Indian students in multiple settings, collected samples of their work, and interviewed them and their parents, teachers, and peers. Despite the fact that my research appeared to be moving along smoothly, I had the nagging sense that I was missing something. Eventually, I realized that the ways in which these adolescents constructed meaning in their lives went well beyond their experiences with reading and writing. They also frequently used visual art and dance and music to express ideas, images, and feelings and to explore issues of significance to them. This finding is supported in other research (e.g., John, 1972; More, 1989; Suina & Smolkin, 1994; Swisher & Deyhle, 1989, 1992) that addresses the significance of visual approaches to learning for American Indian students. According to Swisher and Deyhle (1992), this visual orientation reflects an important way in which Indian children "come to know and understand the world" (p. 84).

Although I recognized the importance of these experiences, initially I did not grant them the same authority I accorded those related to reading and writing. Art, dance, and music all fell outside of my conception of literacy, which was the focus of my study. Yet, after I listened to the adolescents' explanations and interpretations of their engagements with these other sign systems (Leland & Harste, 1994; Siegel, 1984; Suhor, 1984), it became clear that the transactional process of meaning making mirrored those used in reading and writing and that the syntactic and semantic properties were similar. That is, while the symbols and texts of these experiences differed from those of language-based literacy experiences, the transactional relationship between "the reader, the text, the poem" (Rosenblatt, 1978) were much the same. I realized that to ignore the significance of other sign systems would result in a less full, less accurate understanding of the role of literacy—all literacies—in the lives of these American Indian adolescents. Thus, I decided to expand the focus of my study to include the influence of multiple sign systems—language as well as art, music, and dance—in the lives of the adolescents.

THE STUDY

This research was carried out through ethnographic techniques of data collection and analysis. For approximately 7 months (August to February 1994), I gathered data through participant and nonparticipant observation in a variety of settings (e.g., classrooms, hallways, homes, and community events); interviews with students, parents, teachers, and members of the local American Indian community; and examination of artifacts, such as samples of students' writing and drawing. To analyze the data, I employed the constant comparative method (Glaser & Strauss, 1967) through which I identified categories in the data. This process revealed patterns in the adolescents' uses of literacy that suggested that literacy served important personal and social purposes in their lives. In keeping with my desire to provide an interpretive perspective (Erickson, 1986) that would accurately reflect the understandings of my participants, I searched for confirming and disconfirming evidence during the entire period of data collection and analysis.

This chapter describes the role of literacy in the lives of Brad, introduced above, and his peers Amy, Daniel, Kelly, and Zonnie, all of whom identify themselves as Indian as well as Lakota and/or Dakota. Zonnie is also part Navajo, and both Daniel and Amy are part white. Yet, all agree with the sentiment of another American Indian student, who contends that being Indian "is more than just how much Indian blood you have." In the following sections, I show how these adolescents draw upon language, music, dance, and art, often within single literacy events, to construct and represent their personal understandings. In addition, I examine how different cultures—Native culture as well as popular culture and school culture—influence their understandings.

CONSTRUCTING MEANING
USING MULTIPLE SIGN SYSTEMS

For Brad and for Amy and Daniel, visual art represents a medium for expressing personal meaning. Through their drawings they construct and communicate various images, knowledge, and ideas. Drawing also represents a means of expressing strong feelings, as revealed by Amy, an assertive yet sensitive 11-year-old girl. Unlike many of the American Indian students at her school, she speaks openly and frequently about Native culture and feels a sense of responsibility for informing others about Lakota traditions. Amy is also easily hurt by others' careless comments and actions, as was the case one afternoon at the end of the school day.

On her way to the after-school Title V/American Indian Literary Club,[2] Amy was knocked down in the hallway by an older student. Her books flew in all directions and, although she was physically unharmed and viewed the incident as unintentional, she came away with hurt feelings. At the club meeting, still visibly upset, she described the incident to her peers. They listened for a moment, then moved on to other interests, while Amy sat and stared into space. I talked with her for a few minutes and suggested that she might try writing about what happened. She agreed, pulled out a sheet of paper and a pencil and began to write. Later, as I drove her home, she showed me the paper. She had begun writing then scribbled out the words. Below that she had drawn a series of five faces—all her own—with tears running down the cheeks and mouths turned downward in sadness. She had tried writing about her feelings with words but, she explained, "I feel better when I can *draw* my feelings."

Likewise, Daniel, a generally cheerful 13-year-old, draws to express his emotions: "Usually if I'm angry, I just, like, draw mean pictures and if I'm happy I draw peaceful pictures." Peaceful pictures, according to Daniel, are generally scenes of sunsets, forests, and water, which he associates with pleasant experiences, such as spending time with his father. "Me and my dad, we take walks by the river together and he shows me what different plants and trees can be used for, the traditional ways." By contrast, mean pictures include ominous-looking faces of comic strip characters, such as the one shown in Figure 12.2, which Daniel drew on his language arts folder.

Daniel explains that he is influenced in his drawing by the comic strips he reads each week in *Indian Country Today*, a national newspaper that his family picks up or that he reads in the school library. These comic strips, such as *The Redskins* and *Around the Rez*, have "lots of Indian humor," contends Daniel with a chuckle. "I change them to look the way I want. Like this dude (Figure 12.2) I made kinda goofy and also mean 'cause I was *mad.*"

Elsewhere on his language arts folder Daniel has combined letters and an icon—a heart symbolizing love—to signify "Mom" and the warm relationship he has with his mother (see Figure 12.3).

Figure 12.3 is significant in that it represents with simplicity the many instances in which Daniel and his Indian peers draw upon more than one

FIGURE 12.2. Daniel's "Mean Picture"

FIGURE 12.3. Integration of Symbols

symbol system in single meaning making, or literacy, events. By themselves, neither the letters *M-o-m* nor the symbol, or icon, for a heart would communicate the same meaning as does the interweaving of the two. Similarly, when Daniel writes his name on school assignments, he underlines the letters spelling his name with a series of eagle feathers, which symbolize his Indian identity (see Figure 12. 4).

LITERACY AND NATIVE CULTURE

Like these examples, in which different symbols (e.g., letters and icons) are interwoven to create fuller personal meanings, the integration of different sign systems, such as music and dance, is also common in the American Indian students' literacy experiences. This integration is clearly demonstrated at local powwows, important social and cultural events in which many of these adolescents participate as singers and dancers. Daniel and several of his Indian peers, both boys and girls, are members of the Ihanktowan Dakota Singers, a drum group established by Daniel's father. The songs they sing have been handed down through history, explains Daniel, and the lyrics of the songs tell stories. The cultural and historical meanings behind these stories is further communicated by the drumbeat,

FIGURE 12.4. Daniel's Signature

and both the lyrics and the drumbeat are reflected and reinterpreted in the movements of the dancers. The power and richness of these multitextual events are revealed by Kelly, a 13-year-old girl, who describes the personal meaning she derives:

> When I hear the music—well, really, I hear it *and* I feel it inside (tapping her chest)—it just moves me to begin dancing. It's like I can't help it. I've always danced since I can remember. . . . And, like, I know the dance steps—I mostly fancy dance—but . . . the way I move the rest of my body is the way I feel from the sound of [the] music and the drumbeat and also from the meaning of the songs 'cause they have special meaning to my people. . . . It's like, when I dance, I do it the way it's supposed to be but I express my own feelings and my own reaction to the music and everything.

Kelly's description of her experience dancing at powwows suggests a transaction between herself and the multiple texts contained within the drumbeat, the melody, and the lyrics. She "reads" these texts, much as one reads printed text, and infuses into her experience understandings of the cultural significance as well as her own past experiences and her current interpretations. This personal meaning-making experience is quite similar to the transactions that occur when one reads print. As Rosenblatt (1983) explains:

> The benefits of literature can emerge only from creative activity on the part of the reader himself. He responds to the little black marks on the page, or to the sounds of the words in his ear, and he "makes something of them." The verbal symbols enable him to draw on his past experiences with what the words point to in life and literature. The text presents these words in a new and unique pattern. Out of these he is enabled actually to mold a new experience. (p. 278)

For Kelly and other American Indian youth, the melding of new experiences through dancing and singing at powwows is grounded in their cultural understandings. That is, the meanings they create grow from their knowledge of Native culture and history, knowledge that has been passed down to them by parents, grandparents and elders in the community. Their experiences are also influenced by the highly social nature of powwows, which is reflected in the lively conversations and sharing of food with friends and family and the selling of handicrafts. In addition to this cultural context in which Daniel and Kelly construct personal understandings through the language of song and dance, there are other cultural contexts which shape the nature of their literacy experiences.

LITERACY AND POPULAR CULTURE

As American Indian youngsters, Daniel and Kelly and their peers share, in varying degrees, a view of the world that is shaped by Native beliefs. Yet, as young adolescents growing up and attending school in a predominately white, mainstream environment, their lives are also strongly influenced by both popular culture and school culture. Like most young adolescents, these American Indian students watch television and go to movies, listen to the radio, and read teen magazines. They wear T-shirts advertising athletic companies and sports teams, argue the merit of sitcoms, and expound upon the jingles of well-known TV commercials. "Hey, have you had your break today?" one American Indian student asks another, giving him a playful karate chop on the arm. Popular culture is thus revealed in many aspects of the adolescents' lives and impacts their experiences with literacy, as the examples of Zonnie and Amy reveal.

At age 14, Zonnie is a prolific poet whose writing is strongly influenced by ballad, rock, and country music. Like the lyrics of country music, her poems tell of love and heartbreak. Yet, many of her poems describe, not male-female love relationships, but relationships within her own family. Zonnie's exceptional closeness to her mother is reflected in the following poem, written in the form of a letter.

Dear Mom,
I'm proud of the days I spent with you,
Laughing and talking about every dream we had.
Life is so kind to you but seems so mean to me.
As you go on with your life
Living to see me accomplish mine,
I love you for being my mother
Because you are the only one who treated me kind.
And if I start to cry
It is because I know you are in my heart.
So please, Mom, don't leave
For I don't know what to do when you are gone.
But remember, I will always love you
Even if you moved on with your life.
Love, Me.

Zonnie's poetry is influenced not only by the lyrics of country music but also by the rhythm and melody typical of this kind of music. She explains that she makes up her own country melodies and hums them to herself while creating her poems. The melodies and rhythms she hears in her head are reflected in the rhythm and flow of her poetry.

Whereas Zonnie's expression draws upon the lyrics and melodies of popular music, Amy's literacy experiences are sometimes inspired by commercial marketing and television. At age 11, her reading selections are still reflective of preadolescence. For example, in a corner of her bedroom sits a small bookcase with her books and magazines, including the *Boxcar Children* series, *Highlights Magazine*, books of Indian legends, and *Barbie Safari*, a book about the popular doll which Amy describes as "really goofy!" Amy also reads poetry, generally from books checked out at the public library, and writes her own poems. She explains that her ideas for poems, as well as for stories and even inventions, come from a variety of sources: "It just seems that if I look at something, something just pops into my mind. . . . Like a commercial, [or] maybe a movie or a drawing." Recently, she says, she got ideas for an invention from a television commercial about a shampoo cap for toddlers.

Amy also describes how she combined ideas from two sources—a movie on television and the view from her bedroom window—to create a poem, entitled *Out My Window* (Figure 12.5). Amy explains that both the decision to write a poem and the idea for this particular poem came, not only from her observation of a bees' nest and birds in her backyard, but also from watching the movie *Clarissa Explains It All:*

> My inspiration was actually a show on Nickelodeon. It was *Clarissa Explains It All.* She [Clarissa] needed to write a poem—but I did not

FIGURE 12.5. Amy's Poem

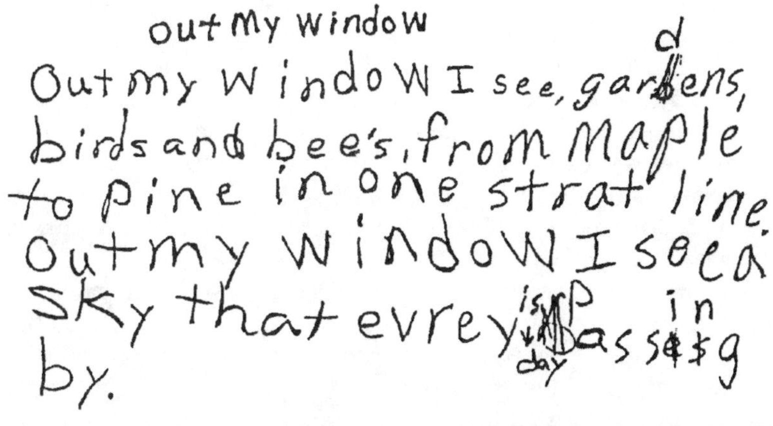
out My window
Out my window I see, gardens,
birds and bee's, from Maple
to pine in one strat line.
Out my window I see a
sky that evrey day is passing
by.

copy this off, because she had a really different perspective—and she was looking out her window. . . . That's how I got inspired.

As Amy talks, it becomes clear that getting "inspirated" to write actually does involve more than something just popping into her mind. In fact, she makes a point of storing words and images in her mind for future use. Sometimes, she says, when she is looking for inspiration,

> if I can't think of anything else, like getting inspired by a TV show or something, I'll look back in my memory and try to find that word that I memorized. And then I'll remember what I put down for that that I memorized and then I'll kind of like do another idea on that, but a different one.

LITERACY AND SCHOOL CULTURE

Just as both Native culture and popular culture exert a strong impact on the lives and literacy experiences of these American Indian adolescents, so too does the culture of school.

School culture, which manifests itself in curricula and materials, methods of instruction, the physical environment, and standards of appropriate behavior, is reflective of mainstream culture. Both school culture and mainstream culture are based upon the knowledge and perspectives of the dominant class, which traditionally have been privileged over the knowledge and experiences of minority groups. The values and expectations of school culture are not foreign to these American Indian students who participate daily in a public middle school. Yet, that is not to say that they have fully assimilated into either mainstream or school culture. In fact, many feel alienated, invisible, and uneasy at school. Sometimes, as the introduction to Brad suggests, meaningful engagements with literacy in school—both authorized and unauthorized—can serve to mitigate such feelings. In that example, Brad finds solace in composing visual images representative of his Native culture. In so doing, he mentally removes himself from the classroom and rejects, at least for the time being, a school-sanctioned literacy experience (completing a worksheet on subjects and predicates).

Similarly, Zonnie carves out spaces during the school day for her poetry. Though a more academically acceptable form of literacy than Brad's drawings, Zonnie's poems, carefully protected in a special notebook, are not part of her school literacy experiences. They are personal and private, unlike the poetry written to satisfy assignments given by her teachers.

"Some of the poetry that I write is private because it's just my feelings and other poetry that I write is just for some kind of thing . . . that teachers tell me I should do," says Zonnie. The functions, or purposes, of her personal poetry and of poetry written for school differ. As a friend observes, and Zonnie confirms, "she uses [her personal] poems to express her feelings about friendships, her parents, and ways she looks at the world." By contrast, assigned poetry fulfills a school obligation, and expectations for its format, style, and even its content are often determined by the teacher. While such assignments are less personally meaningful to Zonnie, completion of them—and of any school assignment—is a highly enforced expectation in school. Zonnie plans to continue on to college, and she recognizes the importance of fulfilling this expectation now as a means to her goal.

These examples of Brad and Zonnie are not intended to suggest that the only school literacy experiences of value to them or to their Indian peers are those that take place "underground" or that lack intrinsic value. In fact, the students also show evidence of purposefully shaping school assignments to meet important personal and social needs. For example, following a language arts skills lesson on giving directions, Amy's class was told to write a "how-to" paragraph. Amy chose to write about how to get dressed for a powwow, thereby addressing not only her personal need to make connections between Native culture and school, but also her social need to inform others about Native customs while complying to school assignments.

Like Amy, Zonnie and Brad sometimes shape school assignments to explore or address significant issues in their lives. At the time of this study, Zonnie's father had just returned home after a lengthy imprisonment, an important event in her life, which she chose to write about in her language arts class. Most writing assignments in this class follow the teacher's lessons on different topics and skills. Zonnie explains that, after teaching about cause and effect in literature, the teacher "would just have us make up our own cause and effect story. . . . I wrote about my dad and how he got in prison. Like cause and effect of what happened." (See Figure 12.6 for an excerpt from her narrative.)

Finally, Brad, described by his teachers as a nonreader and an unwilling writer, becomes unusually engaged in literacy assignments when he is able to make personal connections to the topic. A gentle boy, Brad is easily upset by perceived slights from peers and teachers, which he interprets as evidence of racial discrimination and prejudice. Normally tentative about writing, Brad became quite involved in a writing assignment on the life of Martin Luther King, Jr., in which he focused on the injustices King experienced. Likewise, his interpretation of prejudice in the novel *To Walk a Sky Path* (Naylor, 1993) prompted him to write in his literary journal (see Figure 12.7).

FIGURE 12.6. Excerpt from Zonnie's Writing Assignment

Cause & Effect

This is a story about a man, who never had a chance to live with his wife and children as much as he wanted too.

The man did nothing to deserve what had happened to him. He was put in prison for killing another man. And they sentenced him for 10 years in prison. It was hard to except what he did. Because, he had learned he'd did nothing.

Alternative forms of literacy, such as expression through art, generally are not encouraged in Brad's classes. His language arts teacher explains that she does not allow drawing as a form of expression during the students' writing time "because it's hard to control. . . . I'm really careful with that." Brad, for whom drawing represents an important means of communicating ideas and images, is thus limited to written language as a legitimate means of sharing his knowledge in school.

CONCLUSION

As this chapter shows, literacy in its multiple forms is an integral part of life for these American Indian young adolescents. In addition to the central role of reading and writing in their lives, they also explore personal understandings through music, art, and dance, often using more than one of these sign systems in a single literacy event. Furthermore, they are influenced by and purposefully apply their knowledge of different cultures—Native culture, popular culture, and school culture—to construct meaning. Ironically, however, despite the richness and breadth of literacy in the lives of these adolescents, they are often perceived—both individually at their school and more globally as members of a minority group—as less-than-capable literacy users. Low test scores, failing grades, and high dropout rates among American Indian students locally and nationwide provide ample "evidence" to support this deficit view (see Deyhle, 1995; Reyhner, 1992).

The disparity between the findings of this study and widespread negative assumptions about the literacy of American Indian students poses a challenge for schools. The challenge centers on broadening our theoretical and pedagogical conceptions of literacy so that learning through multiple sign systems becomes the norm in schools for *all* students. By providing regular and integrated opportunities for students to learn through art, music, and dance, as well as through reading and writing, we create broader contexts for students to construct and express their knowledge. Equally as important is the issue of literacy assessment. It is essential that assessments be designed and implemented in ways that accurately reflect students' diverse capabilities and cultural knowledge and that the results of alternative assessments become the basis on which we judge students.

Yet, while implementing such changes is critical in terms of legitimizing students' multiple forms of expression and cultural backgrounds, it is not without potential hazards. In attempting to support students' cultural

FIGURE 12.7. Brad's Journal Entry

To Walk The Sky Path

I beleave that the pielote is very preadis, he did not want Billie's grandpa to help him, he would have died if grandpa did not help.

understandings through various sign systems, we run the risk of appropriating their experiences in ways that could be antithetical to our purposes. That is, in creating opportunities for learning that are reflective of students' home cultures and forms of expression, we risk assuming ownership of their experiences and thus diminishing the authenticity and personal meaning of those experiences. A case in point occurred a few years ago when a public high school in Rapid City, South Dakota, attempted to make powwows an official extracurricular activity. School officials viewed this move as a symbol of support for American Indian students. However, members of the local American Indian community protested on the grounds that placing powwows under the authority of the school as an after-school activity was inappropriate and would alter the cultural significance of powwows.

Likewise, if Native singing and dancing were to become part of their school curriculum, it is unlikely that Daniel and Kelly and their peers would create the kinds of personal and cultural meanings described earlier. In fact, many of these students become uncomfortable when singled out in class for their knowledge of Native culture. While they are proud of being Indian and do wish that Native perspectives were reflected more in their schooling experiences, they resist being placed in the limelight. Most, however, respond positively to teachers' genuine interest in their lives when it is expressed privately and with sensitivity and respect. "Appreciation and respect are the antecedent attitudes for teaching Indian children," note Garcia and Ahler (1992). "Neither . . . are possible without knowing the children's cultural and environmental backgrounds" (p. 14).

In addition to listening with respect to their students, teachers might learn about their home backgrounds through, for example, attending powwows and other American Indian community events (when it is appropriate to do so) and talking with parents. Understanding students' lives outside of school and the forms of expression they use can enable teachers to recognize and support students' literacy capabilities in school. As literacy educators, by recognizing the role of multiple sign systems in literacy learning, we do not diminish the value of reading and writing, but rather we encourage and legitimize the varied ways of knowing of *all* students.

IF SCHOOLS/SOCIETY SHARED OUR PERSPECTIVE ON LITERACY, HOW MIGHT PEOPLE'S LIVES BE DIFFERENT?

A broadened perspective on what constitutes literacy, as described in this chapter, would validate the many different ways in which individuals construct meaning. By legitimizing multiple sign systems—language as well as art, music, and so forth—in schools, our view of who excels, who is bright and capable, would be broadened. Such a change would allow us to focus and build upon the strengths of students who previously have been judged on a single, narrow standard of literacy and been found lacking. In addition, encouraging the multiple ways of knowing of each student within a class would result in a richer learning environment for all students as they share their strengths with one another. Outside of school, appreciation for multiple ways of knowing could have a significant impact on the workplace, on government, and on society's attitudes about diversity.

NOTES

1. All names of participants in this chapter are pseudonyms except for Zonnie and Daniel, who chose to have their actual names used.

2. The Literary Club, which I organized and facilitated during 16 weeks of this study, was developed as a means of "giving back" to my research participants. During our weekly meetings, held in the school library and computer room, the students read, wrote, drew pictures, used the computers, and talked about issues of importance to them. See Noll (in press) for a full description of the club.

REFERENCES

Deyhle, D. (1995). Navajo youth and Anglo racism: Cultural integrity and resistance. *Harvard Education Review, 65*, 403–444.

Eisner, E. W. (1994). *Cognition and curriculum* reconsidered (2nd ed.). New York: Teachers College Press.

Erickson, F. (1986). Qualitative methods in research on teaching. In M. C. Wittrock (Ed.), *Handbook of research on teaching* (pp. 119–161). New York: Macmillan.

Freire, P., & Macedo, D. (1987). *Literacy: Reading the word and the world.* New York: Bergin & Garvey.

Garcia, R. L., & Ahler, J. G. (1992). Indian education: Assumptions, ideologies, strategies. In J. Reyhner (Ed.), *Teaching American Indian students* (pp. 13–32). Norman: University of Oklahoma.

Glaser, B., & Strauss, A. (1967). *The discovery of grounded theory.* Chicago: Aldine.

Goodman, K. S. (1982). *Language and literacy: The selected writings of Kenneth S. Goodman.* Boston: Routledge.

Graves, D. H. (1988). *Writing: Teachers and children at work.* Portsmouth, NH: Heinemann.

John, V. P. (1972). Styles of learning—styles of teaching: Reflections on the education of Navajo children. In C. Cazden, D. Hymes, & V. P. John (Eds.), *Functions of language in the classroom* (pp. 331–343). New York: Teachers College Press.

Leland, C. H., & Harste, J. C. (1994). Multiple ways of knowing: Curriculum in a new key. *Language Arts, 71,* 337–345.

More, A. J. (1989). Native Indian learning styles: A review for researchers and teachers. *Journal of American Indian Education, 24,* 15–28.

Naylor, P. (1993). *To walk a sky path.* New York: Dell.

Noll, E. (in press). Construyendo una "zona de la seguridad" para estudiantes indios americanos. (Building a "zone of safety" for American Indian students.) *Educación.*

Reyhner, J. (Ed.). (1992). *Teaching American Indian students.* Norman: University of Oklahoma.

Rosenblatt, L. M. (1978). *The reader, the text, the poem: The transactional theory of the literary work.* Carbondale: Southern Illinois University.

Rosenblatt, L. M. (1983). *Literature as exploration.* New York: Modern Language Association.

Siegel, M. G. (1984*). Reading as signification.* Unpublished doctoral dissertation. Indiana University, Bloomington.

Smith, F. (1983). *Essays into literacy.* Portsmouth, NH: Heinemann.

Suhor, C. (1984). Towards a semiotics-based curriculum. *Journal of Curriculum Studies, 16,* 247–257.

Suina, J., & Smolkin, L. B. (1994). From natal culture to school culture to dominant society culture: Supporting transitions of Pueblo Indian students. In P. Greenfield & R. Cocking (Eds.), *Cross-cultural roots of minority child development* (pp. 115–130). Hillsdale, NJ: Erlbaum.

Swisher, K., & Deyhle, D. (1989). The styles of learning are different, but the teaching is just the same: Suggestions for teachers of American Indian youth. *Journal of American Indian Education,* 1–14.

Swisher, K., & Deyhle, D. (1992). Adapting instruction to culture. In J. Reyhner (Ed.), *Teaching American Indian students* (pp. 81–95). Norman: University of Oklahoma.

13

Exploring Children's Written Literacy

Two Young Voices From a Native American Community

ELBA I. REYES

In American schools today, thousands of students are being identified as having deficits in literacy skills. Many of these students are marginalized from general education as they are pulled out of the classrooms in order to receive special education services and are considered to be at risk for academic failure. Often, teachers strive to find ways to "teach literacy" to at-risk students, guided by standardized tests that examine specific literacy competencies in uniform ways. As a result of being unable to master the specific literacy skills, nonmainstream students become disempowered, uninterested in school, and ultimately fail. Yet, within their personal social communities, these same students engage in successful literacy practices not evident in school (Taylor & Dorsey-Gaines, 1988).

This chapter pursues the idea that students possess literate abilities that standard school measures fail to identify and standard instruction fails to develop. Using the written work generated by two at-risk students during their participation in a research project, this chapter demonstrates that teachers' expectations—and resultant student performance—are improved when students' multiple literacies are taken into account.

TEACHER AWARENESS AND STUDENT LITERACY ABILITIES

Students who are considered *literate* are students who can demonstrate that they can master school curriculum as illustrated in academic reading and writing tasks. However, other students may possess the literacy skills

What Counts as Literacy: Challenging the School Standard. Copyright © 2000 by Teachers College, Columbia University. All rights reserved. ISBN 0-8077-3972-3 (paper), ISBN 0-8077-3973-1 (cloth). Prior to photocopying items for classroom use, please contact the Copyright Clearance Center, Customer Service, 222 Rosewood Drive, Danvers, MA 01923, USA, telephone (508) 750-8400.

being taught in school but do not reveal them in school tasks (Gallego & Hollingsworth, 1992). Thus, within the school context, teachers are not aware of what the *nonliterate* students know and conclude that those students are not literate. Erickson (1996) suggests that students often do not demonstrate what they know when school experiences are perceived to be unconnected to the students' real, practical life experiences or are viewed as something they "do" for the teacher. The applicability or practicality of what students are exposed to in school literacy is sometimes so far removed from their ways of learning or reasons for learning that they never make the connection and thus do not "perform" well in school.

If one of the objectives of education is to prepare a critical and literate democracy that will continue to transform society as suggested by Freire (1991) and Delpit (1992), then at question is the relevancy of school to the practical lives of the students. At present, such relevancy and integration is lacking for many students who "perceive classroom writing as an activity totally separate from their lives" (Stewart, 1992, p. 280). Teachers must learn to integrate students' knowledge and experiences into school curriculum in ways that will enable students to transform their own forms of literacy so that their voices can be heard. Teachers also need to explore a process that can connect school and students' experiences in ways that reflect students' ideas about communication and their personal literacy and that reflect the students' literacy ability (Englert & Mariage, 1996).

The notion that students may have abilities that surpass teachers' awareness and that are not demonstrated through school literacy tasks is not new (Hubbard, 1989). As a special education teacher in an urban school in New York City, I was privileged to observe many examples of my fourth-grade students' personal literacy when they wrote notes back and forth to each other, wrote personal lists (e.g., "wat I wont for xmas"), or left confidential notes on my desk (e.g., "mis, I ned to tel you somting"). The notes they were writing were relevant to them. Their communication had purpose and expressed meaning. When engaged in their personal literacy activities, the students did not hesitate to write. However, when their general education teachers were asked about these students' writing abilities, the typical response was that the students could not read very well, much less write. On one occasion, two third-grade students were practicing reading aloud the stories they had chosen from the school's library to read to the kindergarten classes later that week. They prompted each other for voice intonation and projection, helped each other figure out words they did not know, and encouraged each other's efforts. At one point, their teacher walked over to our area and commented to me, "My, I didn't know they could read."

"Oh, I can't read," rejoined one of the girls. "I can't read when it's for school. This is for fun."

For this student, because of her repeated school failure, school literacy was viewed as something one did not enjoy and had no practical application. Teachers' instructional practices and expectations of students' performance are influenced by preconceptions of their students. Sometimes those preconceptions are based on stereotypic information that result in low expectations and low student performance.

CHANGING PRECONCEPTIONS

The influence of the effects of such preconceptions was clear in designing this study of Native American children and their teachers. Our interest was initially in the identification of testing measures that could be easily used by school personnel for locating potentially gifted students (Reyes, Fletcher, & Diaz, 1996). But what we learned about students' literacy went far beyond the objectives of the study.

Our study was conducted in an elementary school situated in a small rural city with a nationally known horse racing industry and adjacent to a major reservation. The Native American students, who represented 22 percent of the school's student population, were bused into town each day from the reservation. All the Native American students in the third and fourth grades participated in the project's creative writing activity. However, teachers in that school predicted that the creative writing measure would not yield usable information because, in their estimation, most of these students were *nonwriters*. The teachers, who were not from the students' community, emphasized that the students' culture did not include a written tradition and shared their preconceptions that the Native American students did not have good literacy skills due to the lack of a written language.

Yet, upon my visits to the reservation I found evidence to the contrary. Children from the reservation are from a culture with rich community literacy and are exposed to print from early childhood. Over 90 percent of the children on the reservation attend some type of preschool program where they are exposed to print in both their native and English languages. They also have other literacy experiences. They see announcements and flyers announcing the various religious events and other community activities in the reservation's stores or posted on bulletin boards in the reservation's community center. They visit the public library which is housed in the community center and is staffed by community members. The library is not only a place for reading books, but also a place to work on projects, to gather, talk, and share. A community newsletter is distributed cost-free to every home on the reservation. The children on the reservation are exposed to other public forms of communication such as community literacy events in which community members discuss important issues, plan events, engage in political discourse, and tell stories similar to those told at social and family gatherings. It was evident that the students' sociocultural experiences stemmed from a community with a clear sense of the purposes for communication. Furthermore, the teachers needed to incorporate into the classroom students' ways of and purposes for communicating.

Therefore, for the creative writing activity to be viable for the research project, it needed to be made relevant for the students in the study, and there needed to be a purpose for writing—a purpose for communicating that would enable the students to express their literacy in their own voices. On the reservation, stories are used to teach and learn and to communicate values and tradition. To build on that experience and then expand the concept to written stories, the project staff introduced the story writing activity along with a discussion of why people might write their stories instead of just telling them. We led a class discussion about animal stories, animals that could do things no one thought animals could do. "I know a story about a talking bear," offered one student. "I know a joke about . . . ," began another student, which sparked a lively discussion and oral sharing of a variety of animal stories. The students were then told that we were interested in the animal stories they could write and that these stories would be shared with others. The students were asked specifically to write a story about a flying monkey. They were guaranteed that we were not going to grade their spelling or punctuation—that we were just interested in their story.

Initially, many of the students were reluctant. As I walked around the room to attend to raised hands, the common comment was "Miss, I can't write." One student's comment, that he could "make the letters and some words" but couldn't write, exemplified the dilemma other students experienced. Clearly, the students understood that literacy was different from being able to "make the letters and some words" on a blank sheet of paper. It was also clear that these students' past failures in school-based literacy had reinforced their sense of inadequacy. My final prompt was, "If you were to make up a story to tell and then wrote it down to be able to share with other kids, what would that story be?" As the students started writing, I sat down to work on an article I had been developing as a way of participating in this community of writers and to model the authoring process.

Why did these students engage in written discourse with the project staff even though their teachers predicted that the same students could not write? There was no magical event that took place. There was no obscure scientific method used. However, consistent with the recommendation from the tribe for schools to be more mindful of the lives of the students on the reservations, which is echoed by other Native Americans (Byrd, 1997), I was visible to the students in their community: I attended social events, talked with their families in the center, and learned what they regarded as important. Then, I applied what I had learned to the classroom. For example, on the reservation, teaching and learning occurred based on an apprentice model. The children were encouraged to learn by observation and imitation rather than by exclusive direct instruction and questioning. Children were encouraged to participate in events when they felt ready and every participation was considered a successful event. The process I used in the classroom mirrored that community learning process: some of the children chose to orally talk about the stories as others listened. As I sat down to write, they also wrote what they felt was relevant to our discussions.

Students' writings were first read by the project's scoring team, two graduate students and myself. This was done to familiarize ourselves with the students' work and to develop our workshop for training the teachers in the holistic scoring process. As we read the students' stories, we found ourselves wanting to share some of the stories with the other scorers. We laughed when we read some, and were touched by the feelings conveyed in others. We discovered that the students' work was representative of diverse genres of written literacy, including genres that incorporated their cultural experiences (e.g., chanting, story of grandfather, stories with a moral, jokes, and so forth.). The following two examples represent expressions of literacy by students who were considered to be nonwriters by their teachers.

The first piece, written by a third-grade girl, conveys her understanding of the fable genre that is popular within her culture.

> The flying Monkey was disprechiated by his famely and frinds. The monkey always found a quite place and wach the blue sky and white flufy clouds. Most of the time he was alown, none wanted to play with him they thout he was too brown too small to everything. they hat him to much. He disaided to fly away too an other forest were every one like him how he was and his ability to fly.

The second story was written by a fourth-grade boy, who had been in special education since second grade and whose literacy skills were "severely deficit" according to both general and special education teachers. He had been one of the most reluctant to start his story. But his poignant message reached the hearts of everyone who read it.

> Once upon a time there was a monky who could not do any thing. One day he went to the forest and he found a old airplan and he fixed it and flew it around. Then he realized he could do any thing he wanted if he put his mind to it.

It was evident that these students had ideas they wanted to communicate and that they had the tools they needed in order to communicate through their written work—but not in school.

CHANGING TEACHERS' PRECONCEPTIONS

As part of the research project, teachers were brought together to review the students' work and discuss the feasibility of using the creative writing ability measure. During that workshop, the teachers were asked to read the two pieces above. They were asked to suspend any mastery criteria they normally used to grade student writings. Rather than focus on the "errors" in the students' work, on what the students could *not* do, the teachers were directed to listen to the students' voices and to the messages in the stories. After the initial reading, teachers' comments included: "She's always been so quiet. I never knew she had those thoughts." "I didn't know she knew any stories—that she knew how to write, how to spell." And, "But he's always been a troublemaker—well, maybe, more of a class clown. He never writes." That sentiment was echoed by another teacher: "He refuses to write. I had him for two years and I never knew."

The next activity for the teachers centered around the question, "What did these students tell us about their literacy abilities?" The focus of this activity was to identify the students' literacy abilities and to ascertain the tools the students used to convey their messages. Although several teachers identified spelling and capitalization errors, others determined that the students had learned many of the competencies found in the school-based literacy curriculum. In the first story, for example, teachers observed that the student had a good understanding of the function of prefixes, as demonstrated in her word *disappreciated*. The teachers agreed that the students' writings could help inform the teachers on how to develop future literacy lessons based on these students' actual abilities and needs. Although the idea of using students' works to guide future instruction was not a new concept for the teachers, what was new was the application of this practice with Native American students.

The young authors of the two writings underscored the precept that schools must be relevant if teachers are to know what students already know (Reyes, 1996). Others would maintain that for these students, school is perceived as separate and disparate from their daily practical experiences within their personal communities. In his work on "funds of knowledge," Moll (1992) has documented that although the reality of our students' world outside the classroom is rich in learning, in communication, and in literacy, often that reality has no relation with what goes on in school. His work has demonstrated that when teachers incorporate the community's funds of knowledge into the school's curriculum by integrating the community's worldview regarding the reasons for and ways of learning, more school-type learning occurs. Numerous written samples in this study illustrate students' ability to employ the mechanics of writing in appropriate ways. Erickson (1996) would postulate that these students had chosen not to participate in school, not to demonstrate their abilities. Those abilities the students manifest outside school may not be considered "school knowledge" by them and, thus, not be transferred into the classroom environment. What is important to consider is that students had the ability do what teachers thought they could not.

One evening, as I was reporting the project's progress at a tribal meeting, I read the first story to those present. Around the table everyone was smiling and nodding, "Yeah, that's good." "Yeah," agreed her proud Grandpa, "That one. Always has a *good* story." (His emphasis.) The student's family and neighbors were very aware of her skills. She had learned them within the sociocultural context of her community and made them evident within that community. Glau (1990) exhorts teachers to make curriculum relevant to the daily lives and activities of the students, to discover and build upon their knowledge. This occurs when teachers respect the reality of the students as individuals. It includes respecting a worldview that was developed within a context of society that may be different from the teachers' (Olson, 1992).

TRANSITION: FROM KNOWLEDGE TO LEARNING

Deloria (1994) tells us that education is a process of transition from one state of being and knowing to another. Within our students' community cultural experiences, their education is guided by those concerned with the children's personal growth and ability to become responsible members of that community. Transition is designed to respond to the community's views and values. The students' concepts of education are shaped by this worldview and the values springing from that view. Their perceptions of literacy, then, also spring from that view. So, in order to assist students in their educational transition and in gaining an understanding of the ethos of success in school literacy, teachers need to gain an understanding of the ethos of the students' personal and community literacy by exposing themselves to the "funds" of that literacy. Teachers will find that although there may not be a long history of written literacy, there is, nonetheless, a tradition of literacy experiences (Byrd, 1997). To obtain such understanding they need access to the source of the information.

Gaining access to community knowledge and to a student's experiences is an ongoing process of discovery. It is also a challenging process because teachers carry with them their preconceptions based on their own experiences, that is, their own ways of knowing. One excellent way for teachers to access students' knowledge about literacy is by contacting the leaders of the students' community who are responsible for the youths' educational growth. Teachers might explain that they want to assist the students to succeed in school by understanding and incorporating the students' knowledge and experiences into school activities. They might share proposed class activities and solicit recommendations for incorporating the students' culture. They might ask whether there may be other persons within the community who might be interested in helping develop future lessons and even in participating in the classroom to implement the lessons. Teachers must keep in mind that gaining access to the community's funds of knowledge requires that the community develop a trust in what the teachers are doing over time.

Gaining access is not enough, however. Designing and implementing effective literacy instruction in multicultural classrooms requires continual revision of ideas regarding how persons in other communities perceive learning and knowledge, and ideas about students and how to assist them to succeed in school. At the end of the project, as I left the reservation for the last time, I was asked by the tribal elders to present a final summary of my findings at one of their council meetings. During that meeting, the council members shared their understanding and efforts to assist the children make the transition into a new society of computer literacy and video technology, parenting workshops, and community reading and writing programs. At the same time, they were also implementing a community-wide project to teach their children their traditions and native language, oral and written, "so that they don't forget." That comment echoed the sentiments of one of the students who also prized the value and importance of tradition and who had a clear purpose for writing his stories. Additionally, a final comment made by a tribal member underscored the dialectic and reciprocal nature of the transition process from community to school to society: He wondered when "the school would come to us ready to listen."

CONCLUSION

In order to know what students know, we need to provide opportunities for them to be able to express that knowledge. In this study, the students informed us of their knowledge of literacy, including literacy that is valued in school. Furthermore, the students demonstrated that they had learned many of the mechanics of writing valued in typical school literacy curriculum although that knowledge was not being applied in school tasks. The teachers had not been aware of their students' personal literacy and that each writing represented a *voice* the student was capable of sharing. As we explore our students' literacy and try to understand better their abilities and their message, let us search and listen for their voices, and not merely read the words on the paper.

IF SCHOOLS/SOCIETY SHARED OUR PERSPECTIVE ON LITERACY, HOW MIGHT PEOPLE'S LIVES BE DIFFERENT?

The main tenet of this chapter is that the literacy traditions of a community culture represent and express the worldview, perceptions, and ways of knowing of that culture. Teachers who can understand, accept, and integrate those community literacies into their classroom instruction will not only provide their students with enriched opportunities to participate in varied literacies, they will also assist their students, the future adults of this society, to develop better understanding and respect for each other.

Although that tenet appears to be a worthy undertaking, it may not be a popular or readily acceptable one. School administrators may insist that the "school way" is the only way. This means that educators must understand the pedagogical soundness of what this chapter proposes. Some teachers may even resent the suggestion that extra efforts in terms of additional time and work must be made to understand students' community literacies. This means that educators must be ready to examine their commitment to the education of all of society's children. Still, if they come to understand the pedagogical foundations of including others' ways of knowing into classroom practice and if they seek ways of learning and incorporating communities' funds of knowledge into classroom literacy, they will find that their experiences as educators and their students' experiences as learners will be greatly enhanced.

REFERENCES

Byrd, H. B. (1997). In the oral tradition: Understanding and serving American Indian children with special needs. *Multiple Voices for Ethnically Diverse Exceptional Learners, 2*(1), 43–51.

Deloria., V. Jr. (1994). *Indian education in America.* Boulder, CO: American Indian Science & Engineering Society.

Delpit, L. (1992). Acquisition of literate discourse: Bowing before the master? *Theory Into Practice, 31*(4), 296–302.

Englert, C. S., & Mariage, T. V. (1996). A sociocultural perspective: Teaching ways-of-thinking and ways-of-talking in a literacy community. *Learning Disabilities Research and Practice, 11*(3), 157–167.

Erickson, F. (1996). Inclusion into what? Thoughts on the construction of learning, identity and affiliation in the general education classroom. In D. L. Speece & B. Keogh (Eds.), *Research on classroom ecologies: Implications for inclusion of children with learning disabilities* (pp. 91–107). Mahwah, NJ: Erlbaum.

Freire, P. (1991). On education and the taste for democracy. *The Writing Instructor, 10*(13), 116–120.

Gallego, M. A., & Hollingsworth, S. (1992). Multiple literacies: Teachers' evolving perception. *Language Arts, 69*(3), 206–213.

Glau, G. R. (1990). Returning power: Native American classroom (dis)comfort and effective communication. *The Writing Instructor, 10*(1), 51–58.

Hubbard, R. (1989). Notes from the underground: Unofficial literacy in one 6th grade. *Anthropology and Elementary Quarterly, 20*(4), 291–307.

Moll, L. C. (1992). Bilingual classroom studies and community analysis: Some recent trends. *Educational Researcher, 21*(2), 20–24 .

Olson, G. A. (1992). History, "praxis," and change: Paulo Freire and the politics of literacy. *Journal of Advanced Composition, 12*(1), 1–14.

Reyes, E. I. (1996). Constructing knowledge in inclusive classrooms: What students know and teachers need to know . In D. L. Speece & B. Keogh (Eds.), *Research on classroom ecologies: Implications for inclusion of children with learning disabilities.* Mahwah, NJ: Erlbaum.

Reyes, E. I., Fletcher, R., & Diaz, D. (1996). Developing local multidimensional screening procedures for identifying giftedness among Mexican American border populations. *Roeper Review, 18*(3), 91–107.

Stewart, D. C. (1992). Cognitive psychologists, social constructionists, and three nineteenth-century advocates of authentic voice. *Journal of Advanced Composition, 12*(2), 279–290.

Taylor, D., & Dorsey-Gaines, C. (1988). *Growing up literate: Learning from inner-city families.* Portsmouth, NH: Heineman.

PART III

Personal Literacies

We defined *personal literacies* as:

> the critical awareness of ways of knowing and believing about self that comes from thoughtful examination of historical or experiential and gender-specific backgrounds in school and community language settings, which sometimes stands as critique of both school literacies and community literacies.

Lisa Delpit's classic article on "Acquisition of Literate Discourse: Bowing Before the Master?" opens Part III. This article helps us understand that beyond school and even community, there is a personal spirit, a critical soul that may experience life differently than either our mainstream culture or community-based cultures. Other authors in Part III extend Delpit's ideas to show how personal experience and understanding may require a third literacy. That literacy has been expressed artistically through the language of poetry. It is up to us, as educators, to allow that voice to be developed in prose-based experiences as well.

14

Acquisition of Literate Discourse

Bowing Before the Master?

LISA D. DELPIT

A friend and colleague who teaches in a college of education at a major midwestern university told me a story of one of her graduate students. The young woman, whom I will call Marge, received from a private foundation a special fellowship designed to increase the numbers of faculty holding doctorates at black colleges. Marge applied to the doctoral program at my friend's university and traveled to the institution to take a few classes while awaiting the decision.

Apparently the admissions committee did not quite know what to do with her, for here was someone who was already on campus with a fellowship but who, based on GRE scores and writing samples, they determined was not capable of doing doctoral level work. Finally, the committee agreed to admit Marge into the master's program, even though she already held a master's degree. Marge accepted the offer. My friend—I'll call her Susan—got to know Marge when the department head asked her to "work with" the new student who was considered "at risk" of not successfully completing the degree.

Susan began a program to help Marge learn how to cope with the academic setting. Susan recognized early on that Marge was very talented, but that she did not understand how to maneuver her way through academic writing, reading, and talking. In their first encounters, Susan and Marge discussed the comments instructors had written on Marge's papers, and how the next paper might incorporate the professor's concerns. The next summer, Susan had Marge write weekly synopses of articles related to educational issues. When they met, Marge talked through her ideas while Susan took notes. Together they translated the ideas into the "discourse of teacher education." Marge then rewrote the papers referring to their conversations and Susan's extensive written comments.

Chapter 14, Acquisition of Literate Discourse: Bowing Before the Master?, by Lisa D. Delpit was originally published in *Theory into Practice, 31*, 296–303. Copyright © 1992, College of Education, The Ohio State University. Reprinted with permission.

Susan continued to work with Marge, both in and out of the classroom, during the following year. By the end of the year, Marge's instructors began telling Susan that Marge was a real star, that she had written the best papers in their classes. When faculty received funding for various projects, she became one of the most sought-after research assistants in the college. And when she applied for entry into the doctoral program the next fall, even though her GRE scores were still low, she was accepted with no hesitation. Her work now includes research and writing that challenge predominant attitudes about the potential of poor children to achieve.

This story is one of commitment and transformation. It speaks to many of the issues that fuel the work I do in education and literacy development. It shows how people, given the proper support, can "make it" in culturally alien environments. It makes clear that standardized test scores have little to say about one's actual ability. And it demonstrates that supporting students' transformation demands an extraordinary amount of time and commitment, but that teachers *can* make a difference if they are willing to make that commitment.

I begin with this anecdote because it is one story among many that has led me to challenge certain beliefs often expressed among educators. I have encountered a certain sense of powerlessness and paralysis among many sensitive and well-meaning literacy educators who appear to be caught in the throes of a dilemma. Although their job is to teach literate discourse styles to all of their students, they question whether that is a task they can actually accomplish for poor students and students of color. Furthermore, they question whether they are acting as agents of oppression by insisting that students who are not already a part of the "mainstream" learn that discourse. Does it not smack of racism or classism to demand that these students put aside the language of their homes and communities and adopt a discourse that is not only alien but has often been instrumental in furthering their oppression? In this article I hope to help dispel that sense of paralysis and powerlessness and suggest a path of commitment and action that not only frees teachers to teach what they know but to do so in a way that transforms and liberates their students.

LITERACY AND DISCOURSE

This article got its start as I pondered the dilemmas expressed by educators. It continued to evolve when a colleague sent a set of articles to me for comment. The articles, authored by literacy specialist James Paul Gee ("Literacy, Discourse, and Linguistics: Introduction" and "What Is Literacy?"), are the lead articles of a special issue of the *Journal of Education* (1989) devoted solely to Gee's work. The papers brought to mind many of the perspectives of the educators I describe. My colleague, an academic with an interest in literacy issues in communities of color, was disturbed by much of what she read in the articles and wanted a second opinion.

As I first read the far-reaching, politically sensitive articles, I found that I agreed with much that Gee wrote, as I have with his earlier work. He argues that literacy is much more than reading and writing but, rather, it is part of a larger political entity that he calls a "Discourse." Discourse in this sense is construed as something of an "identity kit," that is, ways of "saying-writing-doing-being-valuing-believing," examples of which might be the Discourse of lawyers, the Discourse of academics, or the Discourse of men. He adds that one never learns simply to read or write, but to read and write within some larger Discourse, and therefore within some larger set of values and beliefs.

Gee maintains that there are primary Discourses, those learned in the home, and secondary Discourses, which are attached to institutions or groups one might later encounter. He also argues that all Discourses are not equal in status, that some are socially dominant—carry with them social power and access to economic success—and some nondominant.

The status of individuals born into a particular Discourse tends to be maintained because primary Discourses are related to secondary Discourses of similar status in our society (for example, the middle-class home Discourse to school Discourse, or the working-class African American home Discourse to the black church Discourse). Status is also maintained because dominant groups in a society apply frequent "tests" of fluency in the dominant Discourses, often focused on its most superficial aspects—grammar, style, mechanics—so as to exclude from full participation those who are not born to positions of power.

These arguments resonate in many ways with what I also believe to be true. However, as I reread and pondered the articles, I began to get a sense of my colleague's discomfort. I also began to understand how that discomfort related to some concerns I have about the perspectives of educators who sincerely hope to help educate poor children and children of color to become successful and literate, but who find themselves paralyzed by their own conception of the task.

There are two aspects of Gee's arguments that I find problematic. First is Gee's notion that people who have not been born into dominant Discourses will find it exceedingly difficult, if not impossible, to acquire such a Discourse. He argues that Discourses cannot be "overtly" taught, particularly in a classroom, but can only be acquired by enculturation in the home or by "apprenticeship" into social practices. Those who wish to gain access to the goods and status connected to a dominant Discourse must have access to the social practices related to that Discourse. That is, in order to learn the "rules" required for admission into a particular dominant Discourse, individuals must already have access to the social institutions connected to that Discourse—if you are not already in, do not expect to get in.

This argument is one of the issues that concerned my colleague. As he put it, Gee's argument suggests a dangerous kind of determinism as flagrant as that espoused by the geneticists: Instead of being locked into "your place" by your genes, you are now locked hopelessly into a lower-class status by your Discourse. Clearly such a stance can leave a teacher feeling powerless to effect change, and a student feeling hopeless that change can occur.

The second aspect of Gee's work that I find troubling suggests that an individual who is born into one Discourse with one set of values may experience major conflicts when attempting to acquire another Discourse with another set of values. Gee defines this as especially pertinent to "women and minorities," who, when they seek to acquire status Discourses, may be faced with adopting values that deny their primary identities. When teachers believe this acceptance of self-deprecatory values is *inevitable* in order for people of color to acquire status Discourses, then their sense of justice and fair play might hinder their teaching these Discourses.

If teachers were to adopt both of these premises suggested by Gee's work, not only would they view the acquisition of a new Discourse in a classroom impossible to achieve, they might also view the goal of acquiring such a Discourse questionable at best. The sensitive teacher might well conclude that even to try to teach a dominant Discourse to students who are members of a nondominant, oppressed group would be to oppress them further. And it is this potential conclusion that concerns me. While I do agree that Discourses may embody conflicting values, I am also aware of many individuals, like Marge, who have faced and overcome the problems such a conflict might cause. I hope to provide another perspective on both of these premises.

OVERCOMING OBSTACLES TO ACQUISITION

I begin with the stories of two successful African American men because I believe one remedy to the paralysis suffered by many teachers is to bring to the fore the real people whose histories directly challenge unproductive beliefs.[1] Clarence Cunningham, now a vice chancellor at the largest historically black institution in the United States, grew up in a painfully poor community in rural Illinois. He attended an all–African American elementary school in the 1930s in a community where the parents of most of the children never even considered attending high school. A school picture of a ragtag group of about 35 children hangs in his den. As he shows me that picture, he talks about the one boy who grew up to be a principal in Philadelphia, the one who is now a vice president of a major computer company, one who was recently elected attorney general of Chicago, another who is a vice president of Harris Bank in Chicago, and another who was the first black pilot hired by a major airline. He points to a little girl who is now an administrator, another who is a union leader. Almost all of the children in the photo eventually left their home community, and almost all achieved impressive goals in life.

Another colleague and friend, Bill Trent, who is a professor and researcher at a major research university, has told me of growing up in inner-city Richmond, Virginia, "the capitol of the Confederacy" in the 1940s and 1950s. His father, a cook, earned an eighth-grade education by going to night school. His mother, a domestic, had a third-grade education. Neither he nor his classmates had aspirations beyond their immediate environment. Yet many of these students completed college, and almost all were successful, many notable. They became teachers, ministers, an electronics wizard, state officials, and career Army officers. Among them also were tennis ace Arthur Ashe and the brothers Max and Randall Robinson, the national newscaster and the director of Trans-Africa, respectively.

How do these men explain the transformations that occurred in their classmates' and their lives? Both attribute their ability to transcend the circumstances into which they were born directly to their teachers. First, their teachers successfully taught what Gee calls the "superficial features" of middle-class Discourse—grammar, style, mechanics—features that Gee claims are particularly resistant to classroom instruction. And the students successfully learned them.

These teachers also successfully taught the more subtle aspects of dominant Discourse. According to both Trent and Cunningham, their teachers insisted that students be able to speak and write eloquently, maintain neatness, think carefully, exude character, and conduct themselves with decorum. They even found ways to mediate class differences by attending themselves to the hygiene of students who needed such attention—washing faces, cutting fingernails, and handing out deodorant.

Perhaps more significant than what they taught is what they believed. As Trent says, "They held visions of us that we could not imagine for ourselves. And they held those visions even when they themselves were denied entry into the larger white world. They were determined that, despite all odds, we would achieve." In an era of overt racism when much was denied African Americans, the message drilled into students was, "The one thing people can't take away from you is what's between your ears." The teachers of both men insisted that they achieve because, "You must do twice as well as white people to be considered half as good."

As Cunningham says, "Those teachers pushed us, they wouldn't let us fail. They'd say, 'The world is tough out there, and you have to be tougher.'" Trent recalls that growing up in the "inner-city," he had no conception of life beyond high school, but his high school teachers helped him to envision one. While he happily maintained a C average, putting all his energy into playing football, he experienced a turning point one day when his coach called him inside in the middle of practice. There, while he was still suited up for football, all of his teachers gathered to explain to him that if he thought he could continue making C's and stay on the team, he had another thought coming. They were there to tell him that if he did not get his act together and make the grades they knew he was capable of, his football career would be over.

Like the teachers chronicled elsewhere in this volume, these teachers put in overtime to insure that the students were able to live up to their expectations. They set high standards and then carefully and explicitly instructed students in how to meet them. "You can and will do well," they insisted, as they taught at break times, after school, and on weekends to insure that their students met their expectations. All of these teachers were able to teach the rules for dominant Discourses, helping students to succeed in mainstream America even though those students not only were born outside the realms of power and status but had no access to status institutions. These teachers were not themselves a part of the power elite or members of dominant Discourses. Yet they were able to provide the keys for their students' entry into the larger world, never knowing if the doors would ever swing open to allow them in.

The renowned African American sociologist, E. Franklin Frazier, also successfully acquired a Discourse into which he was not born. Born in poverty to unschooled parents, Frazier learned to want to learn from his teachers and from his self-taught father. He learned his lessons so well that his achievements provided what must be the ultimate proof of the ability to acquire a secondary dominant Discourse, no matter what one's beginnings. After Frazier completed his master's degree at Clark University, he went on to challenge many aspects of the white-dominated oppressive system of segregation. Ironically, when he received his degree from Clark, Frazier also received a reference from its president, G. Stanley Hall, who gave Frazier what he must have thought was the highest praise possible in a predominantly white university in 1920: "Mr. Frazier . . . seems to me to be quite gentlemanly and *mentally White*" (emphasis added, quoted in

Platt, 1991, p. 15)—no better evidence of Frazier's having successfully acquired the dominant Discourse of academe!

These stories illustrate that despite the difficulty entailed in the process, almost any African American who has become "successful" has done so by acquiring a Discourse other than the one into which she or he was born. And almost all can attribute that acquisition to the work of one or more committed teachers.

ACQUISITION AND TRANSFORMATION

But the issue is not only whether students can learn a dominant secondary Discourse in the classroom. Perhaps the more significant issue is, Should they attempt to do so? Gee contends that for those who have been barred from the mainstream, "acquisition of many mainstream Discourses . . . involves active complicity with values that conflict with one's home and community-based Discourses" (p. 13). Undoubtedly, many students of color do reject literacy, for they feel that literate Discourses reject them. Kohl (1991) writes powerfully about individuals, young and old, who choose to "not—learn" what is expected of them rather than learn that which denies them their sense of who they are:

> Not-learning tends to take place when someone has to deal with unavoidable challenges to her or his personal and family loyalties, integrity, and identity. In such situations there are forced choices and no apparent middle ground. To agree to learn from a stranger who does not respect your integrity causes a major loss of self. The only alternative is to not-learn and reject the stranger's world. (pp. 15–16)

I have met many radical or progressive teachers of literacy who believe that in order to remain true to their ideology, their role must be to empower and politicize their most disenfranchised students. Some of these teachers seek to empower by refusing to teach what Gee calls the superficial features (e.g., grammar, form, style) of dominant Discourses.[2] Believing themselves to be contributing to their students' liberation by deemphasizing dominant Discourses, they seek instead to develop literacy solely within the language and style of the students' home Discourse.

Feminist writer bell hooks (1989) writes of one of the consequences of this teaching methodology. During much of her postsecondary school career she was the only black student in her writing courses. Whenever she would write a poem in black southern dialect, the teachers and fellow students would praise her for using her "true authentic voice" and encourage her to write more in this voice (p. 11). hooks writes of her frustration with these teachers who, like the teachers I describe, did not recognize the need for African American students to have access to many voices, and who maintained their stance even when adult students or the parents of younger students demanded they do otherwise.

I am reminded of one educator of adult African American veterans who insisted that her students needed to develop their "own voices" by developing "fluency" in their home language. Her students vociferously objected, demanding that they be taught grammar, punctuation, and "standard English." The teacher insisted that such a mode of study was "oppressive." The students continued venting their objections in loud and certain tones. When asked why she thought her students had not developed "voice" when they were using their voices to loudly express their displeasure, she responded that it was "because of who they are," that is, apparently because they were working-class, black, and disagreed with her. Another educator of adults told me that she based her teaching on liberating principles. She voiced her anger with her mostly poor, working-class students because they rejected her pedagogy and "refused to be liberated." There are many such stories to recount.

Several reasons can be given as to why students and parents of color take a position that differs from the well-intentioned position of the teachers I have described. First, they know that members of society need access to dominant Discourses in order to (legally) have access to economic power. Second, they know that such Discourses can be and have been acquired in classrooms because they know individuals who have done so. Third, and most significant to the point I wish to make now, they know that individuals have the ability to transform dominant Discourses for liberatory purposes—to engage in what Henry Louis Gates calls, "changing the joke and slipping the yoke" (quoted in Martin, 1990, p. 204), that is, using European philosophical and critical standards to challenge the tenets of European belief systems.

hooks (1989) speaks of her black women teachers in the segregated South as being the model from which she acquired both access to dominant Discourses and a sense of the validity of the primary Discourse of working-class African American people. From their instruction, she learned that black poets were capable of speaking in many voices, that the Dunbar who wrote in dialect was as valid as the Dunbar who wrote sonnets. She also learned from these women that she was capable of not only participating in the mainstream but redirecting its currents: "Their work was truly education for critical consciousness. . . . They were the teachers who conceptualized oppositional world views, who taught us young Black women to exult and glory in the power and beauty of our intellect. They offered to us a legacy of liberatory pedagogy that demanded active resistance and rebellion against sexism and racism" (p. 50).

Acquiring the ability to function in a dominant Discourse need not mean that one must reject one's home identity and values, for Discourses are not static but are shaped, however reluctantly, by those who participate within them and by the form of their participation. Many who have played significant roles in fighting for the liberation of people of color have done so through the language of dominant Discourses, from Frederick Douglass to Ida Mae Wells, to Mary McCloud Bethune, to Martin Luther King, to Malcolm X. As did hooks's teachers, I believe today's teachers can help economically disenfranchised students and students-of-color both to acquire the dominant Discourses and to transform them. How is the teacher to accomplish this? I suggest several possibilities.

WHAT CAN TEACHERS DO?

Teachers must acknowledge and validate students' home language without using it to limit students' potential. Students' home Discourses are vital to their perception of self and sense of community connectedness. One Native American college student I know says he cannot write in standard English when he writes about his village "because that's about me!" Then he must use his own "village English" or his voice rings hollow even to himself.

Jordan (1988) has written a powerful essay about teaching a course in black English and the class's decision to write a letter of protest in that language when the brother of one of the students was killed by police. The point must not be to eliminate students' home languages but rather to add other voices and Discourses to their repertoires. As hooks (1989) and Gates (1986) have poignantly reminded us, racism and oppression must be fought on as many fronts and in as many voices as we can muster.

Teachers must recognize the conflict Gee details between students' home Discourses and the Discourse of school. They must understand that students who appear to be unable to learn are in many instances choosing to "not-learn," as Kohl puts it, choosing to maintain their sense of identity in the face of what they perceive as a painful choice between allegiance to "them" or "us." The teacher, however, can reduce this sense of choice by transforming the new Discourse so that it contains within it a place for the students' selves. To do so, they must saturate the dominant Discourse with new meanings, must wrest from it a place for the glorification of their students and their forebears.

This is what noted educator Jaime Escalante did when he prepared poor Latino students to pass the tests for advanced calculus while everyone else thought they would do well to learn fractions. In a line from the movie chronicling his success, *Stand and Deliver* (Musca & Menendez, 1988), he entreated his students, "You *have* to learn math. The Mayans discovered zero. Math is in your blood!" And this is what those who seek to create what has been called "Afrocentric" curricula do. They seek to illuminate for students (and their teachers) a world in which people with brown and black skin have achieved greatness and have developed a large part of what is considered the great classical tradition.

They also seek to teach students about those who have taken the language born in Europe and transformed it into an emancipatory vehicle. In the mouths and pens of Bill Trent, Clarence Cunningham, bell hooks, Henry Louis Gates, Paul Lawrence Dunbar, and countless others, the "language of the master" has been used for liberatory ends. Students can learn of that rich legacy, and they can also learn that they are its inheritors and rightful heirs.

A final role teachers can take is to acknowledge the unfair "Discourse-stacking" that our society engages in. They can discuss openly the injustices of allowing certain people to succeed, based not upon merit but upon which family they were born into, which Discourse they had access to as children. The students, of course, already know this, but the open acknowledgment of it in the very institution that facilitates the sorting process is liberating in itself.

After acknowledging the inequity of the system, the teacher's stance can then be, "Let me show you how to cheat!" And, of course, "to cheat" is to learn the Discourse that would otherwise be used to exclude them from participating in and transforming the mainstream. This is what many black teachers of the segregated South intended when they, like the teachers of Bill Trent and Clarence Cunningham, told their students they *had* to "do better than those white kids." We can again let our students know they can resist a system that seeks to limit them to the bottom rung of the social and economic ladder.

Gee may not agree with my analysis of his work, for, in truth, his writings are so multifaceted as not to be easily reduced to simplistic positions. But that is not the issue. The point is that some aspects of his work can be disturbing for the African American reader, and reinforcing for those who choose—wrongly, but for the "right" reasons—not to educate black and poor children.

Individuals *can* learn the "superficial features" of dominant Discourses, as well as the more subtle aspects, and if placed in proper context, acquiring those linguistic forms and literate styles need not be "bowing before the master." Rather, the acquisition can provide a way both to turn the sorting system on its head and to make available one more voice for resisting and reshaping an oppressive system. This is the alternative perspective I want to give to teachers of poor children and children of color, and this is the perspective I hope will end the paralysis and set teachers free to teach, and thereby to liberate. When teachers are committed to teaching all students, and when they understand that through their teaching change *can* occur, the chance for transformation is great.

NOTES

1. The stories are based on conversations with Clarence Cunningham and Bill Trent in April 1991.

2. Gee's position here is somewhat different. He argues that grammar and form should be taught in classrooms, but that students will never acquire them with sufficient fluency to gain entry into dominant Discourses. Rather, he states, such teaching is important because it allows students to gain "metaknowledge" of how language works, which in turn "leads to the ability to manipulate, to analyze, to resist while advancing" (p. 13).

REFERENCES

Gates, H. L. (1986). *Race, writing and difference.* Chicago: University of Chicago Press.

Gee, J. P. (1989a). Literacy, discourse, and linguistics: Introduction. *Journal of Education, 171*(1), 5–17.

Gee, J. P. (1989b). What is literacy? *Journal of Education, 171*(1), 18–25.

hooks, b. (1989). *Talking back.* Boston: South End Press.

Jordan, J. (1988). Nobody means more to me than you and the future life of Willie Jordan. *Harvard Educational Review, 58,* 363–374.

Kohl, H. (1991). *I won't learn from you! The role of assent in education.* Minneapolis, MN: Milkweed Editions.

Martin, R. (1990). Black writer as Black critic: Recent Afro-American writing. *College English, 52,* 203–205.

Musca, T. (Producer), & Menendez, R. (Director). (1988). *Stand and deliver* [Film]. Burbank, CA: Warner.

Platt, A. M. (1991). *E. Franklin Frazier reconsidered.* New Brunswick, NJ: Rutgers University Press.

15

Family Literacy in the Autobiographies of Chicana/o Bilingual Teachers

RENÉ GALINDO

Studies of family literacy examine the family as a social context for literacy by looking at the uses of literacy within the different roles that individual family members play, how the family operates collectively, and how the family uses its collective resources to support each other in literacy tasks (Auerbach, 1989). The everyday literacy experiences of Mexican-origin families have recently been investigated. Vásquez (1992) documented analytic strategies that Mexican-origin families employed during their interpretation of texts. These strategies included linking one text to another, using personal experience to interpret a text, and comparing and evaluating texts. She concluded that analytic strategies associated with print-based literacy activities practiced in schools clearly underlies the analytic strategies used by Mexican immigrant families. Letter writing by both adults and children to relatives in Mexico was another important family literacy event, and the need to keep in touch with relatives and friends was the impetus for learning to write in Spanish for many adults (Delgado-Gaitan, 1990; Farr & Guerra, 1995). Literacy practices in Spanish are also an integral part of the religious activities of Mexican immigrant families in Chicago (Farr, 1994). Prayer books used during religious events, catechism workbooks, and religious magazines were all read in their homes. In relation to Gallego and Hollingsworth's (1992) notion of multiple literacies, the family literacy of the Chicana/os described here falls between personal and community literacy and presents the family as an immediate, small, local, and crucial community that mediates between personal and community literacies.

Family uses of literacy may also be studied through autobiographies in which family experiences are viewed as biographical "funds of knowledge" (Moll & Greenberg, 1990). Life history research (autobiography and

What Counts as Literacy: Challenging the School Standard. Copyright © 2000 by Teachers College, Columbia University. All rights reserved. ISBN 0-8077-3972-3 (paper), ISBN 0-8077-3973-1 (cloth). Prior to photocopying items for classroom use, please contact the Copyright Clearance Center, Customer Service, 222 Rosewood Drive, Danvers, MA 01923, USA, telephone (508) 750-8400.

biography) has a long tradition in the social sciences (Bertaux, 1981; Langness & Frank, 1981; Plumer, 1983) but has only recently gained currency in educational research where examples of its use include examining connections between teachers' practices and philosophies and the broader contexts of their lives (Foster, 1990; Goodson, 1992). Autobiographies have also been used to document preservice teachers' positive and negative attitudes towards literacy (Bean, 1994) and college freshmen's reports of their progressive loss of enthusiasm for reading across their years of schooling (Evans, 1993).

The data for family literacy examined here come from autobiographical essays written by Chicana teachers about their impressions and interpretations of the family literacy events and practices that they experienced as children or adolescents. These data document the critical family contexts and the efforts parents and grandparents undertook to help their children acquire Spanish literacy before bilingual education was implemented in public schools. The Chicana teachers identified their families as participants in a variety of literacy events for a wide range of functions.

The autobiographies make possible analyses of the role of literacy in the everyday lives of the families, and how children's access to literacy identified them as family members. Consequently, personal literacy and personal identity will be examined in light of family literacy and family identity. The view of identity taken here is a relational one: it exists in social relationships that are specific to time, place, and situation and that are forged in the context of ongoing relationships that exist in time and space (Sommers, 1994). The discourse basis of a relational view of identity was highlighted by Bakhtin (1986) through his emphasis on dialogue and intertextuality and was echoed in Taylor's (1985) statement, "I become a person and remain one only as an interlocutor" (p. 276). Children's access to literacy, as oral discourse, plays a key role in their participation in networks of family social relationships that provide access to the family roles that are constitutive of family or community and personal identity (Heller, 1987).

MEMORIES OF FAMILY LITERACY

The examples of family literacy analyzed here are drawn from autobiographies of 10 Chicana/o bilingual teachers (8 female and 2 male) about their literacy practices. These autobiographical essays, averaging around 10 to 12 pages, were written in a graduate level course and examined connections between literacy, culture, and education in their life histories. All of the teachers were originally from the Southwest. They were born in the

United States and raised in rural and urban bilingual homes. The teachers' parents were all native Spanish speakers, whose fluency in English varied. All but one of the teachers represented the first generation in their families to complete both high school and college. The texts selected from the teachers' autobiographies for this chapter are intended to illustrate the range and variety of literacy practices experienced as well as the different literacy roles that adults and children played in the home and community. The literacy practices described include such everyday events as the recreational reading of newspapers, occupational reading, and record keeping. The teachers did not participate in the events but, as children, observed carefully what the adults read or wrote. Even though they are separated from these events by many years, these observations remain vivid memories. Anna, for example, recalls her father, a farmer by trade, engaged in occupational literacy.

> I can recall my dad sitting at a white marble-like dining room table reading either seed catalogs or articles about farm machines. He sat at one end of the table wearing a long-sleeve khaki shirt and khaki pants. His dark wavy hair held the impression made by his hat. He would read his magazines quietly. Occasionally, a furrow would form across his forehead as though he were in deep thought. Then he would reach for his pencil and his notes. I sat across from him and peered from my magazine, always wondering what he was writing about. However, I did not stop to question him. This seemed a very special quiet time and was not the moment for interruptions. As I grew older, I realized that he was calculating how many acres had already been planted, the cost of seeds, how certain machinery was repaired, and so forth.

Extended family members, such as grandparents, were also important role models for literate practices. The grandmother in the example below was a widow who operated a store and at one time also a restaurant. She was very proud of being the only one of her siblings to finish eighth grade and felt that her literacy abilities in Spanish and English enabled her to provide for her family.

> As a young child, I would sit quietly on a chair and watch [my grandmother] figure her bills at the end of the week. I would watch her as she wrote letters and made notes to remind herself of events or appointments. She had books that were kept on a shelf behind the glass doors of her secretary [desk] that she often referred to and sometimes wrote in. She had books in English and in Spanish. I

would sit and watch her take care of her business or watch her do her chores and wait for her to answer my questions about the olden days when my dad was a little boy.

In the next example, the author's focus is on the physical characteristics of a book. Her mother's romance novels are this teacher's earliest book-related memories and became one of the texts through which she acquired literacy. These romance novels are called *fotonovelas* and are similar in format to comic books except for the use of actual photographs accompanied by quotation bubbles.

> My first memory of books was my mom's Spanish-language romance novels that were in a comic book form. I would look at the pictures and try to figure out what possibly could be going on. My mom would read the romance novel to me in Spanish. After she put the book down, I remember always trying to read the words to myself. I carried the comic novel with me wherever I went. The comic novel was written on low-grade paper with brown pictures. No color was in the novel. I tried to teach my young sisters how to read by reading to them and sharing my comic novel with them.

The following memory of a father's literacy practices with newspaper reading calls attention to the particular locations where family literacy occurred. Such locations—here called *literacy places*—include objects and people that are specific elements of settings for literacy events. Literacy places are endowed with affective value through memories of family engaged in literacy practices in a particular place. In the example below written by Norma, the father's desk serves as a literacy place because it was the primary setting for the father and daughter's literacy events and because it was the repository for the father's literacy artifacts. The place and events created and reproduced family ties.

> Having only attained a sixth-grade education in Mexico, my father was able to expand his knowledge and acquisition of English grammar and literacy skills by reading newspapers and listening to the evening news. He would sit at his brown mahogany desk for hours reading the paper from cover to cover and clipping out store coupons. Instead of reading to me, he would teach me to write. I would repeat the letters as he was teaching me to write my name. I loved sitting at his desk and going through his drawers. He kept his letters, bills, and church bulletins neatly secured with rubber bands. His tattered black prayer book was always kept in the top drawer

and he would read it frequently. . . . I had the privilege of sitting
there during the day when [my Dad] was at work to compose my
stories or do my illustrations.

In Norma's case, access not only to social networks but to a specific location held implications for identity in terms of viewing herself as a literate
family member.

Lucia's autobiography identifies the kitchen table as an example of
another literacy place. The table was a central gathering place usually associated with extended visitors. During homework time, however, the kitchen
table became a center of family literacy. The grandfather, reading the newspaper and drinking coffee, sat with the children at the table as they did
their homework, while their mother worked a swing shift in a local hospi-
tal as a nurse's aide.

> Homework was accepted without complaint. Every night, after
> supper, we were expected to do our homework at the kitchen table.
> Even though [my family] was unable to help us [directly with our
> homework] because they never had the opportunity to finish grade
> school, I think this made them feel all the more dedicated in assist-
> ing us as best as they could in our education. [My grandfather often
> engaged us in critical discussions of current events during our
> homework sessions.]

This example of the kitchen table as a literacy place involved intergenerational uses of literacy. The fact that two literacy events co-occurred
within this literacy place; doing homework and newspaper reading served
to indicate the importance of literacy in serving both educational and
informative-recreational functions. The newspaper was a valuable literacy
resource for many families providing current events for family discussions
and comics to be enjoyed between parents and children. Two teachers wrote
about their grandfathers and another wrote about her father initiating
discussions with them regarding current events they had read in the newspapers. The adults challenged them to take critical perspectives regarding
the reporting of news. Here is an example written by Silvia.

> My grandfather was the first person whom I remember reading to us.
> He didn't read storybooks, but would read newspapers, magazines,
> or whatever print was available. He would read an article and turn it
> into a story. He spoke Spanish but would often read from an English
> newspaper, then translate it into Spanish for us. He delighted in
> reading Jehovah's Witnesses pamphlets and questioning their view

of the Bible. He would often question us to see if we were listening to his stories. As I recall those precious times, we could never get away without analyzing and critiquing each and every story.

Through these discussions—and sometimes even heated debates—adult family members participated with their children or grandchildren in critiques of the way current events were presented in newspapers. The adults became critical readers, providing opportunities for the children to learn to adopt critical perspectives on the reporting of current events. The parents of one teacher also introduced her to the recreational function of literacy related to the genre of the Sunday morning comics. The final line in Clara's narrative in the following excerpt makes reference to the dominant model of parent-child storybook reading.

Every Sunday morning [I engaged in] the ritual of sitting on [my parents] laps and having the comics read to me. They read Hugo, Little Nancy, Red Rider, and Dick Tracy to me. Brenda Starr and Rex Morgan, M. D. were considered too sophisticated for a 3-year-old. A year or two later I could hardly wait to learn how to read. I wanted to read about that mysterious and fantastic redhead. News events were read to me if they felt they would be of value or interest to me. They shared the gossip of the local town paper. Reading to me was a great event even though it was not with books.

Besides literacy interactions between adults and children, siblings and other children interacted with each other around print materials during play activities of various sorts. Sometimes the activities took the form of reader's theater or acting out stories. Susanna writes:

My sister and I would make up scavenger notes for one another. Sometimes she and I would play teacher and student or grocery store. We would often write grocery lists or do a written assignment. Many times the ground or sand served as our chalkboard. We wrote on anything we could write on. We wrote on the boardwalks with slate. We created oral stories and fashion shows using the pictures we cut out of old magazines or catalogs for our props. We would often cut out the pictures of the models and read the description of the outfits from the catalogs. However, I don't remember actually writing words for the stories we invented.

In these examples, children created opportunities for themselves to be involved with literacy apart from the supervision of adults. Another example of children interacting with each other around literacy involves a different kind of play, related to the appropriation of roles associated with public libraries. Here's Lisa's recollection:

> During the summer months when school was out, I played the role of librarian for the kids in my neighborhood. This was the summer between my fifth and sixth grades. My dad had a trailer parked in front of our house. I set up the library right there inside of it. I devised my own system of check-out. I alphabetized all the books I had, which were quite many. I made check-out pockets for the insides of the books. I let kids come into my trailer library to read books and to check them out if they wanted to take them home. Kids would come on their bicycles to read in my library. They would bring other books that they wanted to donate to the library collection of books. I had collected the paperback books from school clubs very similar to those that are currently circulated in schools (Troll, Scholastic, and See Saw). I read every book that I had in my library and was able to discuss or recommend particular books to the neighborhood kids. I even had requests for Spanish books. Since most of the kids could only read English, they were more than willing to sit and listen to me read to them in Spanish. That was a great summer. They sat in amazement at the different sounding storytelling.

As any good librarian, Lisa was familiar with the books and was able to make recommendations to the patrons as well as conduct story reading sessions. As such she could be considered a "book expert" in the neighborhood. These examples of literacy play illustrate that literacy was a common enough feature in their lives that it could also become an object of play. Unlike the serious family role models that the literacy events provided these teachers to-be, imaginary roles were made possible by literacy play with siblings and other peers. Additionally, some parents also contributed to the literacy development of their children by giving books as gifts.

> Some books were gifts from our parents. They always made the effort to give us books rather than other things for presents. Some of them were purchased with coupons from milk cans or S & H Green Stamps. I remember a special group of books my sisters, brothers, and I received on Christmas. I can still recall the curious package under the Christmas tree. As we tore away the wrappings, a set of Golden Books fell before our feet. With hearts beating rapidly we reached out excitedly to examine the books. The set contained

twelve traditional stories. We were impressed with the colorful illustrations and the wonderful stories. We read them over and over until the pages were worn. A few of the survivors still remain on my bookshelf.

There were two examples of encyclopedias as treasured gifts in the autobiographies. One was the story of a new set bought by a father for his family (in the only family with a college-educated parent); the other was about a used set given to a teacher's family by her aunt. Margarita came from a large family and had limited economic resources.

I remember visiting a favorite aunt who had an updated set of the World Book of Knowledge, which I found entertaining. I would sit in her library and read for hours at a time from these books. I especially loved the illustrations. My aunt would often ask my parents to let me spend the night so that I could have more time with her books. She eventually bought a new set of encyclopedias for her family and gave the old set to me. I was elated and thought she was the most wonderful person in the world. This was the beginning of a wonderful relationship. She would always show up at our house with a box of books for me. She would find them at thrift stores, garage sales, and even in my cousin's bookshelves. For Christmas one year she bought me a new set of the Nancy Drew mystery books.

Another aspect of family literacy involved parents acting as direct instructors of literacy. The autobiographies contained three examples of the alphabet and name writing. For example, some parents took it upon themselves to teach their daughters the alphabet in English in order to help them in the English-only education of the public schools. The parents also improvised materials for the lessons.

I remember speaking only Spanish when I first went to school as a first grader. I did not go to preschool or kindergarten. I went to school reluctantly because I didn't know anyone else who could speak Spanish with me. I felt totally isolated. My dad began to try to help me learn English the best he could. He used teeny tiny plastic letters to teach me the English alphabet. They were so tiny that they were smaller than his thumb fingernails. They remind me of the letters used to label items in the grocery shelves. He made do with what he could get. I liked their tiny nature and it seemed more like fun play than serious work. He didn't teach me the alphabet song. I don't think he knew it. He taught me to say the letters in order. As he drilled me on each letter name, he played a game of cards with me. If I could say the name, I kept the teeny tiny card. He kept it if I didn't. It wasn't long before I could keep the entire set. He also made me write down the letter before I could keep it.

In the following example, the father and mother both taught the alphabet to two of their daughters.

My father lovingly cut three-inch letters out of blue-gray cardboard and placed them on the kitchen wall. Both of my parents took turns teaching my sister and me the English alphabet and sounds. After we learned them, they then took turns instructing us in reading. Mary was five and I was four. Mary was preparing to enter first grade. I suppose my parents did not want to repeat the lessons the following year; therefore, I was taught along with my sister. My parents both had strong New Mexican Spanish accents and as a result we too had a strong accent when we read. However, I don't ever remember hearing or noticing our accents until high school when someone pointed them out. We were young and enjoyed reading so it didn't make a difference. We had no problem under-standing what we were reading and that was what counted. I believe we were taught to read in English first because we were to start a monolingual English elementary school. At that time there was no Spanish literature or instruction available in elementary schools in our area.

Only two teachers discussed the topic of gender and literacy. One teacher related the topic of gender and literacy to family expectations re-garding gender roles. In this family, the boys were expected to learn at a young age to hunt, chop wood, fish, maintain the cars or trucks, build and repair furniture, and do plumbing and basic electrical tasks. In addition, they learned to plant and till the soil for gardens and crops. They also cared for livestock and slaughtered and processed meat. Girls also learned many of these skills in addition to learning how to cook, clean the house, quilt, sew, and embroider.

Just as gender determined [our] place[s] in [our] family, it also played a part in regard to experiences with literacy. Traditionally, the boys in my family attended school and learned to read and write until they were of an age to work. The tradition was for them to work for the railroad as my father did. They would go to school, but I cannot recall ever seeing my three older brothers studying or doing homework. The girls were allowed more time to spend on literacy events. The older ones were encouraged to continue their educations as long as they wished. It was acceptable for them to quit school and get jobs before they had graduated from high school.

The examples above point to the active role that parents played in their children's development of literacy. Besides teaching the alphabet, parents and members of the extended family served as literate role models engaging in literacy for a variety of purposes. These included the uses of Spanish literacy. The autobiographies provide examples of literacy events in which Spanish literacy was acquired and highlight the important role that informal education played in the instruction and maintenance of Spanish literacy. These literacy events were limited to home and community settings such as church services, especially since bilingual programs did not exist in the schools. Parents took this task upon themselves while engaging in personal letter writing or religious instruction.

LETTER READING AND WRITING

A key literacy event that introduced several bilingual teachers to literacy in Spanish was personal letter reading and writing. The need to be able to read letters from relatives written in Spanish was the impetus and opportunity for the teachers to learn to read in Spanish. Letters served to keep contact with family members who had moved away either to different states or to Mexico. One teacher, as an adolescent, exchanged letters in Spanish with a pen pal in Brazil. The teachers as children had access to letters through their parents or grandparents. One teacher, in her primary school years, started copying her mother's handwriting. She asked her mother for help in forming the letters and over time was copying entire letters her mother had written. She eventually wrote a personal letter to her uncle who in turn mailed back a response and she was able to read it. Terry recalls learning to read in Spanish by reading letters sent to their grandmothers.

I learned most of my Spanish from my grandmother because my mom and dad usually spoke to us in English. In fact, when I was student teaching, I called my mom to tell her that I would be teaching in a bilingual classroom. There was a long pause at the end of the line. Her response was, "I've never heard you say one word in Spanish." Well, I may not have been speaking Spanish, but I was certainly listening and learning. My grandmother received mail from her daughter in California. She would sit in her Lazy-Boy chair and scan the letters she received. Then, she would remove her glasses, rub her eyes, and say, "*Leéme la carta, mi hija. Casi no puedo ver* (Read me the letter, my daughter, I almost can't see)." She would lean back on her chair and close her eyes, while I would sit next to her and read the letters. I honestly thought she couldn't see well. However, I now recall her helping me with words I couldn't read, and she had her eyes closed! Was this her way of teaching me to read in Spanish?

These teachers also served as scribes for their families, functioning as language and literacy brokers, writing in a language in which their parents or neighbors had limited or no literacy ability. Patricia, who was in sixth grade, wrote so many letters dictated to her by her parents that she asked her father to purchase a typewriter. Her brother was in the armed services in Alaska, and Patricia was selected to be the writer because of her English literacy skills. Her experience typing letters benefited her later in high school as she notes, "One of my assets in high school was the ability to type fast. I would be awarded certificates all the time for accuracy and speed." Letty also helped an elderly neighbor by writing notes requesting stamps to the mailman. Still another teacher wrote in Spanish for her parents because they had limited education. Her father encouraged her to take Spanish classes in high school in order to be able to write letters for him. The father was able to read letters in Spanish from his sister in Mexico, but felt uncomfortable expressing himself in writing.

By reading and writing personal letters, the teachers not only served as scribes in their houses but also had access to their extended families. The use of Spanish literacy to communicate with family members across geographic space underscored the need for the Spanish language in maintaining family ties. Their access to literacy in Spanish further contributed to the teachers' being able to see themselves as biliterate Chicanas.

RELIGION

Beside letters, religious texts played a principal role in the acquisition of Spanish literacy. While the literacy event of reading and writing letters took place at home, reading religious texts took place both inside and outside the home. Patsy notes the responsiveness of the Catholic church to the bilingual needs of the congregation.

The church was the only institution that was responsive to the language needs of the community. Because the priests used Spanish and English, relatives like my great-aunt were not left out. They also saw to it that Spanish missals and prayer books were available to the community. This provided me with access to print in three languages (Spanish, English, and Latin). The use of the Spanish language in church also served to affirm the language of our lives and provided language models outside of those of my own community.

In contrast to the church, several teachers wrote about other community contexts including schools that were hostile to Spanish and in which they experienced discrimination.

The local school taught English and the Anglo culture. There was never a mention of the northern New Mexico culture. Children were reprimanded when caught speaking Spanish or talking about their culture. No one dared write or read in Spanish because of repercussions. My friend and I would sneak under the slide and bushes to talk to one another in Spanish. We were often caught and reprimanded. Although some of the teacher's aides and teachers were Hispanic, they never spoke to us in Spanish. Instead they would say, "You are in school now, you must speak English, Spanish is not allowed in our school." It was made quite clear that our language and our culture were not acceptable in a school environment. Interactions with religious texts took place across the yearly cycles of Lent and the weekly cycle of church services or family Bible readings. The reading materials included Bibles, handwritten prayer and song books, and church missals used during Catholic mass.

Interactions with religious texts were of two types. The first was learning to read from church missals as one followed along with the readings and the second was participating in group readings. For three teachers, following along in the church missal was their first memory of reading. Missals were available in both Spanish and English. Besides the church services, literacy events involving religious print materials took place at home. Lupe's earliest memories of reading center around his family's weekly Bible reading time. Every Sunday evening the family sat around the living room with the parents and older siblings taking turns reading passages from the Bible and offering their interpretations.

My earliest recollections of being read to center around my family's weekly Bible study nights. Since both of my parents were brought up as devout Christians and, having attended Catholic schools in northern New Mexico, it was expected by my grandparents that they, as "good" parents, initiate their children in the ways of the Catholic faith. Each Sunday evening the entire family would gather in our living room and my parents and elder brothers and sisters would take turns reading passages out of the family Bible and offer their interpretations of these passages. Even though my younger siblings and I were too young to read or really understand what was being said, those children who were older took time to ask us questions about the Bible, in general, which kept us consciously involved in the evening's events. The atmosphere for these sessions was a somber one; as I grew older and was expected to be more responsible for my actions, I grew to appreciate their efforts more and more. [My older siblings' interactions] often helped me to escape my father's wrath when he felt I wasn't being serious enough about what was being said.

In another case, Dina's grandmother gathered the children around an altar she had set up in her bedroom and recited a mass and prayed the rosary with them. She then passed a Spanish Bible around and had the children read portions that she had previously selected. The younger ones learned to read from the older ones, and the grandmother provided words that they were unable to read. After the reading, the grandmother related the passage to some aspect of the children's lives, or she drew a moral lesson from the passage.

Susana's interactions with religious texts focused on the physical characteristics of the book, and the nature of the writing made a memorable impression on her.

Our family was extremely religious and observed Holy Week with the strictest obedience. Children were not allowed to play or participate in loud activities during Holy Week. The only activities allowed were religious activities, reading, and writing. Most of the religious reading material was in Spanish. I can still recall the leather-bound *handwritten* books that had been handed down for generations. They contained Lenten prayers and *alabados* (Lenten songs). The yellowing pages made a crackling sound with the turn of each page as my sister and I read the pages. The ink seemed to run together at one point or another. At times the handwriting became almost illegible.

Susana further commented on these old books by writing,

> The leather-bound handwritten books that were written in sixteenth century Spanish were also a means of keeping our culture intact. There were certain rituals that accompanied our reading such as fasting, praying the rosary, and practicing only good deeds toward our fellow men. Literacy during this time was special as it allowed me to read my ancestors' written language and gave value to my culture.

Teachers began to see themselves as biliterate from their early years through the acquisition of Spanish literacy taking place at home as well as at church. Religious literacy, unlike the literacy of letter writing, presented the uses of Spanish in the authoritative texts of Bibles and prayer books. As such, it introduced the dimension of inspired and spiritual texts to family literacy. Adults' interactions with the authoritative texts of religious faith demonstrated to the children how to interpret and apply these texts to their lives. Participation in religious literacy for the teachers established family membership within the particular element of the family's faith that connected the family to a larger community of faith represented by the local churches.

DISCUSSION: LIVED LITERACY

Family literacy for teachers was embedded in their childhood memories of literacy practices, special texts, and family relationships that were reaffirmed in literacy events often connected with specific settings in their homes used routinely through daily living. These affect-laden memories of place are encompassed in the term *literacy places*. The memories of these places were affectively charged due to the role of literacy in the activities that established family bonds between caregivers and children. The role of home settings in the production of such memories can be understood by looking at literacy places as *literacy chronotopes*. Bakhtin (1981) used the term *chronotope* to describe how the settings of narratives fuse the central components of time, place, and action that give narratives their meanings (see Galindo & Brown, 1995, for an example of the function of chronotopes drawn from the personal narratives of an Amish writer). This fusion of narrative meaning enables the chronotope to play a key role in the narrative interpretation of human social life and personal experience. In the case of literacy chronotopes, narrative memories of family literacy fuse place, family members, and family relationships with literacy practices. As in narrative chronotopes, literacy chronotopes are charged with evaluative intensity that reflects the important role that literacy played in the reproduction of family social relationships and family identity that occurred within a particular place. The term *literacy place* is especially relevant to literacy research employing narrative accounts of literacy experiences such as autobiographies or interviews where memories of literacy are recounted because they highlight the settings of narrative events.

The teachers' autobiographies illustrate two broad areas in which Spanish literacy was acquired and used for cultural and family identity: religious texts and family letters. Religious texts were encountered in the two settings of the church and home. In the home, the uses of religious texts were related to the religious instruction that parents supervised for children as well as adults. Parents or grandparents read religious texts with children and demonstrated how to apply the text to their lives by presenting interpretations of the text or by drawing moral lessons from the texts that could be applied to their lives. As soon as the children were old enough to read, they were expected to participate in the oral reading of religious texts and thus signal their family membership. These religious literacy events were routine family activities that reinforced the value of faith in the life of the family and further provided opportunities to acquire Spanish literacy. The authoritative texts, Bibles and prayer books written in Spanish, gave the children an opportunity to see Spanish used in powerful ways during literacy events. In religious literacy, adult family members demonstrated to the children their involvement with literacy in an area of their life that held deep personal meaning for them. For at least one teacher, the church came to be recognized as a strong ally in the fight to maintain cultural identity through the use of Spanish by providing religious texts in both Spanish and English. Besides the home, the church was the only other social unit in the community that acknowledged and supported the bilingual nature of the Mexican-origin population. For one teacher, the handwritten song books contributed an historical dimension to her family identity by linking her present family to previous generations. Another teacher noted that religious literacy integrated her into a social unit greater than the family: the church congregation.

Personal letter reading and writing between relatives were important literacy events in the maintenance and transmission of Spanish literacy. Some of the teachers were originally drawn into these activities as youngsters, either by playing at writing or by reading. Eventually, some of them became the family scribe responsible for taking down what the parents dictated or for reading the letters. The literacy events of letter writing and reading illustrated that the family benefited from the combined literacy resources of all the family members, including the children (Auerbach, 1989; Farr, 1994). In two cases, the teachers were designated as family scribes.

The teachers and their parents occupied a variety of roles during their participation in family literacy events. The parents were teachers showing their young children how to read and write the alphabet or their names. At other times they led discussions of current events and demonstrated to their children how to be critical readers. In a case of reversal of role, being a family scribe put the children in a position of being more capable with literacy than their parents. In one case, the parents depended on their daughter to communicate to their son in English, a language in which the parents had not received any formal education. In another case, the parents could read only in Spanish. They felt uncomfortable writing due to their limited formal education. In still another case, one child functioned as a language mediator for an elderly neighbor who did not know English.

CONCLUSION

In their autobiographies, the teachers discussed the implications of their life stories for developing literacy in the classroom. The first implication is to be aware of the variety of experiences with literacy that students may bring to the classroom. These were never acknowledged in the classroom when they were children. The second implication is to give importance to native language literacy and biliteracy. Looking back at their own lives helped the teachers see the help they provided their families in communicating with others as well as the encouragement they received from their parents regarding Spanish literacy. In their own classrooms, they now encourage and provide opportunities for the biliteracy development of their students not only to ensure future occupational opportunities but—equally important—to reaffirm cultural identity. A third implication is to provide their students access to a wide variety of book and nonbook print materials that serve a wide variety of functions. In their literacy socialization, nonbook print materials such as magazines, newspapers, church missals, and *fotonovelas* proved to be important print resources. A final important implication is to remain aware that family literacy practices are not rigid, but continue to evolve across time. One teacher wrote about observing her parents, who are now retired, engaging in practices with their grandchildren that they had not engaged in with their own children, "The last time I visited . . . I found my dad reading a book to my niece in English! My mother helps her grandchildren with their homework now! We've come a long way with literacy in this family."

As is the case with all data, autobiographical data have their limitations. Specifically, writing about events that occurred many years ago makes the retrieval of some details difficult. However, in writing their autobiographies, the teachers chose the most memorable literacy events, or those that left a strong impression. The details included in the examples presented here show that despite the temporal gap between the occurrence of the event and the writing of the autobiography, the teachers were able to recall many specific details. The broad range of literacy practices, events, and functions of literacy described across the teachers' narratives was the focus of the analyses presented here, but serves only as a beginning. The need continues for details on the literacy socialization of minority teachers. In future studies, interview data that extends information contained in autobiographical accounts can help present a more dynamic picture of the literacy socialization of minority teachers (see Galindo, Aragón, & Underhill, 1996, for an example of the integration of autobiographical and interview data in the development of case studies of Chicana teacher role identity).

The examples of family literacy drawn from these bilingual teachers' autobiographies demonstrate the broad range of literacy events and literacy materials found in their childhood lives. As such, they contribute to more adequate accounts of literacy in the lives of minority families and provide further evidence to dispel deficit perspectives of minority family literacy. Within the families of these bilingual teachers, it is clear that multiple literacies strongly coexisted—the literacy of play between children, community literacy involving both adults and children in religious activities, personal letter writing literacy that connected the teachers' families to a community of relatives and friends in other geographic areas, and school literacy that included both direct instruction in writing and critical discussions of current events. The absence of child-specific literacy materials in some of the teachers' homes did not preclude the absence of caregiver-child literacy-based interactions.

IF SCHOOLS/SOCIETY SHARED OUR PERSPECTIVE ON LITERACY, HOW MIGHT PEOPLE'S LIVES BE DIFFERENT?

There are two important issues from the preceding discussion of family literacy that might work to broaden our understanding of language and teacher education. The first is the conceptual issue of the relationships between literacy, culture, and identity. The Chicana/o teachers documented how their early, memorable literacy experiences were embedded within family relationships. Memories of community and personal literacies for these minority teachers are memories of family members and places, not school literacy. Their own development as human beings with particular identities was shaped and fashioned within literacy places and events. As educators, an important lesson to be communicated to our students is that literacy is more than a technology to be mastered; it can also be central to who we are and how we became social beings.

The second is the methodological issue of autobiographical funds of knowledge for understanding the rich literate environment of Chicano/a family life. The educational and literacy cultural resources, reclaimed through the examples of family literacy recorded here, have yet to be acknowledged by schools. These autobiographical funds of knowledge drawn from minority families can be used to challenge basic questions such as "What counts as literacy?" and "What is the relationship between self and literacy?" This study suggests that minority teachers should examine their own personal and family histories for insights gained from parents, grandparents, aunts and uncles, and other family members regarding other critical questions, such as what it means to be educated. Such questions have traditionally been answered by excluding minority perspectives and experiences from school (Galindo & Olguín, 1996). Such reexaminations are essential since teacher education programs continue to be dominated by nonminority faculty, who often do not recognize the importance of these autobiographical funds of knowledge and who often devalue the personal literacy experiences of teacher candidates when they come from minority backgrounds (Galindo, 1996).

REFERENCES

Auerbach, E. (1989). Towards a social-contextual approach to family literacy. *Harvard Educational Review, 59*, 165–181.

Bakhtin, M. (1981). *The dialogic imagination.* Austin: University of Texas Press.

Bakhtin, M. (1986). *Speech genres and other late essays.* Austin: University of Texas Press.

Bean, T. (1994). A constructivist view of preservice teachers' attitudes toward reading through case study analysis of autobiographies. In C. Kinzer & D. Leu (Eds.), *Multidimensional aspects of literacy research, theory, and practice* (pp. 370–379). Chicago: National Reading Conference:

Bertaux, D. (1981). *Biography and society: The life history approach in the social sciences.* Beverly Hills, CA: Sage.

Delgado-Gaitan, C. (1990). *Literacy for empowerment.* New York: Falmer Press.

Evans, R. (1993). Learning "school literacy": The literate life histories of mainstream student readers and writers. *Discourse Processes, 16*, 317–340.

Farr, M. (1994). En los dos idiomas: Literacy practices among Chicago Mexicanos. In B. Moss (Ed.), *Literacy across communities* (pp. 9–47). Cresskill, NJ: Hampton Press.

Farr, M., & Guerra, J. (1995). Literacy in the community: A study of Mexicano families in Chicago. *Discourse Processes, 19*, 7–19.

Foster, M. (1990). The politics of race: Through the eyes of African-American teachers. *Journal of Education, 172*, 123–143.

Galindo, R. (1996). Reframing the past in the present: Chicana teacher role identity as a bridging identity. *Education and Urban Society, 29*, 85–102.

Galindo, R., Aragón, M, & Underhill, R. (1996). The competence to act: Chicana teacher role identity in life and career narratives. *Urban Review, 28*, 279–308.

Galindo, R., & Brown, C. (1995). Person, place, and narrative in an Amish farmer's appropriation of nature writing. *Written Communication, 12*, 147–185.

Galindo, R., & Olguín, M. (1996). Reclaiming bilingual educators' cultural resources: An autobiographical approach. *Urban Education, 31*, 29–56.

Gallego, M., & Hollingsworth, S. (1992). Multiple literacies: Teachers' evolving perceptions. *Language Arts, 69*, 46–53.

Goodson, I. (1992). *Studying teachers' lives.* New York: Teachers College Press.

Heller, M. (1987). The role of language in the formation of ethnic identity. In J. Phinne & M. Rotheram (eds.), *Childrens' ethnic socialization* (pp. 180–200). Newbury Park, CA: Sage.

Langness, L., & Frank, G. (1981). *Lives: An anthropological approach to biography.* Novato, CA: Chandler & Sharp.

Moll, L., & Greenberg, J. (1990). Creating zones of possibilities: Combining social contexts for instruction. In L. Moll (Ed.), *Vygotsky and education: Instructional implications and applications of sociohistorical psychology* (pp. 319–348). Cambridge: Cambridge University Press.

Plumer, K. (1983). *Documents of life.* London: Allen & Unwin.

Sommers, M. (1994). The narrative constitution of identity: A relational and network approach. *Theory and society, 23*, 605–650.

Taylor, C. (1985). The person. In M. Steven Collins & S. Lukes (Eds.), *The category of the person: anthropology, philosophy, history* (pp. 257–281). New York: Cambridge University Press.

Vásquez, O. (1992). A Mexicano perspective. In D. Murray (Ed.), *Diversity as a resource: Redefining cultural literacy* (pp. 113–134). Alexandria, VA: Teachers of English to Speakers of Other Languages.

16

El Grupo de Las Señoras
Creating Consciousness Within a Literature Club

ROSI ANDRADE, HILDA GONZÁLEZ LE DENMAT, AND LUIS C. MOLL

What would happen if one woman told the truth about her life?
—Muriel Rukeyser, "Käthe Kollwitz," 1973

The focus of this chapter is on the literacies explored in an immigrant women's literature club. We are interested in the limitations and ramifications of the women's use of certain school literacies rather than a discussion of the skills and literate capabilities of the women themselves. What we will demonstrate, however, is the problematic nature of schooled standards of literacy even for those who espouse them.

Macedo (1993) commented on the dominance of an "instrumental literacy for the poor," one that he describes as "a competency-based skill banking approach," but also suggests that it and the "highest form of instrumental literacy for the rich . . . share one common feature: they both prevent the development of the critical thinking that enables one to 'read the world' critically and to understand the reasons and linkages behind the facts" (p. 188). Both types of school literacy promote unquestioned acceptance of the status quo. We find this point key to a discussion of literacies, for it places us all on notice to critique our own schooled and accepted conceptions of literacy. It should not be surprising, then, that when women, much like the immigrant women in the literature club, are placed in situations in which these unspoken canons of unquestioned acceptance operate, they are rendered illiterate. This, we find, is often the case because they do not speak English, but it is also due to the myriad patriarchal traditions, both in their homeland and in this country, that together have served to train these women to also accept those canons as truth.

What Counts as Literacy: Challenging the School Standard. *Copyright © 2000 by Teachers College, Columbia University. All rights reserved. ISBN 0-8077-3972-3 (paper), ISBN 0-8077-3973-1 (cloth). Prior to photocopying items for classroom use, please contact the Copyright Clearance Center, Customer Service, 222 Rosewood Drive, Danvers, MA 01923, USA, telephone (508) 750-8400.*

How, one might ask, do the relationships between literacy, language, and patriarchal traditions manifest themselves? For purposes of this argument, we take one example, that of school-family partnerships. Presently, the call for school-family partnership, often focusing on issues of literacy, has been made far and wide, from school district mandates to research initiatives. Yet the tenets underlying such collaborations have remained largely unquestioned, as have been the guidelines of participation. If we look beneath the facade that such partnerships present, more often than not we find that it is the school that determines the form and quality of parental participation, not the family. It is also the school that determines a successful collaboration. While such partnerships remain the norm, especially in minority and working-class communities, they are problematic for several reasons.

In our own work, we have rejected the deficit model ascribed to language-minority and working-class families that suggests that their households are at the root of educational problems and need to be remediated through school-family "partnerships." We focus, instead, on the claim that capitalizing on household and other community knowledge bases can provide strategic resources for school practices. At the same time, we have remained largely outside of the predominant theoretical models guiding work with parents and families. Our participation has typically ended at the classroom door, where teachers—and rightly so—engage in creating a curriculum that capitalizes on that familial knowledge (see Moll, 1992a; Moll, 1992b; Moll & Greenberg, 1990). In retrospect, we find that our concern for respecting the integrity of children and their families as repositories of knowledge has fallen short. The deficit model remains a guiding dictum with regard to partnerships between families and parents, as evidenced in the proliferation of attitudes and behaviors that foment it. The paucity of intellectual autonomy permitted to parents is quite telling.

Lareau (1989) has suggested that schools shape and limit the participation of parents solely under the conditions made by the school. For parents to choose *not* to abide by those conditions, to fall out of compliance with them, is not permitted. The suggestion that parents have autonomy in their relationship with the school is but an illusion for many minority and working-class parents. Thus, the creation of these partnerships, by the very nature of the relationships between school and parents, is a contradiction.

This chapter is dedicated to a discussion of the multiple literacies that exist in the various communities with which we have negotiated a reciprocal partnership. We suspect that these are not unique communities, but can be found under many different guises throughout this country. Our discussion of the subject of this book, multiple literacies, finds itself situated within the context of a local literature club for Mexican and Mexican American women, *Las Señoras*, established and organized by Hilda González Le Denmat in the southwestern United States. The significance of this literature group is that it challenges several myths often tied to working-class, minority women and their families, as well as prevailing notions of literacy ascribed to them. Often, for example, factors such as poverty, ethnicity, and gender influence how these women's literate capabilities are perceived. Additionally, preconceived notions of how literacy should be standardly defined and measured do not take into account the dynamic nature of literacy, the significance of literacy to the population under scrutiny, nor the nature of multiple literacies as they affect working class Mexican and Mexican American women, in particular, who are the subjects of this chapter. These two points will be elaborated at the conclusion of this chapter.

We begin by describing a typical day of the literature study group.

EL CLUB DE LITERATURA

El Club de Literatura is one of various offerings made to parents and community members at a local elementary school. Although the idea of the program is not unique—family liaisons organize services for families in most district schools—this particular program is distinct for several reasons. The program has been tailored to the needs of the local community, using a Freirian approach to community literacy (Freire, 1992; Freire & Macedo, 1987), by Hilda González Le Denmat, a bilingual teacher with over 10 years of teaching experience. Hilda is interested in promoting the role of mothers in the education of their children, through their own personal development. Her task, however, is not a simple one, for two reasons. First, she must begin with the particular needs and interests of the community in creating the curriculum, rather than simply impose a generic curriculum that is usually better suited to mainstream communities. Second, she must go against the grain of what the school desires: parent participation with a large dose of remediation. Furthermore, the literature study group is unlike school, for several reasons: (1) It does not subscribe to the authority of the teacher; (2) the curriculum is created through collaboration with the participants; (3) all those in attendance are knowledgeable and literate; and (4) the content of the literature remains at a high intellectual level. Additionally, the goal of the study group is not to categorize and label learner's abilities or shortcomings, but to promote the access to knowledge and the process of individual self-discovery, in essence to promote literacy much in the same way as in intellectual groups such as *La Generación del 98*. *La Generación del 98* was a club composed of Spanish writers, such as Unamuno, Azorín, Valle-Inclán, Baroja, and Antonio Machado. The group was formed after Spain's loss of Cuba and the Philippines in 1898. As a group, *La Generación del 98*, not only helped to define an artistic genre, but also discussed political, economic, and social accounts during their many *tertulias*. *Tertulias* were reunions of members to discuss social, political, and economic affairs. *Tertulias* were typically reserved for men and intellectuals as a breeding ground for thought, discussions, and writing.

Las Señoras, as they are respectfully addressed, range in age from their early 20s to late 80s, though most are in their early 30s. The *Señoras* are minority women who speak little or no English, who are struggling financially, whose domestic ties to the home frame their exposure to the world outside the home, and who are often subjugated by fathers, husbands, boyfriends, and the dominant culture of the society in which they live. These factors together serve to seriously constrain the personal development of these women and limit their intellectual and social potential.

The following is a narrative snapshot of the literature study group. The literature study takes place twice weekly during hour-long sessions. The reading of a book may take anywhere from 2 to 8 weeks, depending on the selection. Reading selections are made from Spanish-language literature on the college level.

EL NARANJO O LOS CIRCULOS DEL TIEMPO

The literature club begins by continuing the reading of Carlos Fuentes' (1993) *El Naranjo o los Circulos del Tiempo* (The Orange or the Circle of Time). There are 10 participants today, sitting around two large kidney-shaped tables, joined to form a circle. As is typical, all are women, with the exception of Mario, who is a new arrival to this country. Mario is a welder by trade and originally from Hermosillo, Sonora, Mexico. Mario is also the brother-in-law of one of the women, hence his connection to the group. Another new member, Conchita, is a graduate of the University of Hermosillo with a degree in social work. Previously a high school teacher in Mexico, Conchita is now celebrating a year since her arrival in the United States. She originally entered this country as a tourist, knowing, however, that she would remain in Tucson indefinitely. Conchita has followed her husband's dreams of building a better tomorrow for their young children, leaving behind her status and the security of her position as a teacher, by coming to this country where she is no longer considered a professional, nor even literate. Celestina has been in the United States for a decade and a half, yet still does not speak a great deal of English. Better said, she does not have the confidence to explore her English language abilities. Cristal is a long-time community member who does not have children at this elementary school, but does have two children in high school. Like most members of the literature study group, she is also interested in furthering her personal learning experiences. Such is the variety of the participants' experiences and backgrounds in the *Club de Literatura*.

Reading takes place in many shapes and forms (e.g., silent reading, oral reading, partner reading). However, due to a scarcity of resources, the few books available generally remain in the classroom. The literature study, out of necessity, takes place there also. Hilda reads as well, not to demonstrate that she is in any way a better reader, but to model the act of oral reading and to allay any fears of what the oral reading activity is. The oral reading of the book, as always, happens voluntarily. On this day, Mario offers to read aloud first. Because the group cannot remember the page number on which they had left off previously, the group begins retracing Tuesday's reading. They recall, for example, the encounter between Moctezuma and Cortés, and that the Aztec king feared horses and fair-skinned people. Together, they also recall the history of Quetzalcoatl, the benevolent God, and his promise to return to his homeland. Hilda shares with the group different legends and questions regarding the existence of Quetzalcoatl, who was described physically as being a fair-skinned man, not an indigenous native. How did he arrive? Was he shipwrecked? Was he an alien? These are the questions the group contemplates.

As the group is discussing this text, Hilda brings out yet another book that she has in the classroom. The book represents the life and culture of the Aztecs pictorially. Cristal suddenly remembers that her high school daughter needs to do a report for one of her classes, precisely on the Aztecs. At that same moment, Mario requests that he be able to take the book home to look at it. However, after Cristal shares her daughter's pending assignment, he foregoes his request so that Cristal may borrow the book.

As the reading of *El Naranjo o los Circulos del Tiempo* (Fuentes, 1993) begins anew, the narrator is describing his position as translator to the conqueror and the natives:

> *Yo sé todo esto porque fui el traductor en la entrevista de Cortés con Guatemuz, que no podían comprenderse entre sí. Traduje a mi antojo. No le communiqué al príncipe vencido lo que Cortés realmente le dijo, sino que puse en boca de nuestro jefe una amenaza: Serás mi prisionero, hoy mismo te torturaré, quemándote los pies igual que a compañeros, hasta que confieses donde está el resto del tesoro de tu tío Moctezuma (la parte que no fue a dar a manos de los piratas franceses).*

[I know all of this because I was the translator for Cortés and Guatemuz, because they could not understand each other. I translated at whim. I did not communicate to the defeated prince what Cortés had truly told him. Instead, I put a threat in the mouth of our superior: You will be my prisoner, I will torture you today, burning your feet as well as those of your companions, until you confess where the rest of your uncle's treasure lies (the part that did not fall into the hands of the French pirates).] (p.18)

The narrator, Jerónimo de Aguilar, who is speaking from the dead, is recounting how, having use of the power of language, he was able to distort what Cortés had said. The group pauses to discuss another phenomenon, namely, how in the United States there are those who also lack the power of language or the language of power. The group shares situations in which each has been limited by a lack of English language skills. Conchita, for example, tells of her own frustration when visiting stores, riding the bus, or visiting this very elementary school, where the study group meets, and where Hilda is the Family Liaison for the school. Conchita confides to those in the group that because of a lack of English skills, since her arrival in this country, she has required a translator to communicate her needs. She adds, *"Me siento como una tonta, cuando voy al Walgreens y en lugar de empujar la puerta, la estiro o al reves."* [I feel like a dummy when I go to the Walgreens (drugstores) and instead of pushing the door, I pull or the other way around.]

Once again, the reading resumes as the narrator is describing the Cholula image, which refers to the precolonial town dedicated to Quetzalcoatl as well as to the dress and customs of its inhabitants. In this scene, Cortés and Moctezuma are together once again and the natives bring back the head of a horse. It is already evident in this early encounter that Moctezuma is fearful of the conqueror's power. The group reading pauses. The passage they have read lends itself to a discussion of the introduction of horses in America, as well as the impact of this never-before-seen figure of man and horse representing a disturbing image for the natives. It is an image that Cortés quickly utilized to his own advantage. The discussion of horses and their origins in this continent lends itself to yet another discussion, and that leads to another, in a pattern that characterizes the dynamic of the groups' interactions. Returning to the text, the narrator is now informing the reader that Cortés had the blessing of Marina's presence by his side. Marina was a bilingual native woman. Originally a princess, Marina was given as a slave by her own father. Not only was she a translator of Spanish for Cortés, but she eventually became his lover.

Cortés escuchaba a Marina no sólo como lengua, sino como amante. Y como lengua y amante, prestaba atención a las voces humanas de esta tierra.

[Cortés listened to Marina not only through dialectic language but also through the language of love. And, listening to both, he paid attention to the human voices of this land]. (p. 31)

Cortés had the opportunity to listen to Marina not only publicly, but also in their intimate world. He paid close attention. He came to understand the hate and the fear that other villages held for Moctezuma's empire. The narrator (Jerónimo de Aguilar), on the other hand, in his former role as translator, had informed Moctezuma of the pending danger that the conquerors presented to his kingdom. Moctezuma, the king, however, did not listen to lackeys such as Aguilar: he only spoke and listened to the Gods. This, it has been said, was Moctezuma's undoing. The lesson here is that bilingualism without the power to interpret the language is no asset.

Yo, que también poseía las dos voces, las de Europa y América, había sido derrotado. Pues tenía también dos patrias; y ésta, quizás fue mi debilidad más que mi fuerza.

[I, who also possessed the two voices, the European and the American, had been defeated. Well, I also had two homelands; and this, perhaps, was my weakness more than my strength.] (p. 25)

The subject of Moctezuma's arrogance motivates yet another discussion. "Especially in Mexico," Mario offers, "the politicians do not listen to the people that put them in power." Hilda suggests that in this country it is not any different. The group makes a connection to CTM (Confederación de Trabajadores de México), a political labor organization in Mexico. It is, supposedly, an association for and by the workers. The CTM's leader, Fidel Velásquez, has held the presidential post for over 60 years; at 99 years of age, he has been described as being so decrepit that he can no longer walk on his own. Upon hearing this, the group breaks out in laughter. Yet, it quickly returns to the seriousness of the topic, how those in power have historically been known to listen selectively, often ignoring the poor, among others. The group makes a passing comment on the beauty of the language Fuentes has utilized in *El Naranjo o los Circulos del Tiempo*. (Fidel Velásquez died in late spring 1997, some months after this discussion.)

The group is at this point discussing the complexity of relationships emerging between characters. The narrator is now describing how Marina physically and intellectually extracted the language of power from Cortés. Already bilingual in Mayan and Nahuatl, she became trilingual, as she learned Spanish. As a consequence of Marina's dexterity, the narrator describes his horror at the realization of his own loss of power as a translator. Marina far exceeded his talents, in that while he could only translate, she could manipulate language to its fullest potential. For now she had, suggests Hilda, "la sarten por el mango [the pan by the handle]."

As the group prepares to conclude its hour of reading, two of the participants wonder aloud, "How is it possible for the narrator to continue to say that he is dead, when he is the narrator?" As she has throughout the hour, Hilda takes this opportunity to suggest to the group a possible explanation, suggesting that it is a literary strategy that the author has utilized to pique their curiosity. She explains that an author is able to manipulate language and create situations that in reality are implausible; with the power of language one is able to create such scenarios.

For the group, it is at first difficult to understand this concept. Hilda then suggests that the narrator is but one of multiple voices that the author employs to relay the story. "Now," she adds, in an attempt to bring closure to the discussion, "when your children are at home reading a story, you can explain to them the idea of multiple voices and characters." The reaction of the group is one of fascination at the capacity of language to create and recreate realities. At the end of the reading period, Mario makes yet another request, this time he asks if he can take *El Naranjo* home.

LITERACY AND LANGUAGE OF MINORITY FAMILIES

The function of the literature study group goes far beyond the confines of reading a novel or story. The reading that takes place is but a vehicle for the transformations that occur as a result of the sharing and cocreation of knowledge and experience. What each participant brings to this experience, and consequently takes away, is multifold.

The narrative description of the literature study group is replete with themes for exploration: politics, history, language, social issues, discrimination, issues of gender, education, and ethnicity, among others. Our interest here is not to explore these themes in isolation, but to present them as lived realities that stand in stark contrast to myths often perpetuated about language-minority families, parents and children. In this respect, we find that there are three often held tenets about Mexican and Mexican American minority families regarding literacy: (1) They do not want to learn English; (2) they lack formal education and therefore have little to offer to the education of their children; and (3) they cannot benefit from the same intellectual offerings afforded the middle class. These beliefs are summations of what we often hear and read in the media and in teacher and school reports. We will reexamine these beliefs in light of what we learned from *Las Señoras*.

Do They Want to Learn English?

In this country it is imperative that anyone interested in surviving be able to speak English. However, English instruction often relegated to working-class immigrants (English as a Second Language, ESL) assumes the learner is a *tabula rasa*, to be shaped into the culture and society of the United States via language instruction, rather than a literate individual with vast experiences, individual aspirations, and political consciousness. Such instruction often is, and should be, rejected in favor of more respectful learning settings.

Not unlike the early experience of the *Señoras* in ESL classes, Rosi Andrade recalls as a child being in attendance in her mother's ESL classes, watching her mother repeat nonsensical words and forming basic sentence structures in lesson upon lesson. What most stands out in Andrade's memory was that the pupils were treated as children, the curriculum was that of the school, and yet these were adults. In retrospect, she suggests that the process was one of indoctrination, not education. Additionally, the ESL classes, for what language instruction they offered, made no sense to her mother's reality; she understood English, but had little opportunity to use the language as a homemaker and was in greater need of understanding the social, political, and cultural structure of the United States vis-à-vis her own immigrant status. These more important lessons were learned in conjunction with her daughter who served, not solely as a language translator, but an interpreter of the hidden messages so that her mother could better understand the unfair power relations of language.

Thus, when one suggests that minorities do not want to learn English, they speak from a lack of knowledge. Access to the language of this country is impeded by many institutional obstacles, which not only limit access to English, but also limit the quality of instruction of the language to be used as a tool for social, political, and cultural survival.

Is Lack of Formal Education an Indication That Parents Have Little to Offer to the Education of Their Children?

There is a vast distinction between an individual unable to participate actively in the formal education of a child and an individual uninterested in the same endeavor. Parents of language-minority children often entrust the education of their children to the authority of the school. They do so out of respect for teachers as professionals. On the other hand, school authorities often display an attitude limiting parents' awareness and understanding of their rights as parents of schoolchildren. Their rights are not necessarily withheld, but they are often not made apparent. If parents are unfamiliar with their rights, it is unlikely that school officials will take the time to education them. This is the case with Cristal and her son. Along with other students, Cristal's son was accused of criminal behavior and was later reported to the police and the Juvenile Court system. The serious accusations were questioned by the mother. Shocked by the gravity of the predicament in light of her son's professed innocence, she shared her dilemma with Hilda. After listening to the details of the ordeal, Hilda asked a few questions and was able to discern that the mother was kept in the dark about district policies with regard to parental and student rights.

Following Hilda's advice, Cristal contacted the school and made reference to due process and began to document her plight, including her thoughts and frustrations. Absolutely everything went into the journal. Over the course of almost one year, there were many more false accusations made with no reliable witnesses or evidence. Furthermore, the school principal repeatedly refused to meet or speak with Cristal, referring her instead to the school secretary. Shaken by the ordeal, Cristal and her family eventually hired an attorney. Following this year of great stress and emotional trauma, Cristal and her family were eventually vindicated, in great part due to the documentation she had collected and presented to a court judge. In the end, what truly stands out in this example is that too often there are limitations to the parental involvement offered by the school. It is the school that defines the appropriate involvement, while it is also the school that criticizes lack of parental involvement.

Regarding the *Señoras'* involvement with their children's education, while some teachers were pleased with the indirect influence on the *Señoras'* children through the literature study group, other teachers were intimidated by the academic nature of the activity and suggested that if these mothers really cared about their children's education, they would not be reading, but coming to the classroom to cut paper and trace letters or going to the cafeteria to monitor students.

Can Working-class Parents Benefit from the Same Intellectual Offerings Afforded the Middle-class Adult?

Although this question may seem redundant in light of the activities of the literature study group, it is one that is seldom asked. While the outcome of the study group was not controlled nor predicted by Hilda, the organization was deliberate. In preparing the curriculum for the study group, Hilda had several prerequisites, but first and foremost in the *Club de Literatura* is the acknowledgment that everyone is literate, able to read in the broadest sense of the word, and more importantly capable of applying knowledge and experience to the reading of the text. This dictum breaks from norms that have traditionally kept the *Señoras* from both the experiences of participating in similar dialogic exchanges and from reading these texts, often reserved for the elite male intellectuals. Additionally, like the networking that inevitably emanates from this form of *tertulia*, this experience opens doors through which the *Señoras* begin to see and understand themselves differently and in the process begin to participate in new ways in the home, school, and community.

CONCLUSION

It is difficult to assign a single conclusion to the reading that the *Señoras* do in the literature group. Their responses to the texts were too varied, dynamic, even unpredictable, and included a range of modes of engagement that varied from preoccupation about decoding smoothly to extracting insights about the role of language and social relationships in life. The books became another social environment or context within which to develop new knowledge and experiences—new social identities, if you will.

Neither the teacher nor the *Señoras* could prespecify what would count as reading in any one of the sessions; there were no general rules that defined reading, although regularities or routines emerged to organize and hold together, but not control, reading activities in the group. There was, consequently, no evaluation or punishment for misreading, no competition among readers, no one correct way of dealing with text, and no external control or mandated prescription of lessons, for there was no single model or understanding of what it meant to read.

It is revealing to contrast the *Señoras'* reading practices to what typically occurs within classrooms, especially in regard to the control exercised over what counts as reading with working-class, language-minority students. The reading these students do is usually strictly controlled and defined, not only through the type of text, but what is done with it. Displays of curiosity, mastery, or personal connections are sometimes allowed, but delimited to specific amounts of text, in prescribed ways, and always subject to external testing or evaluation. And from performances within these reduced contexts, judgments are passed and social identities as learners and as human beings are assigned.

Through the literature, the *Señoras* are examining their own historical contexts as women: as daughters, as wives, as mothers, as citizens in their homeland and in this country. As *Las Señoras* begin to peer through the blinds that have previously closed off other understandings and possibilities to them, they are creating a consciousness of themselves as individuals and as a group.

Yet, we do not find similar results from learning to read in schools. As suggested above, the purpose of schooling, be it informal or formal, is primarily to control participation and thought through the use of reading and writing. The unequal footing of parents in family-school partnerships must be challenged in that the school, given its very structure and reason for being, will not go against its own interests. We argue that the intent of schools must not be to indoctrinate parents en masse in training for the menial, but to further the personal development of literacies for parents, school personnel, and children alike. Ask not for family partnership, but for the codevelopment of multiple literacies—the literacies necessary to navigate in the contexts of schools and communities.

IF SCHOOLS/SOCIETY SHARED OUR PERSPECTIVE ON LITERACY, HOW MIGHT PEOPLE'S LIVES BE DIFFERENT?

This is a difficult question to address, because of its many implications; any response might serve to simplify the complexity of the issues at hand. To begin, we realize there are no "miracle cures" to the maladies affecting our schools and society. Our position, in fact, is that literacy is not the cure-all. Instead, we suggest that the focus be on the richness and complexity of multiple literacies. In light of this position, we might state that any orientation that confines the potential of language and language uses is symptomatic of the problem, thus reversing the general trend of culpability from children and their families to elsewhere. That is one foreseeable influence. The other would be to look at individuals' lives with questions in mind: What are the daily experiences affecting families and children and how are they shaping their respective development as individuals? What is the intent of literacy development programs, themselves devoid of understanding and knowing? That is, the messenger can no longer remain inscrutable when delivering the call for literacy. The differences we foresee begin at the institutional level, where a great deal of the problem rests. We are reminded of Macedo's (1993) words on the subject of the "learned ignoramus," of the implicit distinction between the learned and "*il*-learned" often being the power vested in the sanctioned authority.

With respect to the idea of multiple literacies as it is presented in Chapter 1, Rosi Andrade is drawn back to the biographical narrative of "Gallego's Story" there, as she reflects on the many parallels and differences between herself and Gallego. Though hers is also not a "hard luck" story, it is another story that expands on the topic of community literacies. Andrade (1994) has suggested that literacy is like a reflection in the mirror. It all depends on who is looking in and what the backdrop is. Though she grew up speaking, reading, and writing both Spanish and English, she writes,

> My schooling was strictly in English, though in report cards from the schools of this community [a working class Mexican, Mexican American barrio], my perceived progress in reading, understanding, and speaking English was always made a measure of my academic capabilities. Interestingly, though, upon moving from South Tucson in the 4th grade, to what is demographically referred to as a middle class, predominantly Anglo neighborhood in midtown Tucson, my English capabilities were no longer made an issue, nor questioned, in earlier terms, but regarded as a core subject matter like mathematics or social studies. Yet I had not changed, nor had I undergone any academic transformation [from the physical move]. (pp. 19–20)

Andrade's educational life course has been driven, not by a sense of wanting to belong to the mainstream, but by a refusal to do so because of its implications to her own struggle for intellectual autonomy and identity. This intransigence has at times come at a price. Yet, Andrade chooses to maintain separate lives, moving in and out of their linguistic and cultural boundaries, while allowing them to feed and nurture each other intellectually. One does not supplant the other.

Thus, we express a disquieting concern with the subject of literacy, especially as it affects those language-minority populations divested of any authority, like the *Señoras*, for example. Another potential difference, then, might be that the backdrop that so often expunges other literacies from forming part of the reflection, must itself be critiqued as to its intents and purposes that so paternalistically suggest that "other" literacies be dismissed and sacrificed for the simplistic ideal of a common good, a common language, a common literacy. The focus on commonalties is passé; we live and speak in multiplicities. If institutions were to change from imposing disabling constraints on intellectual autonomy, we might see not so much a physical but a psychological transformation in children and families, as they would begin to explore their literacies, their lives in context with the larger social world. We might well conclude what many of us already suspect: that education comes in many shapes and forms, and that formal education is not always the key, but often the problem when it stifles self-worth in a learner and the ability to mobilize all resources at hand. That is why the exploration by *Las Señoras* as they engage in readings and discussions of literature that is of relevance to them as women, as mothers, as wives, as minorities, and as immigrants (to name but a few), while tapping their own linguistic, social, and cultural resources, itself a far cry from more traditional roles prescribed, holds such promise.

DEDICATION

We dedicate this chapter to the memory of Paulo Freire, for the many philosophical seeds he has planted, as well as his penchant to place "the other" in the foreground of both theory and practice.

REFERENCES

Andrade, R. (1994). *Children's constructive social worlds: Existential lives in the balance.* Unpublished doctoral dissertation, University of Arizona, Tucson.

Freire, P. (1992). *Pedagogy of the oppressed.* New York: Continuum.

Freire, P., & Macedo, D. (1987). *Literacy: Reading the word and the world.* Westport, CT: Bergin & Garvey.

Fuentes, C. (1993). *El naranjo o los circulos del tiempo.* México: Aguilar, Altea, Taurus, Alfaguara, S.A. de C.V.

Lareau, A. (1989). *Home advantage: Social class and parental intervention in elementary education.* Philadelphia: Falmer Press.

Macedo, D. P. (1993). Literacy for stupidification: The pedagogy of big lies. *Harvard Educational Review, 63*(2), 183–206.

Moll, L. C. (1992a). Bilingual classroom studies and community analysis. *Educational Researcher, 21*(2), 20–24.

Moll, L. C. (1992b). Literacy research in community and classrooms: A sociocultural approach. In R. Beach, J. L. Greene, M. L. Kamil, & T. Shanahan (Eds.), *Multidisciplinary perspectives on literacy research* (pp. 211–244). Urbana, IL: NCRE/NCTE.

Moll, L. C, & Greenberg, J. B. (1990). Creating zones of possibilities: Combining social contexts for instruction. In L. C. Moll (Ed.), *Vygotsky and education: Instructional implications and applications of socio-historical psychology* (pp. 319–348). New York: Cambridge University Press.

Rukeyser, M. (1973). Käthe Kollwitz. In J. Goulianos (Ed.), *By a woman writt* (p. 374). New York: Bobbs Merrill.

17

A Second-Grade Teacher's Encounters with Multiple Literacies

LESLIE TURNER MINARIK

I have wrestled with my personal understanding of the concept of multiple literacies for weeks that have stretched into months. I actually began my growing understanding of multiple literacies as a participant in an ongoing teacher research group. The research group is composed of five elementary and middle school teachers (Anthony Cody, Mary Dybdahl, Karen Teel, Jennifer Davis Smallwood, and me) and one college teacher (Sandra Hollingsworth), who have been meeting for 13 years to discuss teaching concerns and shifting constructions of literacy and to support each other's teaching through teacher research. We have argued the topic theoretically in our group meetings, but, more important, we have tried to see what multiple literacies really look like in the classroom with our students. I have been stumbling personally because I could not initially see my students through the concept of multiple literacies and that is why I could not translate them into anything meaningful, despite our usually helpful conversations. My only choice now is to begin again by rethinking my definition of literacy and to link that with my experiences with my students.

So I began with the narrow and perhaps most commonly used definition of literacy: the ability to read and write. But another, broader definition explains literacy as extensive knowledge, experience, or culture. Either definition leads to the conclusion that literacy is ultimately about power. As Candy Dawson Boyd (1996) said during a recent presentation, "literacy enables you to act effectively in the world, with the world, and despite the world." It gives us voice. It gives us a chance at success and power. It gives us choices.

The definition of literacy that teachers choose to operate under daily in their classrooms can have a critical impact on how they see their stu-

What Counts as Literacy: Challenging the School Standard. Copyright © 2000 by Teachers College, Columbia University. All rights reserved. ISBN 0-8077-3972-3 (paper), ISBN 0-8077-3973-1 (cloth). Prior to photocopying items for classroom use, please contact the Copyright Clearance Center, Customer Service, 222 Rosewood Drive, Danvers, MA 01923, USA, telephone (508) 750-8400.

dents and serious implications for how they hinder or help them towards access to power and success. In other words, a teacher's personal understanding of literacy directly impacts on the children's development of literacy in the classroom. If I defined literacy solely as school reading and writing success, then every year one-third to one-half of my class would be failing. The measure of school literacy success is defined by whether students can read "on grade level." This is the definition used by many who judge education and students. They are often not teachers who know—on a personal, tacit level—that successful literacy instruction must go beyond standard school methods, particularly for the third of the children who do not speak standard English at home. We teachers may try to ignore what newspapers, district administrators, and state policymakers say, but they are so loud (especially lately in California) that we can still hear them through our closed doors, where we are frantically trying to teach reading and writing. But policymakers are so invested in this standard definition that they cannot see beyond it on multiple levels, even to help students who cannot read and write.

I must share my favorite, true story that has helped shape my personal literacy as a reading teacher. Several years ago, teachers at my school were given a new core reading series. My colleague and I sat through the in-service training on the series, hoping that our students would be able to read it; knowing that if they could, life would be easy, just as the saleswoman/former teacher said. However, we left the in-service knowing—on a gut or personal level—that the saleswoman's projections were wrong and that a significant number of our second-grade students would *not* learn to read from the designated blue book. We just *knew*. So we began to inquire about getting some red books (first-grade level). The answer from downtown administration was a firm "no," the reason being that "the students should be reading on grade level." I believe this response came from the same department that had berated us 2 weeks earlier because our test scores showed that the majority of our students did *not* read on grade level. So we "snuck" into book rooms and acquired books our students could read; soon we began a secret trade market with other teachers.

Things have improved through the years. Downtown administration does not admit that they are wrong, that our personal understandings of literacy instruction might be right, but they do acknowledge that "supplemental books" (i.e., books children can really read successfully) might be appropriate for some students. Unfortunately, the district has not yet approved textbook funding so we can buy them.

What all of this means is that many of my students are still labeled as failures. And by the single standard of school literacy, they are. Jamal and Frank and Lynette struggle through reading each day. Jamal refuses to look at his reader. I cannot get him to follow the words, and his writing is fragmented. His phonemic awareness and spelling skills are so limited that I can barely decipher what he writes even though I have been teaching second grade for 9 years. Frank cannot find patterns. I cannot convey rhymes to him. He cannot write in complete sentences, and he does not seem to be aware of it. Lynette is so insecure with her reading skills that putting her in a large reading group brings tears to her eyes. Aldo always seems virtually in another world, completely tuned out to my voice. Noel and Ivan are like many other boys who avoid reading. They engage in distracting behavior to cover up their poor reading skills. Both seem rather committed to not reading in my class. All of these students look like many of my students in years past if I define success using the narrow definition of school or grade-level literacy. But each one stands out in my mind as a special individual, whose personal literacies define success.

Jamal, in fact, is a great artist. He draws in such detail. He accompanies each drawing with complex, well-articulated stories that he loves to tell me, but cannot write yet. His thinking skills and oral expertise have been well used to make him something of a success in his world. Aldo, for his part, lights up when the subject of the human body or certain science areas comes up in class. His whole demeanor changes. His tone becomes confident and knowledgeable.

Frank is well liked. He has a kind, giving personality. He plays with all the students at recess. When I finally learned to listen to the children on the playground this year, I heard such fun and laughter and saw skills that crossed gender assignments with personal literacies. The girls, for example, play a wonderful hand-clapping rhyming game. When I ventured out to have them teach me, I found Frank there. He could rhyme and create a pattern with the best of the girls. Lynette, on the other hand, is outstanding at basketball: she is diligent about practicing. She is so confident that she is a good teacher of the sport.

I learned that Noel spends hours and hours with his father: fishing, taking care of animals, and growing things. The whole class went over to his house one day for a "field trip." We shared in his personal literacy skills. Noel was like a docent showing us each plant and animal, telling us endless details. The year I had Noel in my class, I did not bother researching much on fishing, plants, or animals. I just asked Noel. So did the other children. I remember that one day I got a copy of *Just Me and My Dad* by Mercer Mayer (1990) and Noel tried to read it on his own.

These students are succeeding. These students possess extensive knowledge and experience. However, to see them as literate, we teachers must be willing to acknowledge the existence of multiple literacies. In other words, we might have to look outside the classroom and beyond the traditional measures. We have to personally embrace such literacies in order to draw upon them for instructional purposes. So these students are at once failing by the narrowly defined measures of school literacy, yet successful in their understanding and acknowledgment of multiple ways of communicating and expressing and decoding community and personal text.

HAVE I DONE RIGHT BY THEM?

Such conclusions, of course, raise further critical questions. The key issue is an obvious one. Is acknowledgment of their success in some areas of literacy sufficient? No! They have the right—and we have the moral obligation to insure that right—to learn to read and write from the perspective of school literacy. There can be no excuses—not even the ones that Jamar comes up with. And in the process, we cannot let them tire us out so much that we give up.

Until I personally redefined for myself the meaning of literacy, it seemed enough to teach them to read and write as best I could with what I was given. There were nights that I did not sleep because of worrying about those who were not succeeding. Or I dreamt about them, their journal writing, their guided reading groups, their assessments. Fortunately, for many students in my classes, there is success with school literacy because they understand how classrooms operate, how schools work, and how the tasks of reading and writing are defined and played out in schools. They can do this regardless of what happens at home or in their community. If there are discrepancies between the two, they bridge them. When they are in the classroom they can follow the school rules. We know this because they pass the tests.

But there are more questions: How do we make the connection between success and failure for those students who do not personally understand the school rules? How have they learned to succeed in the ways they have? How can we use their experiences to build success in school literacy as well as community and personal literacy? As teachers we are obligated to do so. If we are the "power brokers" that Herbert Kohl (1996) says we are, then one way or another we must coax, hook, push, or pull our students into participating with us in the journey toward the literacy defined by school reading and writing success. The usual excuses—not enough time, inappropriate materials for students who do not speak English as their first language, students who come to school underprepared for school—have to be left behind. The fact is that in most cases students come with much knowledge and experience; we just do not see it because we have not been encouraged to look beyond their school literacy.

Now that I can see through the lenses of multiple literacies, I can find ways for all my second-grade students to step toward reading and writing fluency. What I see is that all of my students—including Jamal, Noel, Lynette, Aldo, and Frank—do operate by rules and structure. They can focus, retain information, practice, and master data. They are motivated. Each in his or her own way was successful in some aspect of literacy. They had acquired literate understandings through their personal experiences that went beyond community literacy (e.g., Frank's rhymes) and were applying them in ways that made them happy and able to stretch themselves further. I see now what was failing them: (1) a teacher who had not yet learned to recognize success in other forms, (2) a structure that continued to be alien to them and which they did not need to access to survive in their life outside of school, (3) a curriculum that was not authentic, or motivating enough to hook them into practice and mastery, and (4) role models that had not shown them that the skills or tools they have used to master drawing, debating, and basketball could be applied to reading and writing within a classroom.

I also need to be kind to myself as a teacher. It could be worse. I might have remained blind to multiple literacies and only have been able to watch the children lose all expectations of being able to succeed at anything. Sylvia Ashton-Warner (1996) described children as "volcanoes with twin vents: block the creative vent and the destructive one will blow." We might substitute "fail to acknowledge" for "block" and get the same result. I see it everyday with Jamal and students like him. Recognizing his literate strengths, albeit strengths that do not necessarily fall into the parameters of my assigned curriculum, is the only way I hook him into trying to get to school, to read, to write.

Now as I look around me I see multiple literacies in all my students. And if it is all around me, then it is my responsibility to grab it and pull it into my classroom and use it and build on it and praise it. It is my hook. It can, and must, be the place I start to build for those students who have not been hooked by the standard school literacy. The repetitive practices on the basketball court or soccer field; the clapping, rhyming; the acting on the stage; the story telling that comes from home and the community: these are all forms of literacy. But have they been valued as such? Have we missed an opportunity to build on these and use the learning process as a bridge toward acquiring another kind of standard literacy which would give students access to more opportunities, choice and power? When the next Jamal comes through my door, perhaps I can convince him to use his visual and oral literacy—perhaps to write the story of his picture for us, so that he can publish a book and share it with the class. And maybe I'll let him skip the reading group for a short time or come in at lunch to finish it. Maybe that will be the place I can start with him. And the next time a Lynette walks through my door, maybe I can put her in charge of a PE lesson on basketball. Maybe they could get help to write down the rules and teach them to the class. Maybe I can do that.

IF SCHOOLS/SOCIETY SHARED OUR PERSPECTIVE ON LITERACY, HOW MIGHT PEOPLE'S LIVES BE DIFFERENT?

Speaking as a teacher, I am limiting my response to this question to the possibilities of the classroom and the school site. I imagine a school staff who would value the concept of multiple literacies to such a degree that they would be able to vocalize the worthlessness of restrictive report cards and standardized tests, and the curriculum that is generated to support them. They would be able to rethink the ways in which students are allowed to demonstrate their abilities. I see a celebration occurring of what students can do instead of a critique of what they cannot do. I imagine curriculum programs with broader opportunities for students to react to them, with multiple ways in which students could choose to present their discoveries. The critical skills of reading, writing, oral language, and math would be defined as tools needed to achieve students' goals and would not be the ultimate and sole measure of their worth as human beings. I imagine a rather substantial broadening of what is allowed as curriculum and a total rehaul of the assessment process. Teachers can build on positive attitudes and skills that are valued and respected; it is hard to build on broken self-esteem and failure. I wonder what a school would look like where students were in charge of a significant number of duties and responsibilities based on their life skills?

Yet in the months since I first drafted this chapter, I have seen such possibilities drying up. More and more curriculum is specifically mandated, as less and less time is allowed for teachers to present to students what is interesting or important to them. There is more monitoring to insure that mandated materials are taught. The evaluation measure of literacy is increasingly limited to little more than the standardized test given once a year. All talent and, in some cases, the considerable progress made by students is disregarded unless it is manifested on the standardized tests. Whatever strides have been made in considering teachers as professionals and in encouraging them to reflect and rethink common practice are now being jettisoned and replaced by mandated programs to ensure that class size reduction is getting value for the dollars spent. That means an increase in traditional programs that tend to highlight what many of our non-mainstream students do not do very well and ignores their many talents (community and personal literacies).

I want to be more positive, but nothing encourages me except the possibilities that lie in the following questions: How can teachers who are the most connected to our students and the realities of education have a greater impact on and greater control over education policies, attitudes, and perspectives? How can teachers' personal literacies be expressed so that they can influence literacy instruction? The bottom line is that teachers are responsible for preparing students to face the world with the skills and attitudes that will give them choices. My hope now rests in the fact that small groups of committed teachers may be able to make changes at the site level.

REFERENCES

Ashton-Warner, S. (1996, June). Keynote address given at given at *Literacy for all: Learning from best practices*. Emeryville, CA.

Dawson Boyd, C. (1996, June). Literacy for the 21st Century. Presentation given at *Literacy for all: Learning from best practices*. Emeryville, CA.

Kohl, H. (1996, June). Should we burn Babar? Presentation given at *Literacy for all: Learning from best practices*. Emeryville, CA.

Mayer, M. (1990). *Just me and my dad*. Racine, WI: Golden Books, Western.

18

Conclusion

Implications for Teacher Practice

MARGARET A. GALLEGO AND
SANDRA HOLLINGSWORTH

As we explained in the introduction (Chapter 1), we asked the authors writing for this volume to respond to the following question: "If schools/ society shared our perspective on literacy, how might people's lives be different?" As we anticipated, the authors responded in a wide and rich variety of ways. Their common refrain, however, was this: One static approach to literacy education limits the enormous power of our children to lead us into an increasingly complex future. The authors, along with many of the classroom teachers with whom we have worked over the years, have shown us many ways that classroom instruction might be organized to release the full potential of diverse groups of students. However, all of us are realists. Unfolding the project of multiple literacies in classrooms will not be easy, particularly in light of the current national fever to enforce common standards. Teachers who choose to implement multiple literacy instruction and speak for its benefits need courage.

The current sociopolitical climate in our home state of California, for example, is far from endorsing multiple literacies, as revealed in N. Asimov's article in the *San Francisco Chronicle* (July 16, 1998).

> In a speedy decision intended to resolve how California will teach non-English speakers before children go back to school, a federal judge yesterday rejected a move to block voter-approved Proposition 227 (banning bilingual education).
>
> The decision by Judge Charles Legge in San Francisco means that as of August 2, school districts across the state may no longer teach academics in

What Counts as Literacy: Challenging the School Standard. Copyright © 2000 by Teachers College, Columbia University. All rights reserved. ISBN 0-8077-3972-3 (paper), ISBN 0-8077-3973-1 (cloth). Prior to photocopying items for classroom use, please contact the Copyright Clearance Center, Customer Service, 222 Rosewood Drive, Danvers, MA 01923, USA, telephone (508) 750-8400.

any language but English. Replacing bilingual education will be a required one-year program of intensive English language instruction. The new law also lets parents sue teachers who refuse to teach in English.

Despite the judge's ruling, educators in several Bay Area districts said . . . they will try to find a way around the ban. San Francisco [Unified School District] vowed openly to defy Proposition 227. (pp. A1, A13)

The popular culture and political context in California at the end of the twentieth century thus suggest that Americans not only support, but will legislate, a single standard of literacy in our public schools. So we will close this volume by turning our original question on its head: What can teachers do with a belief in multiple literacies if society does not value the diversity embedded in that perspective? At first, this single-standard movement might cause educators who value cultural and linguistic diversity to panic. This turn of events, however, could force them to abandon a reliance on *language* as the prominent means of recognizing diversity, thereby making the ideas and practices of multiple literacies even more important. So how might teachers still achieve literate diversity without bilingual education?

To be able to organize classrooms for multiple literacies, the authors of this volume agree on one feature consistent with the California ruling: all children should learn the dominant discourse of standard English in school in oral and written forms. Delpit (Chapter 14) argues this case compellingly. Indeed, each of the classic chapters that open each section of this book clearly support the need for learning and teaching school literacy. Yet Resnick (Chapter 2), Ladson-Billings (Chapter 8), and Delpit are not satisfied with simply achieving standard English; they call for teachers and schools to do "more." The other authors support that position. They believe "more" does not mean more of the same, such as the remediation of deficit literacies to meet a single standard of literacy. They advocate instead a variety of literacies. Collectively, the instructional examples offered by the authors of this volume suggest three key strategies that teachers might draw from to develop multiple literacies in contemporary classrooms:

Expand what counts as text in schools
Engage in instructional praxis
Learn about literacy teaching from relational knowing

These strategies were illustrated in unique combinations across the chapters on school, community, and personal literacies.

EXPANDED NOTIONS OF TEXT

The notion of multiple literacies in itself implies expanded notions of text—that is, increasing (and therefore changing) what counts as literacy in the classroom. Several of the authors of this volume described types of literacy that were not constrained by written form. Flood, Lapp, and Bayles-Martin (Chapter 4) use the concept of *visual literacy* to encourage students to create alternative texts. "Students encouraged to explore how visual images can be collected and presented in order to communicate an idea or feeling become authors of a new sort and, in so doing, grapple with the inner workings of communication and creation." Vásquez and Durán (Chapter 10) teach students to become literate through live chats and electronic mail. In after-school arrangements, where the constraints of school are lifted, they were able to change what counted as being literate to include knowing how to collaborate and how to use varying resources, both technological (computers) and personal (community neighbors). Myers, Hammett, and McKillop (Chapter 5) advocate an expanded notion of literacy through technology tools, including sound, image, and video multimedia, to interrupt and expand written text. The authors suggest that personal reflections on text represented by multimedia expressions are important for students' self-identity.

Short and Kauffman (Chapter 3) remind us that although schools have focused primarily on language, children naturally integrate art and music while they learn outside of school. The authors illustrate children's use of alternative sign systems in inquiry projects into art and music as text organized in cycles of learning, learning about, and learning through sign systems to develop multiple literacies. Noll (Chapter 12) and Leland, Harste, and Helt (Chapter 6) also give us compelling examples of how non-mainstream students' use of a variety of sign systems (imagery and pictures) as multiple literacies provided alternative ways of communicating knowledge and expressing themselves. Teachers can draw on all these examples to promote school, community, and personal literacies.

INSTRUCTIONAL PERSPECTIVES OF PRAXIS

We have defined *praxis* as the dialectical relationship between thought and action, subjectivity and objectivity, and theory and practice: one always critiques the other. Instructional praxis requires teachers in multicultural classrooms to be continually critical of politically motivated educational policies and educational theories drawn from research on mainstream populations. In the context of this volume, praxis also requires a deliberate assessment of dominant modes of literacy instruction and the use of effective alternatives, so that children from all cultures and communities can access standard English, while also articulating personal and community literacies.

The actions that teachers might take—even within a conservative societal climate—are described by several authors in our text. Resnick (Chapter 2) critiques schools for promoting literacy as a "collection of skills" and for being too isolated from everyday uses of literacy. She suggests that teachers adopt apprenticeship models (more commonly found out of school), which view literacy as a form of cultural practice. Ladson-Billings (Chapter 8) writes about culturally relevant pedagogy with African American children, and Reyes (Chapter 13) refers to the same notion in her work with Navaho children. Panofsky (Chapter 11) gives an example of instructional praxis in her critique of "best practices" in literacy which imply deficiencies in less dominant community literacy practices.

Finally, Andrade, González Le Denmat, and Moll (Chapter 16) give teachers still another example of praxis—through a distinct kind of work with students' parents. In establishing *El Grupo de Las Señoras*, the teacher helped mothers educate their children through their own critical literacy development. In doing so, the teacher interrupted the dominant school trend toward "remediating" working-class parents. Viewing teaching as praxis can promote multiple literacies: teachers who do so continually seek alternative solutions to dominant—and societally destructive—ideology.

RELATIONAL KNOWING

To go beyond critique of dominant practices and develop alternatives, these chapters suggest that teachers draw upon relational knowing. We described *relational knowing* as a form of knowledge available to teachers through their critical understanding of self and others in relationship. Engaging in reciprocal relationships with students and parents can give teachers a new understanding of the power of relationships—and the value of learning about self and others from those less powerful. For example, when reciprocal relationships are formed, the relational knowing causes educators to reframe their assumptions about the value of the other's knowledge. Suddenly, the teacher may not always know best. Insights from relational knowing also help teachers learn about childrens', parents', and their own lived experiences, in and out of school, and that knowledge helps them develop community and personal literacies. Several authors speak to the use of relational knowing to develop multiple literacies.

Bressler and Siegel's work with parents (Chapter 9) is one example of the kinds of understanding teachers might gain through relational knowing. Through the development of a collaborative relationship, they were able to reposition parents' roles in classroom assessment. Rather than simply presenting students' portfolios to their parents, the parents themselves participated in the actual assessment. This relationship helped teachers learn more about students' out-of-school lives. Galindo (Chapter 15) draws on stories of teachers' past relationships with their families to understand their current classroom practices. The importance of understanding the relationship of lived experience to classroom practice is especially relevant for this group of teachers who share the same cultural minority backgrounds with children in their classrooms.

Minarik (Chapter 17) suggests that one of her best tools for understanding her role as a teacher in attempting to develop multiple literacies are the lessons she learns from her relationships with students. She learned, for example, that one of the factors that contributed to students' failure to learn standard English was "a teacher who had not yet learned to recognize success in other forms"—herself! Gee and Clinton (Chapter 7) validate Minarik's discovery when they suggest that teachers and researchers must change their interactions with nonmainstream students in order to adequately assess their comprehension of instructional material. Without a reciprocal relationship, it may be the teacher who misunderstands the students' meaning, rather than the reverse. Finally, Panofsky (Chapter 11) further validates relational knowing: "teaching [is] an ongoing inquiry in which . . . getting to know one's students would be understood by teachers as a *sine qua non* for children's successful learning in schools."

A FINAL THOUGHT

The nested strategies for (1) knowing self and students in order to (2) thoughtfully critique dominant practices and (3) expand what counts as text in classrooms will bring teachers a long way toward the development of multiple literacies, even in the face of increasingly antidiversity political trends. Without such tools, the California decision could be alarming for the state's teachers who value a healthy multicultural society. From a different view, however, the ruling helps educators rethink an overreliance on language to maintain and develop cultural diversity. Even at the university level in California, student teachers are prepared for diverse classrooms with a heavy dose of linguistic preparation at the expense of broader cultural analyses (see the *CLAD* and *B/CLAD Program Approval Documents*, California Commission on the Credentialing of Teachers, 1993).

School's historic privilege of language, in both its oral and written forms, as the primary mode of classroom communication (both for instruction and as a means of expressing and ranking students' knowledge) has been long documented (cf. Flanders, 1970; Cazden, 1986). The current attack on native language instruction (bilingual education) and its subsequent fallout may require teachers to look elsewhere and seek alternatives to language-laden methods. While we clearly would not support a ban on bilingual education, we believe the ideas and instructional examples in this book will help all teachers realize their instructional "languagecentrism" and promote multiple literacies in their classrooms. This is especially promising for those most affected by the current political climate—the non-English-proficient minority children. We are deeply appreciative of the authors of this volume for all their efforts—and of the teachers who are engaged in projects of praxis for a diverse society.

REFERENCES

Asimov, N. (1998, July 16). Prop. 227 upheld by federal judge: 'No constitutional right to bilingual education.' *San Francisco Chronicle*, pp. A1, A13.

California Commission on Teacher Credentialing. (1993). *Cultural, language and academic learning credential program approval document* [CLAD . . .]. Sacramento, CA: Author.

California Commission on Teacher Credentialing. (1993*). Bilingual cultural, language and academic learning credential program approval document* [B/CLAD . . .]. Sacramento, CA: Author.

Cazden, C. B. (1986). Classroom discourse. In M. C. Wittrock (Ed.), *Handbook of research on teaching*, Vol. 2 (pp. 432–463). New York: Macmillan.

Flanders, N. A. (1970). *Analyzing teacher behavior*. Reading, MA: Addison-Wesley.

About the Authors

Rosi Andrade, a research associate at the Southwest Institute for Research on Women in the Department of Women's Studies at the University of Arizona, holds a Ph.D. in reading. Her interests lie in the social, cultural, and political experiences of minority children and their parents, especially mothers. She has developed a specialty in expanding literacy experiences as a means to personal development and empowerment. She continues to collaborate with many of the same women who formed part of *El Club de Literatura,* as together they promote Leadership through Literacy for community women through popular education. Andrade was born and raised in Arizona, the daughter of a Spanish immigrant mother and a Mexican American father.

Debra Bayles-Martin received her Ph.D. in curriculum and instruction from the University of Texas at Austin. She is currently an Assistant Professor at San Diego State University, where she directs the Community Reading Center, coordinates the Reading Program, and serves as advisor for the Reading Masters Program. Her research interests center on teacher beliefs and knowledge and on interventions for struggling readers.

Darlene Bressler is an Associate Professor of Education in the Department of Education of Houghton College where she teachers courses on literacy education and works with student teachers. A former elementary classroom teacher and reading specialist, she received her Ph.D from the University of Rochester in Rochester, New York. Her research interests include family and community literacy, teacher research, and critical pedagogy.

Kate Clinton is a doctoral student in the literacy program in the Department of Curriculum and Instruction at the University of Wisconsin at Madison. Before coming to Wisconsin, she managed a research project devoted to implementing an after-school program in science education for diverse middle school children, organized by the Hiatt Center for Urban Education at Clark University in Worcester, Massachusetts. Her interests include work on sociocultural approaches to language, literacy, and identity.

Lisa D. Delpit is the holder of the Benjamin E. Mays Chair of Urban Educational Excellence at Georgia State University, Atlanta, Georgia. She received a B.S. degree from Antioch College and an M.Ed. and Ed.D. from Harvard University. Her background is in elementary education with an emphasis on language and literacy development. Originally from Baton Rouge, Louisiana, she is a nationally and internationally known speaker and writer whose work has focused on the education of children of color and the perspectives, aspirations, and pedagogical knowledge of teachers of color. She has used her training in ethnographic research to spark dialogues between educators on issues that have impact on students typically least well-served by our educational system. Her recent work has spanned a range of projects and issues, including assisting national programs engaged in school restructuring efforts; working with the Professional Standards Commission; establishing the Peachtree Urban Writing Project in Atlanta; creating high-standard, innovative schools for poor, urban children; and developing urban leadership programs for teachers and school district central office staff. Her primary effort at this time is establishing the Center for Urban Educational Excellence at Georgia State. Delpit's work on school-community relations and cross-cultural communication was cited as a contributor to her receiving a MacArthur "Genius" Award in 1990.

Richard Durán is a Professor in the Graduate School of Education at the University of California, Santa Barbara. He specializes in research on the acquisition of literacy by second-language learners and families, the use of technology to mediate learning, and innovative methods of assessment. His team's research program in these areas has been supported by the Center for Research on Education, Diversity and Excellence, the Center for Research on Education of Students Placed At-Risk, and the University of California, Office of the President.

James Flood, Professor of Reading and Language Development at San Diego State University, has taught in preschool, elementary, and secondary schools and has been a language arts supervisor and vice principal. He has also been a Fulbright scholar at the University of Lisbon in Portugal and the President of the National Reading Conference. Dr. Flood has chaired and cochaired many IRA, NCTE, NCRE, and NRC committees. Currently Dr. Flood teaches preservice and graduate courses at SDSU. He has coauthored and edited many articles, columns, texts, handbooks, and children's materials on reading and language arts issues. These include the following, which were codeveloped with Diane Lapp: *Content*

Area Reading and Learning, which is in its second edition, and the *Handbook of Research on Teaching Literacy Through the Communicative and Visual Arts.* His many educational awards include being named the Outstanding Teacher Educator in the Department of Teacher Education at SDSU, the Distinguished Research Lecturer from SDSU's Graduate Division of Research, and a member of the California Hall of Fame.

René Galindo, an Associate Professor at the University of Colorado at Denver, received his Ph.D. from the Ohio State University in 1990. A product of the borderlands, he was born in Nogales, Arizona, and worked as a bilingual elementary school teacher in Tucson. His research interests have included Amish literacy and Chicano teacher role identity. His current research project is a language policy study of the debates over the future of bilingual education that is funded by the Spencer Foundation.

Margaret A. Gallego, Associate Professor, San Diego State University received her Ph.D. from the University of Arizona in 1989. Her research interests include expanded notions of literacy, classroom cultures, and issues of social justice, which are represented in published articles and chapters, some of which have been coauthored with Sandra Hollingsworth. Most recently she has served as Project Scientist at the Laboratory of Comparative Cognition at the University of California, San Diego, where she conducted research and evaluation of after-school computer clubs, collectively known as the Fifth Dimension.

James Paul Gee, formerly the Jacob Hiatt Professor of Education in the Hiatt Center for Urban Education at Clark University in Worcester, Massachusetts, is now the Tashia Morgridge Professor of Reading in the Department of Curriculum and Instruction at the University of Wisconsin at Madison. His research centers around the application of linguistics and discourse analysis to issues of language, literacy, culture, and learning. His most recent book is *An Introduction to Discourse Analysis: Theory and Method* (1999).

Hilda González Le Denmat completed her Ph.D. in the College of Education, Department of Language, at the University of Arizona in 1998. She has been an educator in Arizona, developing a weekly literature study group (*El Club deLiteratura*) for Mexican immigrant women. The goal of the literature study group is first to further personal development and then to use that development to affect the lives of participants. This work takes its lead from the work of Paulo Freire in promoting liberatory teaching. She was born in Mexico and immigrated to the United States as an adult. She is living in France with her husband and two daughters, where she hopes to continue her work with immigrant women in the European context.

Roberta Hammett, a Ph.D. graduate of the Pennsylvania State University, is Assistant Professor of Education at Memorial University of Newfoundland. She teaches curricular uses of computers, secondary English education, and graduate courses in multiple literacies. She researches literacy applications and implications of computer technologies. Her web address is WWW.UCS.MUN.CA/~hammett.

Jerome C. Harste is Distinguished Professor of Language Education at Indiana University, where he holds the Martha Lea and Bill Armstrong Chair in Teacher Education. Together with teachers and interns at the Center for Inquiry in Indianapolis, he is exploring how children's literature might support critical conversations about literacy in classrooms.

Christina Helt teaches third grade at Allison Elementary School in Speedway, Indiana. While in the teacher education program at Indiana University-Purdue University at Indianapolis (IUPUI), she was awarded an undergraduate research grant to study the progress of students with learning disabilities in whole language classrooms. Some of the data for this article was collected as part of this project.

Sandra Hollingsworth is Professor and Director of the Office of Research on Educational Reform at San Jose State University. She is currently on assignment as the Director of Reading and Language Arts at the Developmental Studies Center, a nonprofit organization in Oakland, California. A former historian and classroom teacher, Dr. Hollingsworth took her first academic position at the University of California, Berkeley, and her second at Michigan State University. In those locations, she conducted longitudinal research on the impact of teacher education coursework on beginning teachers' professional needs in urban schools. She found that preparing teachers to conduct action research was the most powerful form of teacher education. A former journalist, photographer, and K–12 classroom teacher, Dr. Hollingsworth's current research interests are in creating centers of inquiry in urban schools, the reform of teacher education through urban school–university partnerships or professional development schools, image-based research into alternative assessments of student learning through these partnerships, and policy implications of image-based research concerning rethinking education for Latino and other minority students. She is the 1999 winner of a lifetime research award on behalf of women and minorities from the American Educational Research Association.

Gloria Kauffman is a doctoral student in Language, Reading, and Culture at the University of Arizona. She has more than 20 years teaching experience and is currently teaching an intermediate multiage classroom at Duffy Elementary School in Tucson, Arizona. Her current teacher research interest is how children view themselves as learners in an inquiry-based curriculum.

Gloria Ladson-Billings is a professor in the Department of Curriculum and Instruction at the University of Wisconsin-Madison. She teaches courses in multicultural perspectives on education and culturally relevant pedagogy. Her current research interests are in pedagogy and critical race theory.

Diane Lapp, Professor of Reading and Language in the Department of Teacher Education at San Diego State University, has taught in elementary and middle schools. In fact, Dr. Lapp, who codirects and teaches field-based preservice and graduate courses, spent her recent sabbatical from SDSU team teaching in a public school first-grade classroom. She has coauthored and edited many articles, columns, texts, handbooks, and children's materials on reading and language arts issues. These include the following, which were codeveloped with James Flood: *Teaching Reading to Every Child*, a reading methods textbook in its fourth edition, and the *Handbook of Research in Teaching the English Language Arts*, soon to be released in its second edition. She has also chaired and cochaired several IRA and NRC committees. Her many educational awards include being named as the Outstanding Teacher Educator and Faculty Member in the Department of Teacher Education at SDSU, the Distinguished Research Lecturer from SDSU's Graduate Division of Research, a member of the California Hall of Fame, and IRS's 1996 Outstanding Teacher Educator of the Year.

Christine H. Leland is Associate Professor of Education at Indiana University, Indianapolis (IUPUI), where she directs a cohort of undergraduates in the Learning to Teach/Teaching to Learn program. A former classroom teacher, she is interested in exploring curriculum that seeks to access education for populations of students who historically have not been well served by schools.

Ann Margaret McKillop is Assistant Professor of Education in the Curriculum and Instruction Department at the University of Maryland where she teaches courses in secondary language arts and technology applications in the classroom. Besides student-constructed hypermedia, her interests and research areas include composition, read-response theory, media literacy and interdisciplinary curriculum.

Leslie Turner Minarik teaches second grade at Highland Elementary School in Richmond, California. After working in the business world for 10 years she went back to school to get her teaching credentials. During the program at the University of California, Berkeley, she participated in a research project that evolved into a teacher research group that has met continuously for 12 years. She has spoken at national conferences and published a number of articles related to her classroom experiences and her research. She is currently involved in new teacher support and is teaching literacy courses for her district's Intern Program.

Luis C. Moll, who was born in Puerto Rico and earned his Ph.D. at UCLA in 1978, is a Professor in the Department of Language, Reading, and Culture in the College of Education at the University of Arizona. He has conducted educational research with language minority students for the past 20 years. Among other studies he has analyzed the quality of classroom teaching, examined literacy instruction in English and Spanish, and studied household funds of knowledge and how that knowledge can be documented, analyzed, and applied by teachers to improve classroom instruction. He has served on the editorial boards of several journals, including the *American Education Research Journal, Educational Researcher, Reading Research Quarterly, Journal of Literacy Research, Educational Psychologist, Cultura y Educación,* and *Mind, Culture and Activity.* His most recent project involves the analysis of biliteracy development, how children develop literate competencies in two languages, and the broader social and ideological conditions that mediate such development.

Jamie Myers is an Associate Professor at the Pennsylvania State University, where he teaches English education and critical ethnography. He holds a Ph.D. from Indiana University, Bloomington. His current scholarly interests focus on promoting the collaborative generation and critique of multimedia representations of the self, others, and the world, and how this technology can support the social construction of community knowledge. His e-mail is jmm12@psu.edu.

Elizabeth Noll is an Assistant Professor of Language, Literacy, and Sociocultural Studies at the University of New Mexico. She teaches undergraduate and graduate courses in literacy education, writing, and case study research methodology. Her current research focuses on schooling and homelessness and on oral and written academic discourse.

Carolyn P. Panofsky is Professor of Educational Foundations at Rhode Island College. She teaches courses in issues of diversity in schooling and qualitative classroom research. Before becoming a teacher-educator, she taught reading and writing at colleges in the West and Southwest. Her research addresses the application of cultural-historical theory to contexts of learning in homes and schools. She received her Ph.D. at the University of New Mexico.

Lauren B. Resnick is an internationally known scholar in the cognitive science of learning and instruction. Her recent work has focused on socializing intelligence, the nature and development of thinking abilities, and the relationship between school learning and everyday competence, with special attention to mathematics and literacy. Dr. Resnick's current work lies at the intersection of cognitive science and policy for education and workforce development. She is co-founder and co-director of the New Standards partnership, a consortium of states and school districts setting shared performance standards and building assessments for a standards-based educational system. She founded and directs the Institute for Learning, which focuses on professional development based on cognitive learning principles and the study of effort-oriented motivational systems.

Elba I. Reyes received her Ph.D. from the University of Arizona in the area of special education. Her research has focused on multicultural populations, specifically on identifying learning environments and approaches that facilitate students' learning and that assist them to demonstrate their abilities. Dr. Reyes is presently Director of Special Education for a school district in southern Arizona.

Kathy G. Short has focused her work on literature circles, curriculum as inquiry, and collaborative learning environments for teachers and children. She is a Professor in the Department of Language, Reading, and Culture at the University of Arizona where she works extensively with teachers to develop curricula that actively involve students as authors and inquirers. She has coauthored a number of books including *Teacher Study Groups* (NCTE, 1998), *Literature as a Way of Knowing* (Stenhouse, 1997), *Creating Classrooms for Authors and Inquirers* (Heinemann, 1996), and *Learning Together through Inquiry* (Stenhouse, 1996). In addition, she is coeditor of *The New Advocate*, a journal that connects children's literature and teaching.

Marjorie Siegel is Associate Professor of Education in the Department of Curriculum and Teaching at Teachers College, Columbia University, where she teaches courses on literacy education and qualitative research methods. A former reading teacher, she received an Ed.D. in reading education from Indiana University-Bloomington. Her scholarly interests include the contribution of transmediation (juxtaposing multiple symbol systems) to literacy learning, students' negotiation of multiple literacies, and critical approaches to literacy theory and research.

Olga A. Vásquez, a Ph.D. graduate of Stanford University, is an ethnographer of education in the Department of Communication at the University of California, San Diego (UCSD). She is founder and director of *La Clase Mágica,* an after-school project that partners UCSD and a community institution in a social action initiative to bring about change in the educational experiences of Spanish-English bilingual learners. Professor Vásquez is the lead author of *Pushing Boundaries: Language and Culture in a Mexicano Community* (Cambridge University Press, 1994) and author of *La Clase Mágica: Imagining Optimal Possibilities in a Bilingual Community of Learners* (forthcoming). She has contributed chapters to numerous edited volumes in the fields of education, bilingual education, literacy, and community studies and has published articles in various national and international professional journals.

Index